ART WORK

Edward Hayward

Edited by Lisa Hyde
Designed by Huw Davies

BBC Longman

Published by BBC Books and Longman Group UK Limited

BBC Books
a division of
BBC Enterprises Limited
Woodlands
80 Wood Lane
London W12 0TT

Longman Group UK Limited,
Longman House,
Burnt Mill,
Harlow,
Essex,
CM20 2JE,
England and Associated Companies throughout the World.

First published 1990

Edited by Lisa Hyde
Cover and book design by Huw Davies

ISBN 0 582 05295 5

Set in Goudy Bold 10/12 pt and Helvetica Light Condensed 10/12 pt
Typeset by Ace Filmsetting Ltd
Text printed in England by Ebenezer Baylis and Son Ltd
Cover origination in Hong Kong
Cover printed by Clay's of Norwich

ART WORK

Contents

4 Acknowledgements

5 Foreword by Edward Hayward

GOING ABOUT IT

6 Ideas and Planning
8 Experiment and Research
10 Finishing the Work
12 GCSE: A Teacher's View

SEEING AND BELIEVING

15 What is Art?
18 Art at Work
20 A Painter at Work
22 Things to Do
24 All Times and Places

APPEARANCES

27 Why Portraits?
30 What is Appearance?
32 A Portrait of Two People
34 Image
36 Ideas for You
38 Just for Laughs

STYLE FOR LIVING

41 What is Design?
44 Two Styles, Same Method
46 Research
48 Experiment: The Practical Problems
50 The Customer is Always Right
52 Ideas for You
54 Take Off Here!

POINT OF VIEW

57 Graphic Design
60 The Reader in Mind
62 A Style Develops
64 The Identity in Use
66 Ideas for You
68 Symbols in Art and Design

REFLECTIONS: A WORLD OF IDEAS

70 The Environment
72 A Load of Rubbish?
74 Street Theatre
76 Telling Stories
78 Comics
80 Landscapes

WHERE DO WE GO FROM HERE?

82 Another Medium
84 Another Time, Another Place
86 Another Point of View
88 Extend the Story

STUDY

90 Themes
91 Materials and Techniques
92 Study Sources
93 Galleries, Museums and Art Centres
94 Bibliography

95 Index

Acknowledgements

The author would like to express his gratitude to Joe Connolly, General Adviser, Suffolk Education Authority; Catherine McDermott, Lecturer, Kingston College of Art; Howard Hollands, Lecturer in Art Education, Middlesex Polytechnic; Moy Keightley and Sean McErlain. Also Judy Brooks and Wanda Petrusewicz, assistant producers who worked on the series.

PICTURE CREDITS

P6-7: 1 Royal Collection, 2-6 Ann Carrington; p8-9: Metropolitan Museum, New York, 2 Tate Gallery, London, 3 Ancient Art & Architecture, 4 BBC TV, 5 Metropolitan Museum, New York; p10-11: 1-3 BBC TV, 4 James H Kirkman, 5 BBC Books; p12-13 all BBC TV; p14-15: *The Independent*, 2 Bridgeman Art Library/National Museum Athens; p16-17: 3 Jim Baikie, 4 Robert Harding, 5 Bridgeman/Tate Gallery, 6 Bridgeman/ Galleria degli Uffizi, Florence; p18-19: 1-2 Nikki Wilson, 3 BBC TV, 4 BBC Books/Daniel Thistlethwaite, Middlesex Polytechnic; p20-21: 1,4 Anthony Green/Mayor Rowan Gallery, London; 2 Bridgeman/National Gallery, London, 3,5,6, BBC Books/Daniel Thistlethwaite; p22-23: 1 Sarvat Jabeen, 2 BBC TV, 3 Tate Gallery, 4 Michael Brennand-Wood, 5 Nikki Wilson; p24-25: 1 Picturepoint, 2 BBC TV, 3 Zefa, 4 Wheelwright Museum, 5 Hasse B. Gaenger; p26-27: 1 Mansell Collection, 2 James H Kirkman, 3 Victoria & Albert Museum; p28-29: 4 Bridgeman/British Museum, 5 Picturepoint; p30-31: 1 Picturepoint, 2 Zefa, 3 Alison Watt, 4-6 Bridgeman/Tate Gallery(tl), S & O Mathews (background), Zefa (b); p32-33: 1 BBC TV, 2 Index: Spain/ Bridgeman, 3 Leon Kossoff/Edward Hayward, 4 Picturepoint; p34-35: 1 Picturepoint, 2 London Features International, 3 Lee Bowery/Anthony D'Offay, London, 4 BBC TV, 5 Hulton Picture Company/Bettmann Archive; p36-37: 2 Bridgeman/Tate Gallery, 3 Stillman Drake Collection, 4 Victoria & Albert Museum, 5 Tate Gallery; p38-39: 1 Steve Bell, 2 Bridgeman, 4 Central Television plc; p40-41: 1 Picturepoint, 2 London Transport Museum; p42-43: 1 Picturepoint, 2 National Motor Museum, 3 The American Museum in Britain, 4-5 Victoria & Albert Museum, 6 Phil Gray; p44-45: 1 Next, 2-3 Din Associates, 4 BBC TV; p46-47: 1-2 Din Associates, 3 Japanese National Tourist Board, 4 Benson & Forsyth, 5 Robert Harding; p48-49 all BBC TV; p50-51: 1 BBC TV, 2-3 Din Associates; p52-53: 1 Habitat, 2 Anthony Green, 3-4 BBC Books/Daniel Thistlethwaite, 5 W Boesiger, Editions Girsberger, Zurich: Le Corbusier: Oeuvres Complets; p54-55: 1 Montage: Network, Picturepoint, Zefa, 2 Kobal Collection, 3 Joan Batten, 4 H F Marks, 5 World of Interiors/Max Forsythe; p56 Zefa; p57bl &tr Zefa, others H F Marks; p58: 2 Picturepoint, 3 British Museum; p59 background Zefa, t BBC, b Gatwick Airport; p60-61: 2 Gatwick Airport, 3 BBC TV, 4 Edward Hayward, 5 Toulouse Lautrec Museum, Albi Fabri/Bridgeman; p62-63: 1 RHM Foods Ltd, 2 Assorted Images & BBC TV (portrait of Malcolm Garrett); p64-65: 1, 3, 4, London Symphony Orchestra, 2, 5, Assorted Images; p66-67: Logos: Audi, Volkswagen, W H Smith, Opel, Halifax Building Society, Brooke Bond Tea, 4 *The Face*, 5 J Walter Thompson; p68-69: 1 Bridgeman/Museum of Modern Art, New York, 2 Bridgeman/ Tate, 3 Bridgeman, 4 Zefa; p70-71: 1-3 Andy Goldsworthy/Fabian Carlsson Gallery, London, 4 Picturepoint, 5 Hutchison Library, 6 Moy Keightley; p72-73: 1,4, BBC TV, 2 Picturepoint (Italian straw hat), Robert Harding (Elgin marble), 5 Robert Harding; p74-75: 1 Bridgeman/Christie's, London, 2 John Styles, 3-4 Robert Harding; p76-77: 1 Bridgeman/Sir John Soane Museum, London, 2 Tivi Etook/Gimpel Fils Gallery, London, 3 Zefa; p78-79: 1 Jim Baikie, 2 Rex Features, 3 H F Marks, 4 Tate Gallery; p80-81: 1 Picturepoint, 2 Bridgeman/National Trust, Anglesey Abbey, 3 Victoria & Albert Museum, 4 Bridgeman/United Grand Lodge of England, 5 Bridgeman/Imperial War Museum; p82-83: 1a British Museum, 1b Zefa, 2a Tate Gallery, 2b Bridgeman/Musee d'Orsay, Paris, 3 Victoria & Albert Museum, 4 Bridgeman, 5a Imperial War Museum, 5b D Day Museum, Portsmouth; p84-85: Oriental Museum, Durham, 2 Tate Gallery, 2a Graham Dean, 3 Guy Brett, 3a Mary Evans Picture Library, 4 Picturepoint, 5 Zefa, 5a Lesley Howling (detail); p86-87: 1 Glasgow Art Gallery, 2 Dienst Gemeentelijke Musea, Rotterdam, 3 Graham Dean, 4 Hayward Gallery, London, 5 Graves Art Gallery, Sheffield, 6 Photographie Giraudon; p88-89: 1 Anthony Green/Mayor Rowan Gallery, 2 Bridgeman/National Gallery, London, 3 Bridgeman/Tate Gallery, 4 BBC TV, 5 Bridgeman/ Phillips Collection, Washington D.C.

Front cover:
Television series logo based on electronically animated programme titles, designed by Ian Greenway at the BBC, executed by Mike McGee at the Frame Store, London, and redrawn for this book by Selwyn Hutchinson.

Picture research by Joanne King.

Foreword

Art Work arose from the BBC School Television series of the same name, first transmitted in Spring Term 1989. Although ranging wider than the series, this book's primary aim is to help teachers and students (and their families!) working on GCSE art and design syllabuses. A second broader aim is to suggest an approach to the study and practice of art and design for other people who may feel unsure of their ability to enter this world and perhaps feel a little apprehensive about it.

The main part of the book is divided into seven sections corresponding with some of the major concerns of artists and designers, beginning with a section ('Going About It') about the new thinking in the teaching of Art and Design incorporated in GCSE which has been so widely welcomed. This thinking brings together a methodical approach to practical work, and a consideration of its context in the activity of artists and designers in the real world as well as in past centuries and in non-European cultures. At the end of the main part is a section ('Where Do We Go From Here?') which suggests the importance of the imagination and inspiration in making already competent work individual and special.

Throughout these sections each double page spread is self-contained and the later ones generally contain ideas for looking, thinking and working. At the very end of the book in the final section there are some suggestions for sources of practical and inspirational new ideas ('Study').

Like the series, this book does not set out to be a textbook of techniques and materials – it isn't a 'how to' book. There are many (probably far too many) of those available already. For GCSE students the practical facilities and teaching in the vast majority of school art rooms is not just excellent, but will be geared to your own needs and circumstances. What *is* new in GCSE, and what this book and the *Art Work* television series set out to provide, is the setting of this work in context through observation, thinking and recording of the wider worlds of art and design.

Edward Hayward
London, 1990

GOING ABOUT IT

Ideas and Planning

How do you start? First of all, don't panic! It is far better to take things step by step. Decide on your subject then on the medium you want to use – have you got what you need? If not, what will it cost you? If it turns out to be too expensive look around you and see if there's another solution using another method or medium.

Think what you'd like to achieve, but if you don't feel inspired just relax. Examine the tools and materials around you and recall what has attracted your attention recently. Look at magazines, newspapers and books, particularly art books, and concentrate on views – in the studio, outside it, of the people and objects around you. Examine things close to you in great detail and also consider how distance affects objects. Try to look methodically and observe shapes, colours, textures and patterns. Something will catch your eye and with thought it may well be the start of an idea. From then on, whether it seems promising or if you reject it at once, you have started making decisions and fixing limits.

Experienced artists and designers make shorthand notes – written and pictorial. They scribble down descriptions and sketches of anything that interests them – often no more than doodles, sometimes collected into scrapbooks including photographs, cuttings and all sorts of visual material. Another idea is to have miniature 'art galleries' on the bedroom or studio wall, which can include postcards, cuttings and fragments of your own work. This is nourishment for the eye and the brain, and many artists and designers may browse over their 'galleries' and scrapbooks for years before one idea takes its proper place in their work.

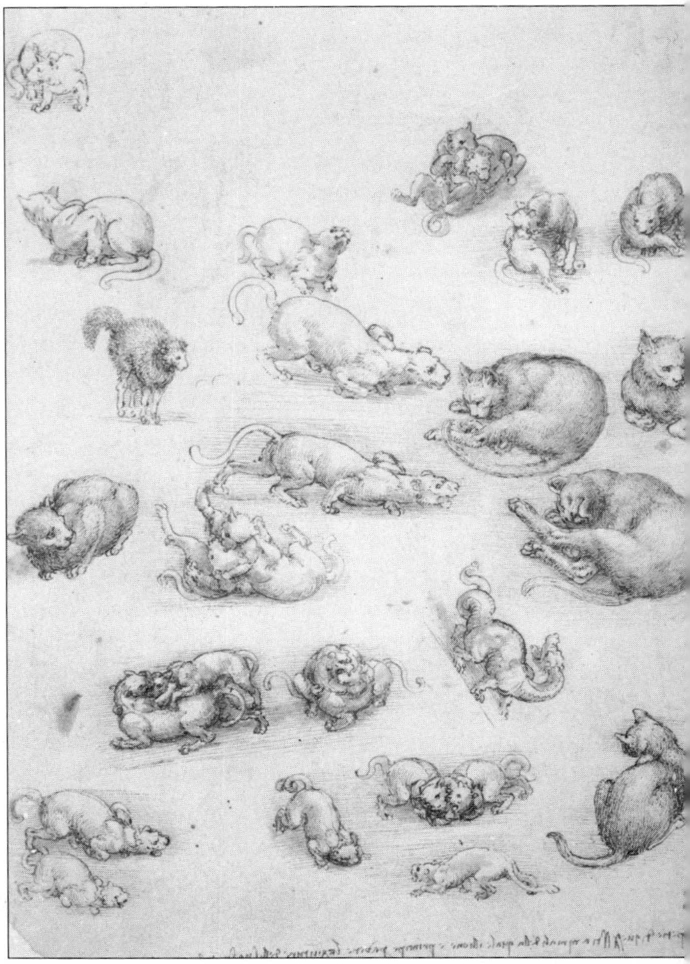

1-2

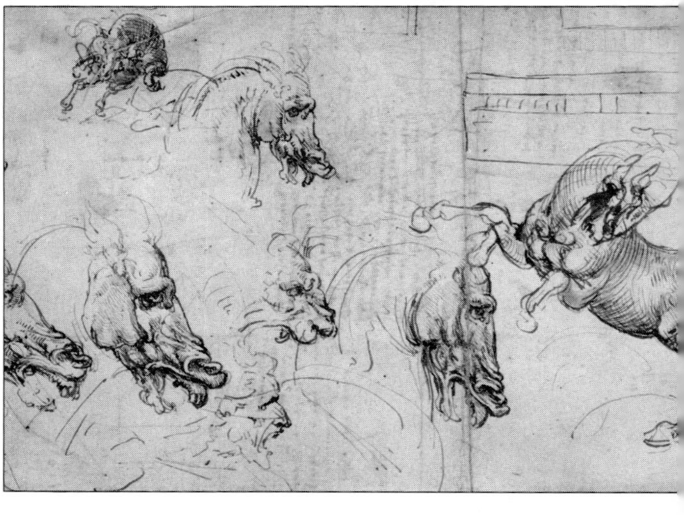

1-2
Pages from the notebooks of Leonardo da Vinci (1452–1519) showing mainly cats (which will often stay still enough for you to study and draw them in a variety of poses). Leonardo's looking and drawing seem to have helped his imagination too. The cats here have led to lions and even a dragon.

3-7
Pages from the scrapbooks of sculptor Ann Carrington.

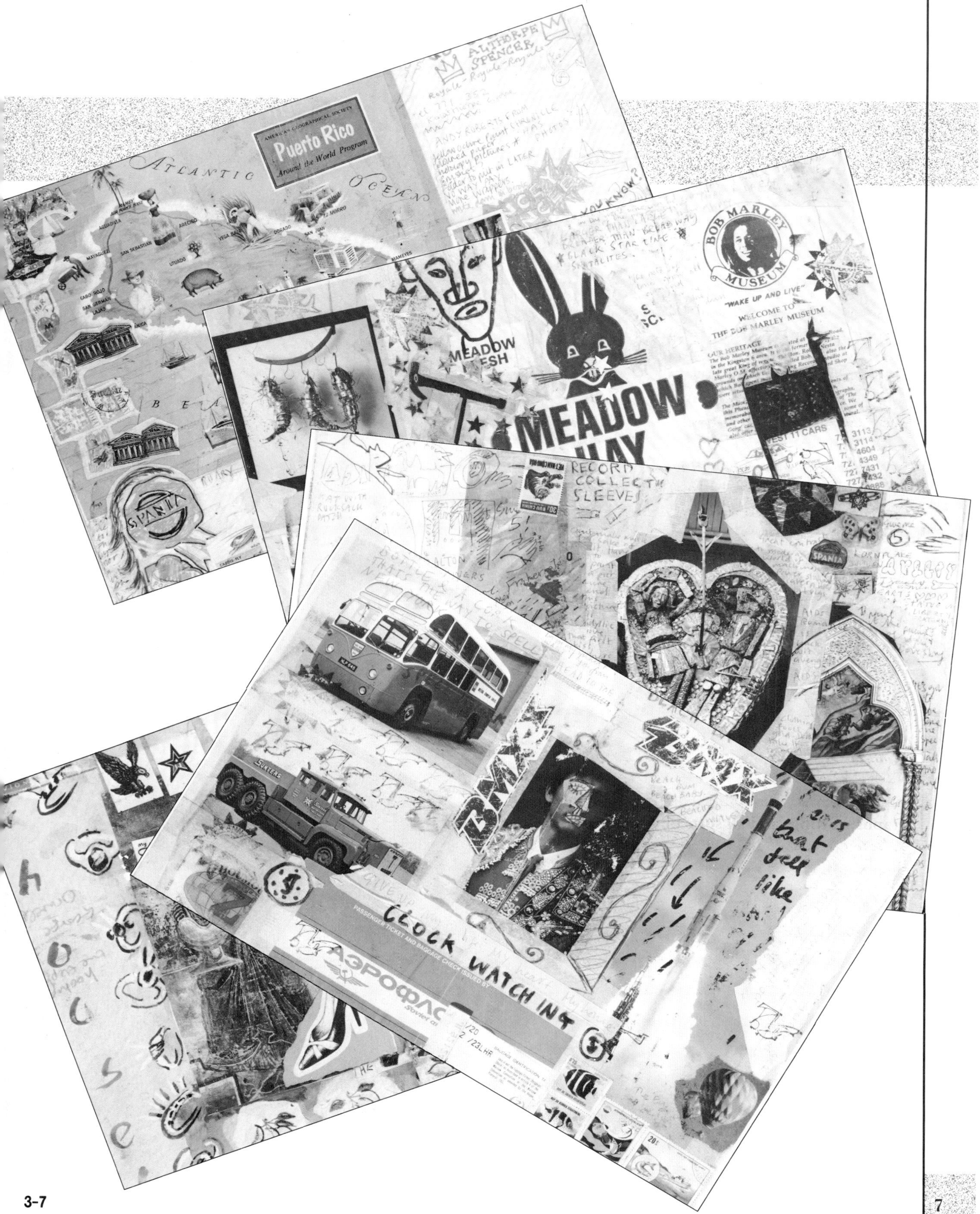
AMERICAN GEOGRAPHICAL SOCIETY
Puerto Rico
Around the World Program
ATLANTIC
OCEANO
ALTHORPE SPENCER
BOB MARLEY MUSEUM
"WAKE UP AND LIVE"
WELCOME TO THE BOB MARLEY MUSEUM
OUR HERITAGE
MEADOW FRESH
MEADOW WAY
RECORD COLLECTN SLEEVES
SPANIA
CLOCK WATCHING
PASSENGER TICKET AND BAGGAGE CHECK ISSUED BY
АЭРОФЛОТ

3-7

GOING ABOUT IT

Experiment and Research

Sketchbooks and scrapbooks aren't just archives. Try describing how a bicycle works. Sooner rather than later you're likely to need a visual aid, such as a mime or a drawn diagram. That diagram, if it's to be useful, has to be honest. Before you can make your diagram you need to know for certain how each piece joins together and how the moving parts move on each other in a way that takes you well beyond your previous knowledge of the theory. A drawing is a form of research, and also a form of experiment. If a thing is drawn right, it should look right.

As you proceed with research on your project you'll try out details, try to get certain colour effects and learn the possibilities of materials as well as the tools available. Gradually you'll build up a scrapbook of ideas around the subject of your work. You'll learn what will or won't work, in which circumstances, and where there are alternatives. Keeping a record of your research and experiments means that you will always have something to fall back on if inspiration falters later.

Of course, a few people say that for them inspiration is the thing. If you are sure this is true for you there's no point in wasting time on the early stages, but that isn't an excuse to be lazy. If anything you need to work even harder to prove yourself!

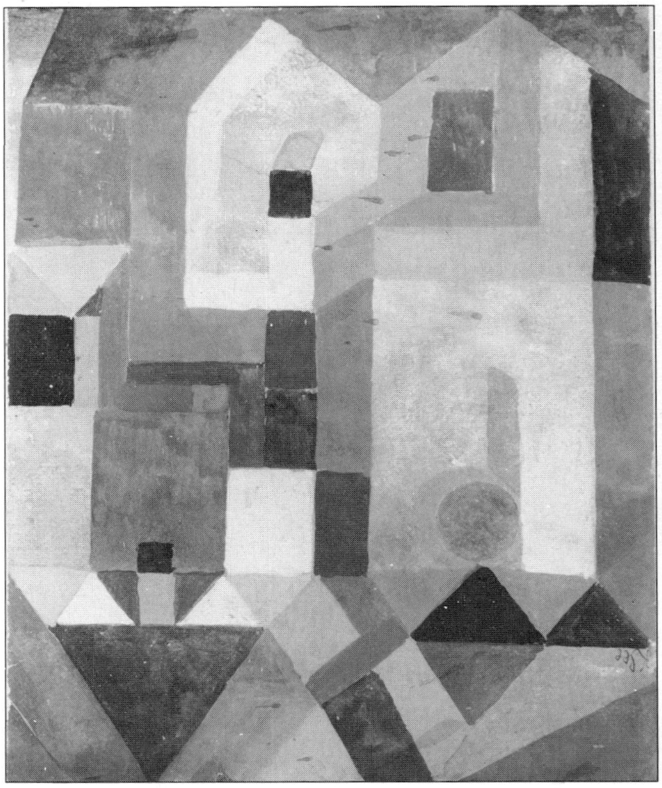

1△

2▽

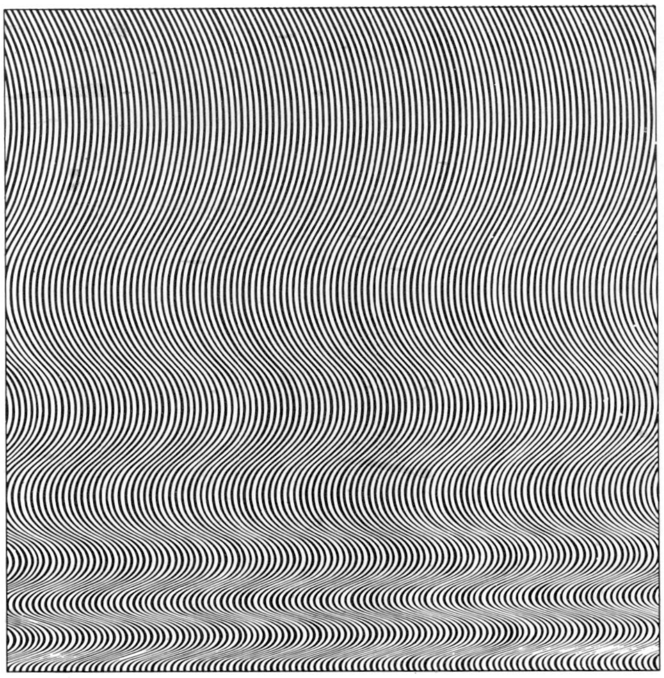

1
'Colorful Architecture', 1917. The Swiss painter Paul Klee believed in freshness and spontaneity. His finished pictures were experiments, particularly in the way he used colours which, when placed next to each other in different ways, made different compositions and evoked different moods.

2
Op (optical) art exploited the effect on the eye of contrasting tones. The contrasts in this Bridget Riley work seem to make the whole picture move.

3
'The Wrestlers', a Third Century BC Greek sculpture with a very ingenious design. But is the sculptor just trying too hard? What do you think of the finished result?

4
Student fashion designer Clive Smith's degree exam work. These designs are an important part of the examined work and are helpful right through the making of the finished garments as well.

5
In Leonardo's time it was forbidden to cut up human bodies to see how they worked, but without a knowledge of anatomy few artists can paint a convincing human figure. Some of his 'research' is genuine, but some had to remain guesswork. Can you find out which is which?

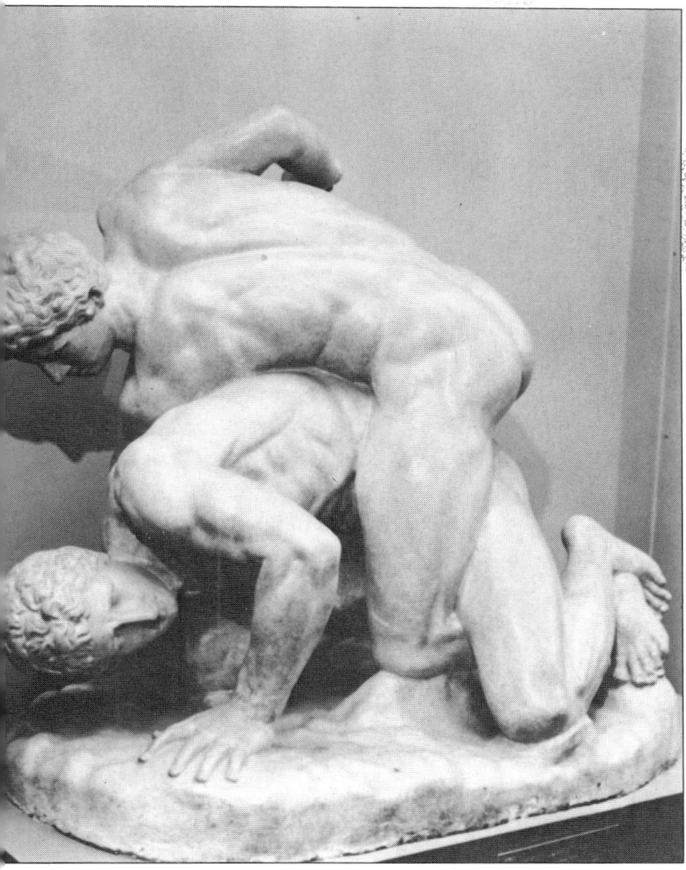

3△

4▽

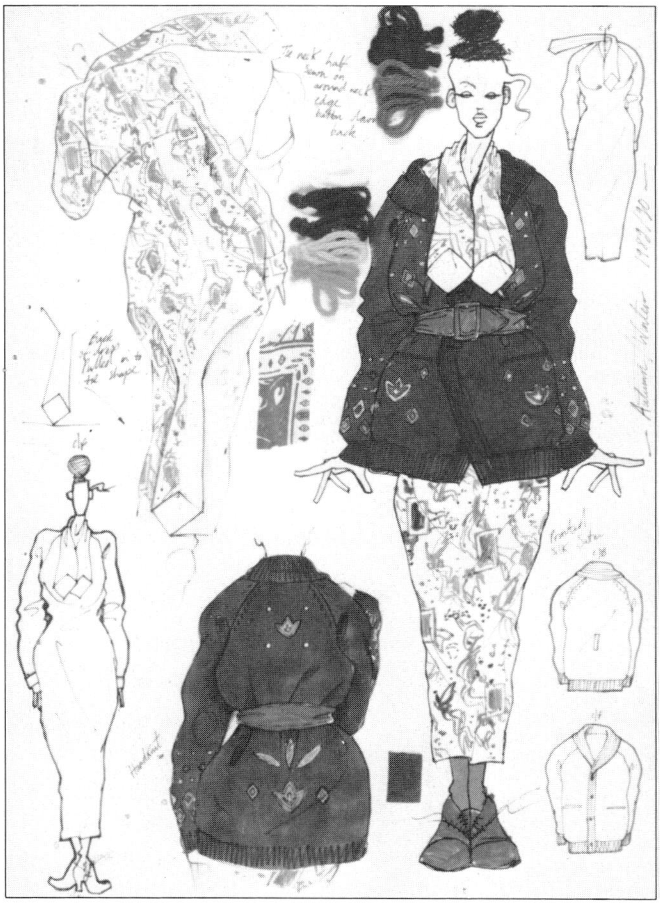

5

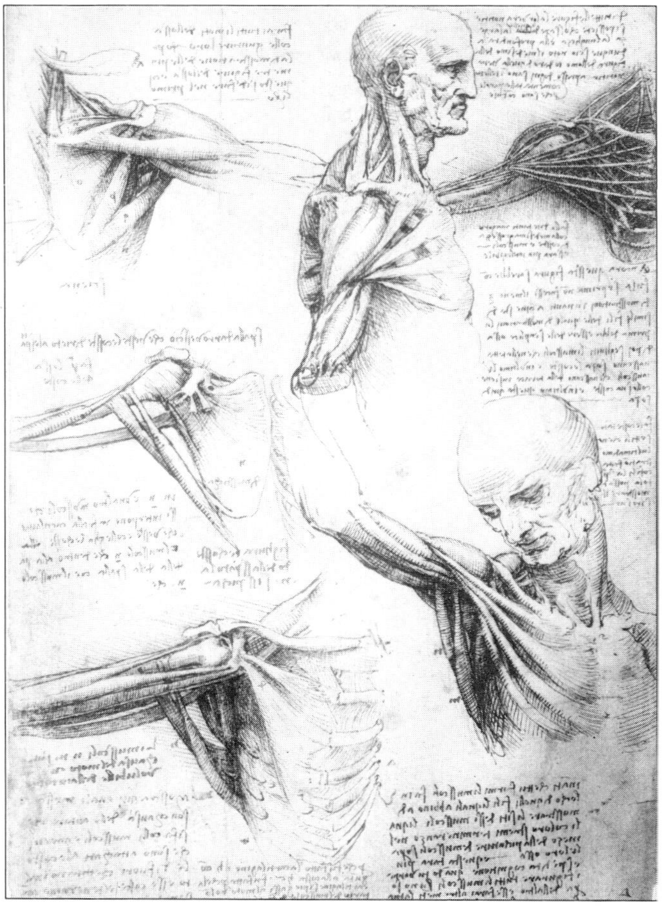

GOING ABOUT IT

Finishing the Work

For most people the 'finishing' stage is the most satisfying. Many artists have a strong practical side and relish working with their hands. Indeed, part of the attraction of the finished work for the viewer and artist is the texture of the paint or the clay, the excitement of seeing one wet colour mixed with another on the surface or seeing patterns on fabric with the tiny irregularities which show they were made by an artist and not a machine. The thinking, research, preparation, planning and experiment stages ought not to rule out late changes. They should just make it easier to understand why something isn't working and what could be done to put it right.

So, for even the smallest project it's useful to plan your resources and the time available to you. The lion's share, perhaps two thirds of the time, has to go into the finished work. But some preparation is rarely wasted. Remember too that certain processes, like the drying of paint, ink and clay take a fixed time – they can't be rushed and must be calculated for.

If you have planned your time and resources well, you will be able to finish the work in time and on budget. But there are two further stages to bear in mind. It would be unfair to show off anything without proper display. Do the best you can to present the final work clean, properly mounted and lit, against an appropriate background. If preliminary work is important, try to find space for that too. Finally, invite people to view and comment on the understanding that you will do the same for them. It's usually possible to find constructive words – kind words which will help improve the performance of any artist or designer the next time round. But if you've approached your work methodically, seriously and honestly, it's almost certain there will be good and positive things to say even about something that doesn't entirely work.

1

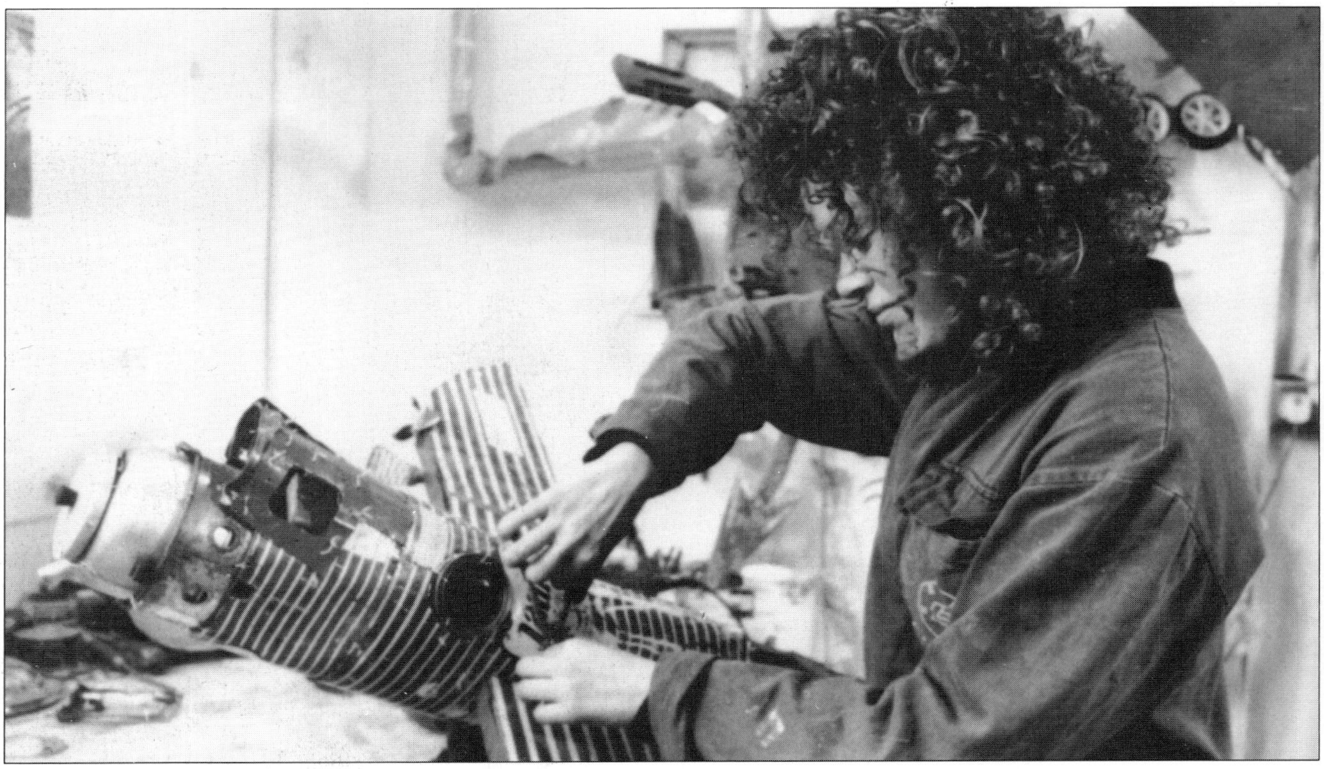

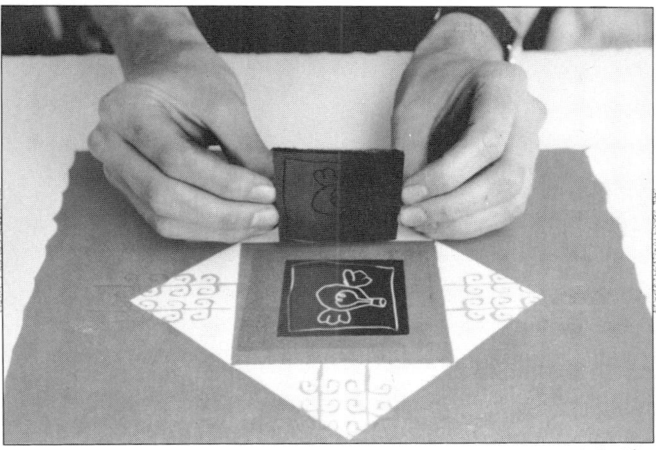

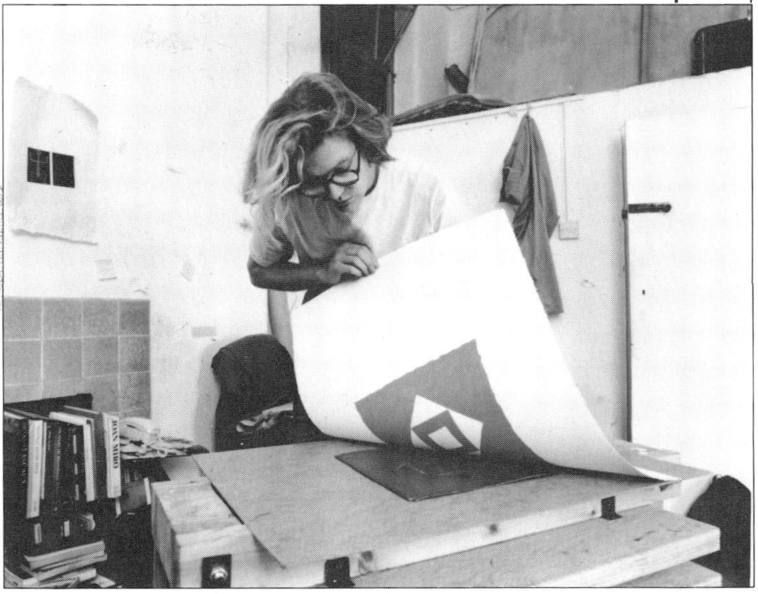

△2-3▷

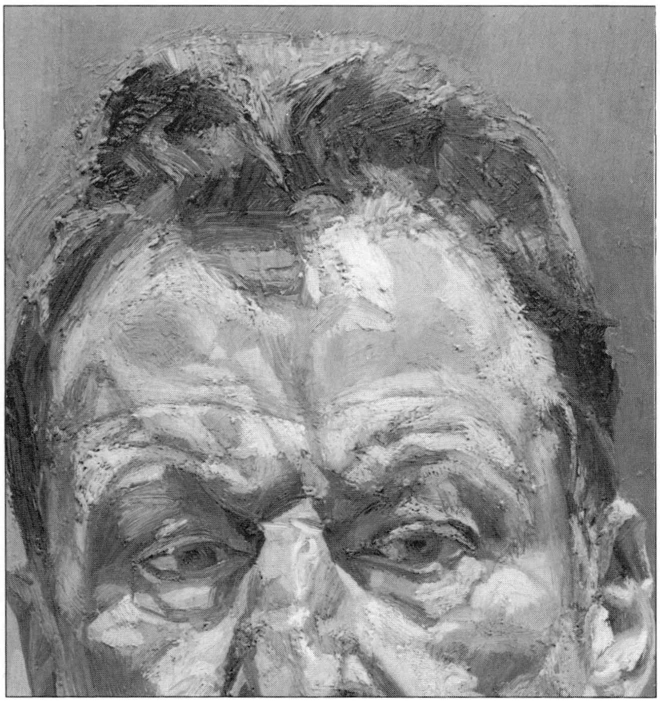

4△

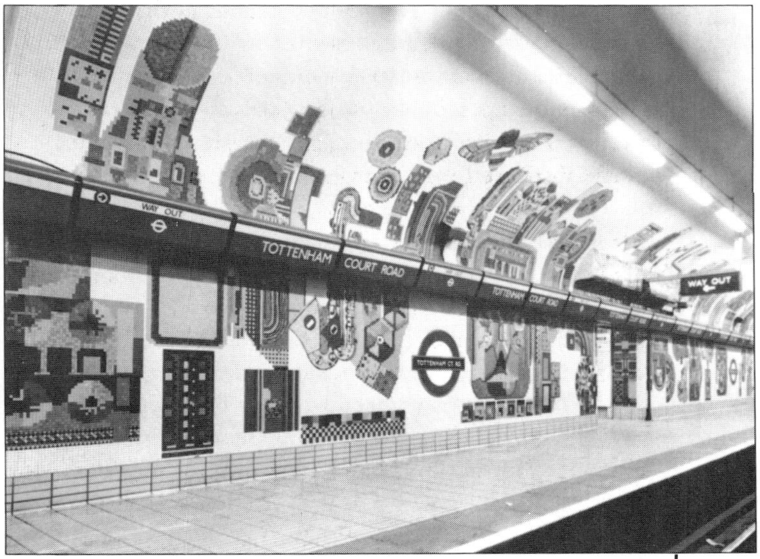

5△

6▽

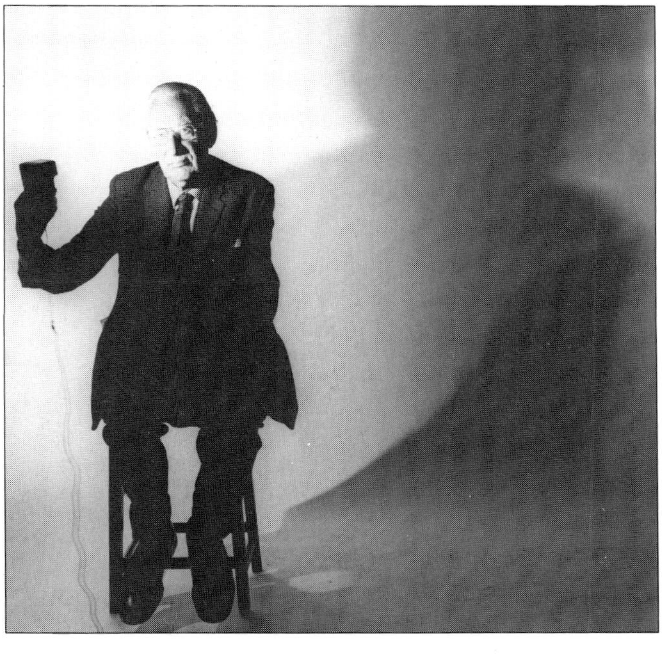

1

Ann Carrington is working on a sculpture of a plane made from the rubbish of our consumer society.

2-3

Dale Devereaux Barker makes printed collages: that means in part he chooses the elements of each composition, and the ink colours he uses, as he goes along.

4

The paint surface on this Lucien Freud has an exciting look to it – you almost feel you want to reach out and touch.

5

Eduardo Paolozzi designed the mosaic decoration for this London Underground station. Colours, shapes and details are all brilliantly eye-catching and shout the excitement of the designer at work.

6

'Bill', one of the participants at a workshop held by portrait photographer Liam Woon at the National Portrait Gallery, London, Summer 1988. Liam Woon often uses backgrounds to say something about his subjects.

GCSE: A Teacher's View

The teaching of art and design aims to establish visual literacy achieved by formal understanding, practical experience and intellectual consideration at all levels and abilities. Fundamental processes involved should include research, observation, analysis, design, organisation and development but not necessarily in a 'linear' or formal method. Opportunities must be provided for instinct, insight and inspired visual concepts. Art and design subsumes a wide range of human enterprise. It may mean working in one or more of many materials or techniques – painting, drawing, printmaking, ceramics, textiles for example; it may be an activity inwardly motivated or externally stimulated by the need to solve problems. It may be practical, making something new or original or it may be contemplative, enjoying what already exists through individual and group activity. It is not necessarily age/skill related.

At GCSE level, pupils may embark on courses selected by the centre, according to available resources, from the syllabus outline distributed by each examination board. In support of GCSE principles – i.e. 'Candidates should be given the opportunity to show what they know, understand and can do' – the available courses would have common assessment objectives, and more specific content instructions according to the nature of the course. Art and Design Unendorsed is intended for those candidates following a broad course, the emphasis which is not determined by specific design based, material based or technique based considerations. Endorsed courses would include any of the following – Drawing and Painting, Graphics, Textiles, 3D Studies and Photography.

There is no model or prescribed programme of activities within any of the available Art and Design courses and centres are encouraged to advise and direct pupils towards courses that encourage a depth and breadth of experience appropriate to the needs of each individual. Each centre is able to compose its own course outline and emphasise the priority of the assessment objectives.

Assessment Objectives

(The assessment objectives are not listed in order of importance.)

Candidates will be expected to demonstrate the ability to:

1 show a personal and authentic response to a stimulus, e.g. an idea, theme or subject;

2 record from direct observation and personal experience:

3 sustain a chosen study from conception to realisation:

4 work independently in realising their intentions:

5 analyse an idea, theme, subject or concept and to select, research and communicate relevant information and to make and evaluate in a continuum;

6 select and control materials and processes in a systematic and disciplined way (taking account of considerations of costs as appropriate);

7 synthesise an idea, impulse and feeling with materials, techniques and processes;

8 use and compose visual elements, e.g. line, tone, colour, pattern, texture, shape, form, space;

9 make informed responses to contemporary and historical art and design through an awareness of artistic qualities, an analysis and evaluation of design, and the forming and expressing of judgements.

Extract from the N.E.A. Syllabus, 1989

Objective 9 relates directly to critical and contextual study. This is an essential course element although its form may be varied according to the centre's objective priority and activities. The intentions of elaborating this objective within the diversity of art and design courses is to encourage an interaction between the experience of the artists' or designers' work and the candidates' own artistic sensibilities which may lead to direct positive influences and an extension of personal awareness.

Art projects should be accessible to a wider range of pupils, becoming more sequential and coherent. Pupils should be able to see their work in relation to that of others instead of in isolation and through realising the arts as an integral and essential part of life develop that essential awareness and sensitivity to the world around them.

Art and Design can be seen as worth studying and practising because it is one of those activities by which we seek to widen our horizons and enrich our lives. Visual education provides the basis of standards rather than the imposition of predetermined standards of good taste.

The breaking down of unreal mental barriers, avoiding the restrictive practices of isolated disciplines and the artificial barriers between subjects, prepares a student to cope more effectively with the complexity of modern life.

The implication is that students will want more and more, to have everything subjectively orientated on a 'personal centre'. It is the role of reducation to develop strengths and involve the individual, so he/she can contribute to society and the environment rather than be a complaisant and apathetic victim.

Frank Barnes
Arts Co-ordinator (Abraham Guest High School, Orrell, Wigan)
N.E.A. Moderator in Art and Design

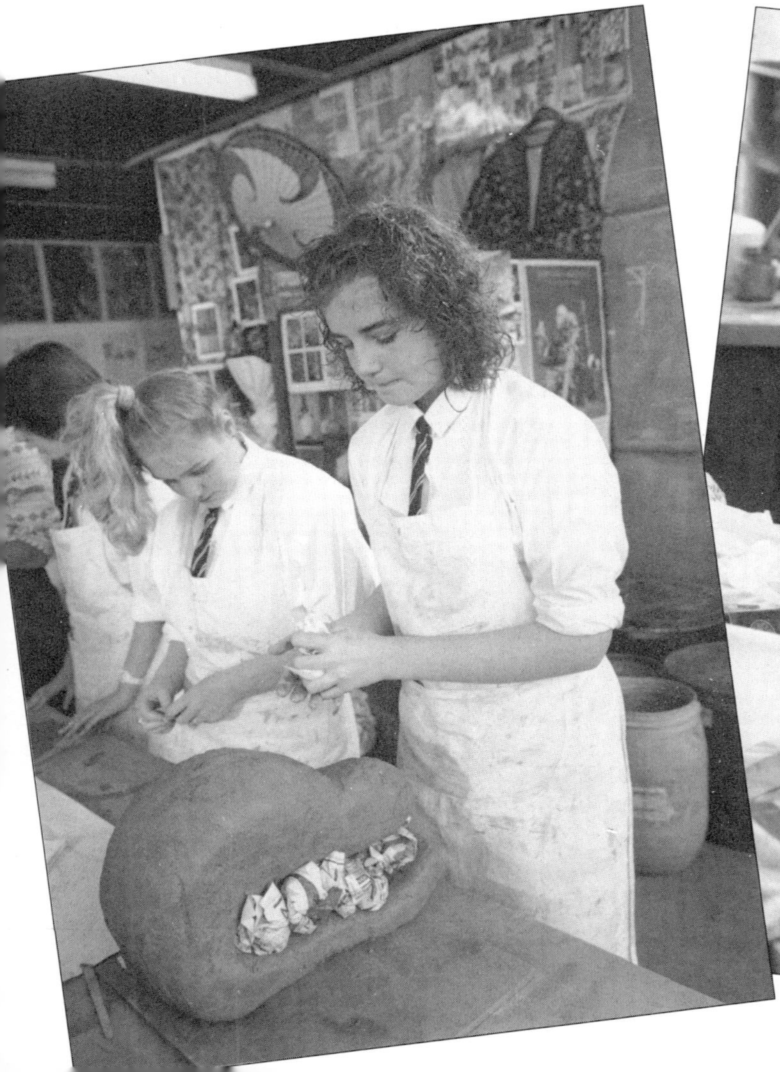

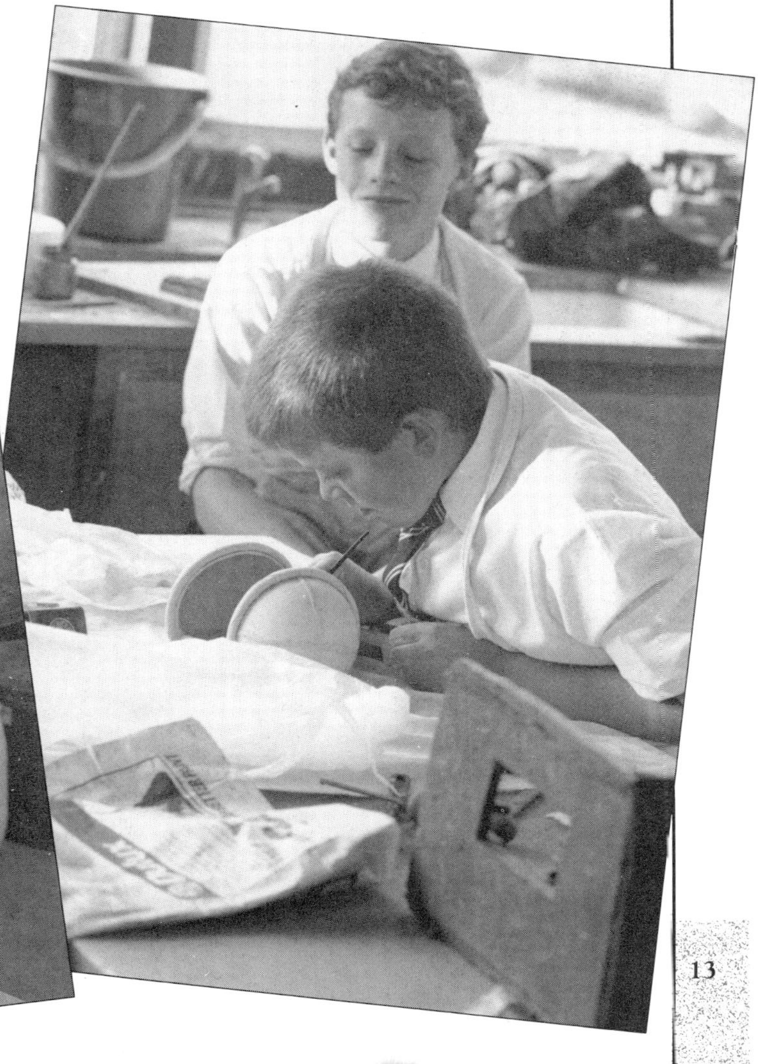

SEEING AND BELIEVING

Dear Sir,

Andrew Graham-Dixon has reflected on the problems undertaken by judging panels for art awards (4 October).

If we agree that there are only five elements in visual composition - form, colour, line, tone and texture - the greatest artists must be those who make the most use of these in their choice of medium, and who bring the most truth, imagination, variety and unity to visual completeness in an expression of universal appeal.

While judges need to employ a sensitivity equal to the best in the work they judge, they face three important questions. First, how closely is it possible to assess whether the final visual expression matches the artists' original conception; second how clearly is it expressed; and third, how deep is the quality of its expression?

Finding an answer to these questions tests the ability of the judges to distinguish an artist's integrity from the affectations and pretensions so often masquerading as the genuine article.

Yours faithfully,

JOY STANLEY RICKETTS

Honiton, Devon

1

What is Art?

People often get worried and angry about art. They may see it as a useless extra appealing mainly to affected highbrows or millionaires. Yet there is scarcely a group of humans, across the world and all the thousands of years of our existence, which has managed without it. Art is one of those things which distinguishes humans from animals. For humans the world of ideas is very important and art can put those ideas over in a way others can understand, usually much better and quicker than by spoken or written words. So a work of art may be about what is beautiful or ugly or about how we should view our world. It may be about life and death or what we are on earth to be or to do. It may help us to look at the deeds or personalities of others and perhaps learn from them. It may try to create a mood, a mood artists know most humans experience, so that viewers can explore their state of mind and learn about themselves.

Artists get through to us by way of the senses, and particularly sight. In almost everything we do we take in a picture and then work out in our minds what we think it means. Our senses and our brain work together to weigh up evidence and come almost instantly to a conclusion, but most of the evidence comes from seeing. An artist tries to present us with the right visual evidence to communicate his or her ideas, in the most persuasive way. 'Art' isn't necessarily the same thing as 'beauty', though a pleasing set of shapes, colours, patterns and textures may be the best way of communicating with the viewer. But artists may want to use their shapes, colours, patterns and textures to make us feel uneasy, overwhelmed, scared, angry, mystified or just to make us laugh. But the ultimate objective is to make us *think*.

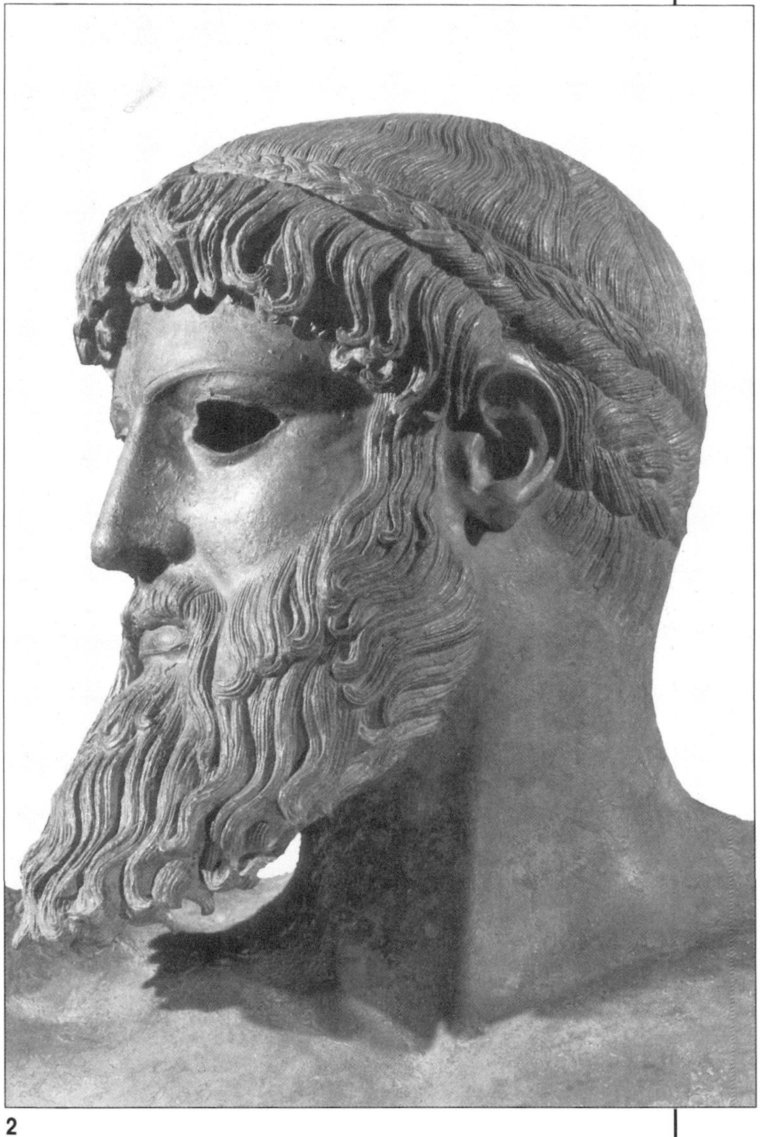

2

1
From the *Independent*, 1988. Do you think this is a good definition of art?

2
Zeus statue, Ancient Greece. What feeling does this give you? Consider the material the artist used. What does it add to the effect? Who was Zeus?

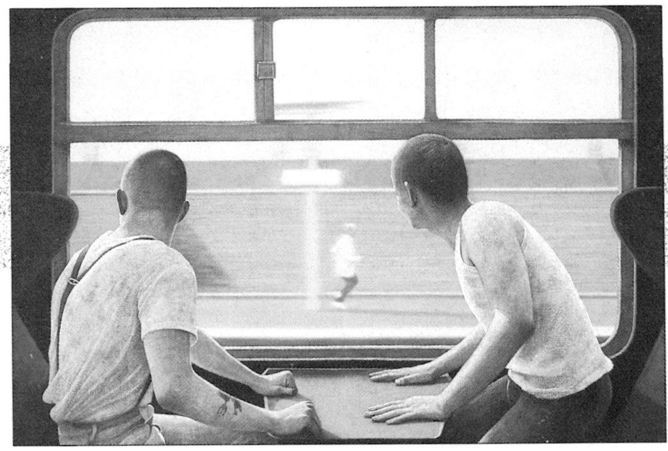

3

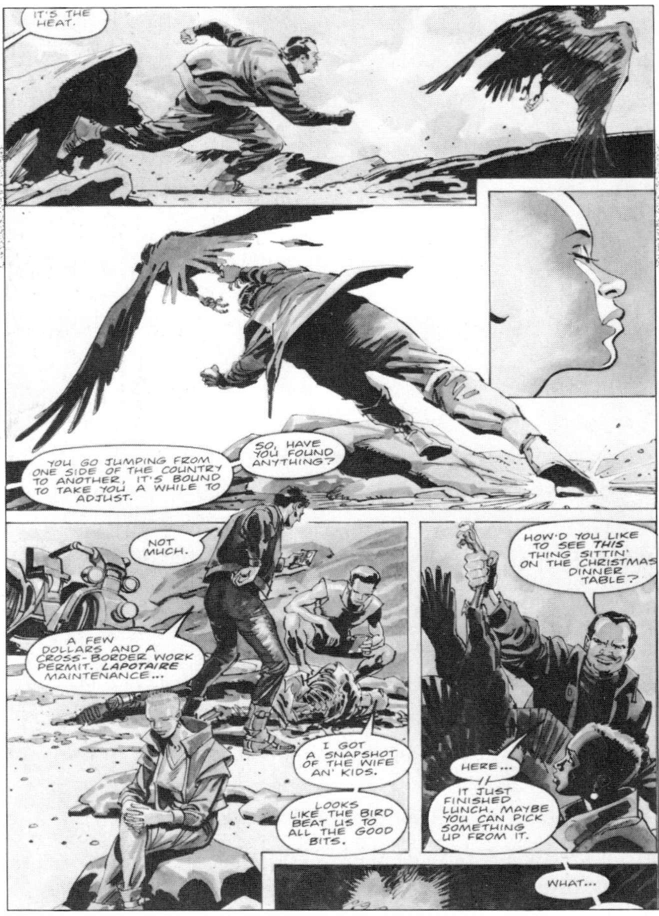

4

3
'Compartments' by Graham Dean. Something has happened here, just out of the picture frame, the edge of the painted story. You couldn't call this 'beautiful'. So what does it set out to do? What's the story? How does the painting achieve it?

4
Comic art by Jim Baikie.

5
Street art.

5▽

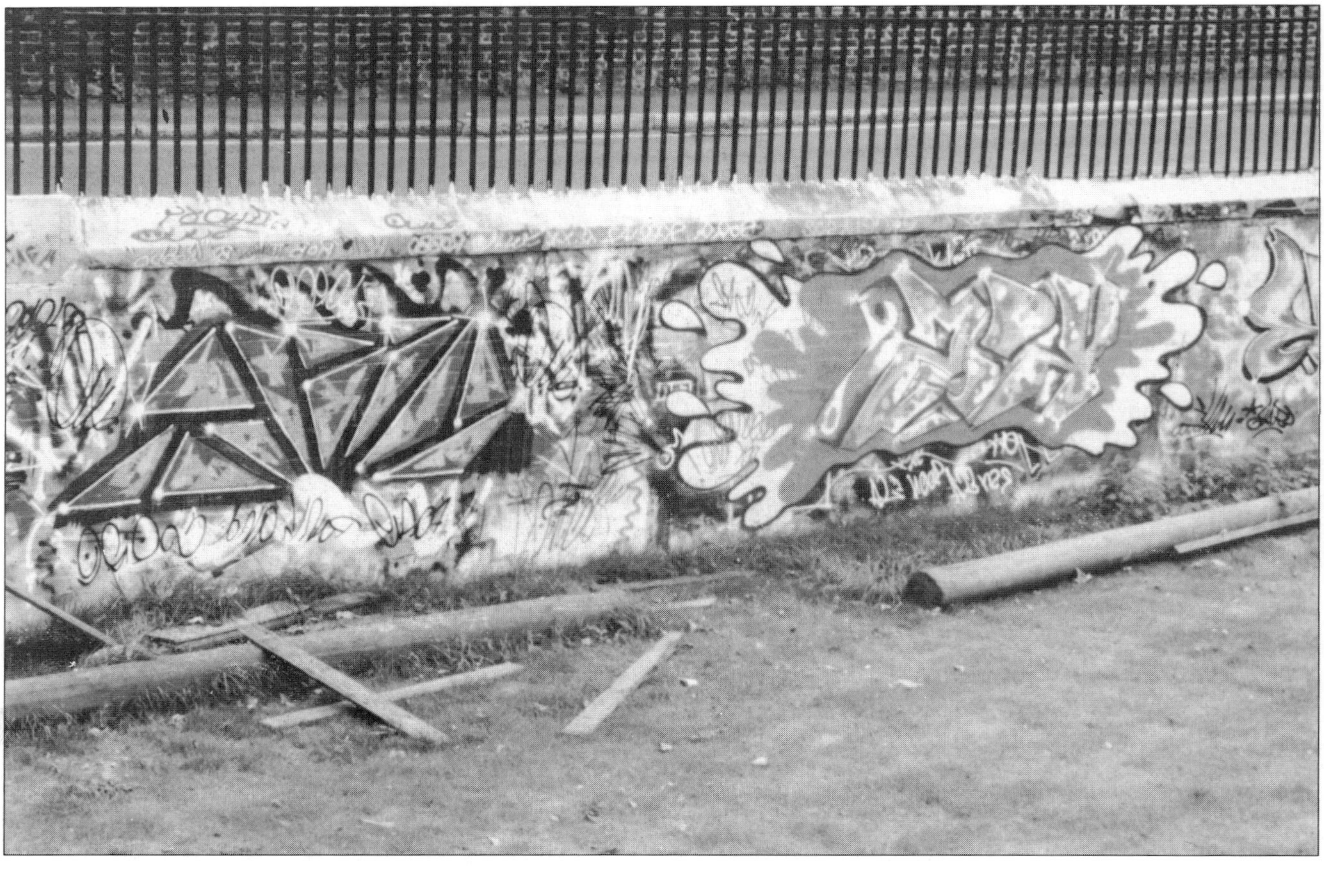

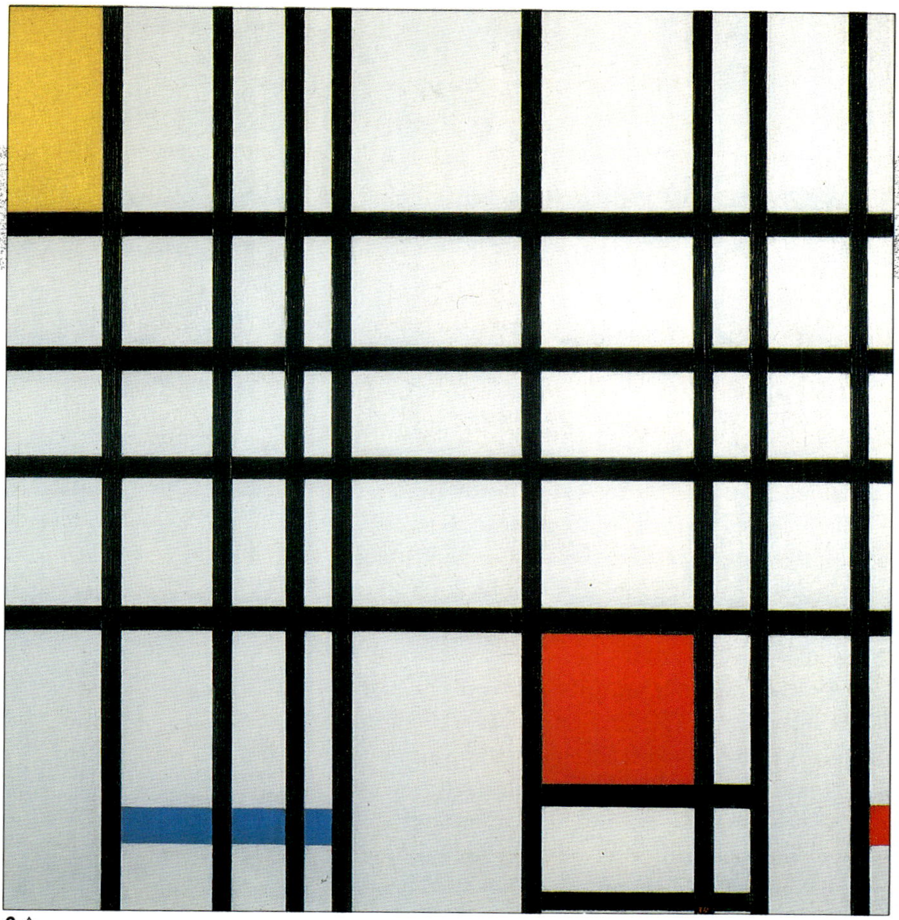

6△

6
'Composition with Red, Yellow and Blue' by Piet Mondrian, 1937.

7
'The Annunciation' by Simone Martini, 1333. Many painters have taken on this scene, which only some Christians would believe actually happened. So what is the artist trying to get across and how does he use his materials to achieve it?

7▽

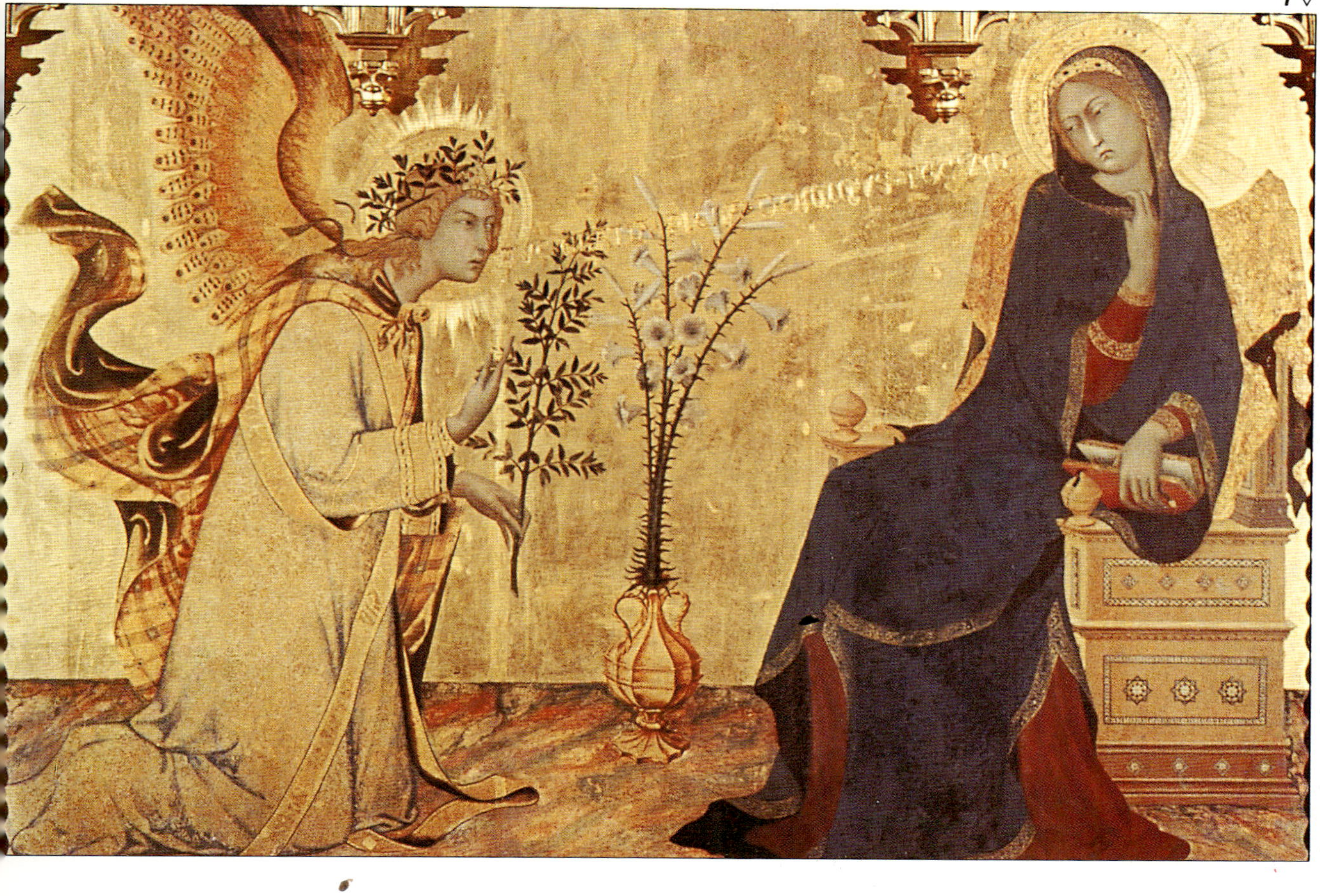

Art at Work

Artists and designers are at work everywhere in our world, so it's important for almost any activity to use our eyes carefully and intelligently. Colours are often used to mean things – red for danger, green for safety and so on. It's often quicker and easier to read colours than words for information. But it's important to recognise that colours can be used dishonestly – that picture on the biscuit package makes them look tempting, but is that because the golden colour has been deliberately exaggerated?

Nikki Wilson is an artist who was brought up and still lives in Wigan. She works with patterns and shapes and her work often takes the form of painted pottery. Her influences come from what she has seen herself here and abroad and what she sees in magazines and books. So her ideas come from her own environment and what she chooses from it, but as well as that she also feeds ideas back into it for others to draw on. Both these activities are important to her development as an artist.

Like many artists she can't make a living from selling her work alone: she has a part-time job as artist in residence at local schools. She isn't a teacher because she doesn't *tell* people what to do and how to do it. But in the course of her work she has found certain things that work or don't work for her. She can talk these choices and experiences over with students as they work, helping them to sort out their ideas and the best way to get them across. In return she gathers ideas for herself, because everyone's experience of seeing is different and everyone's ideas are valuable.

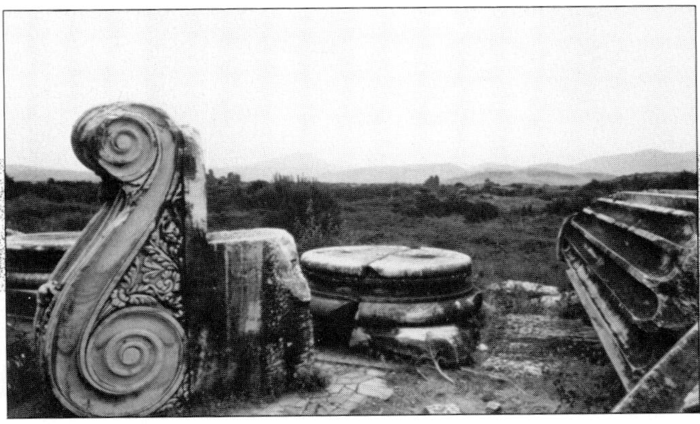

1

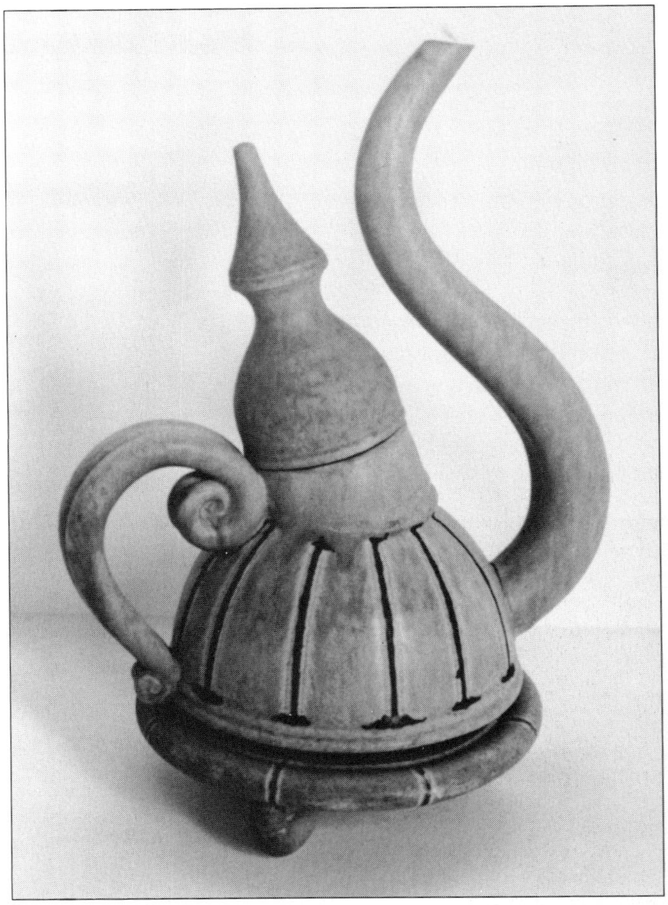

2△

3▽

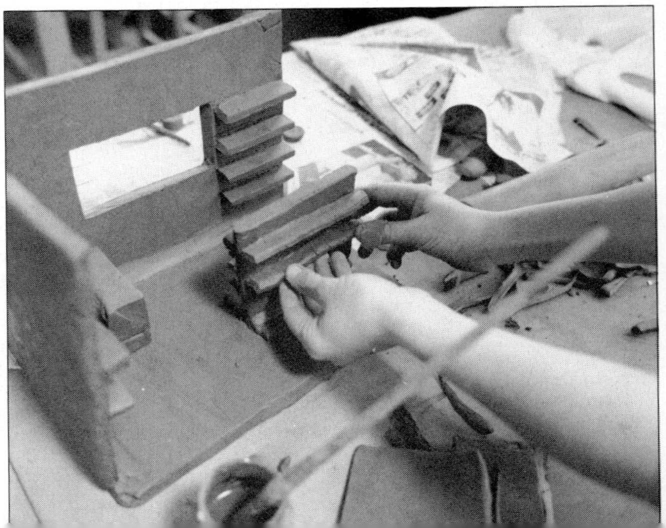

1
Nikki Wilson is fascinated by the scenery and culture of Turkey. These are part of the ruins of the ancient city of Ephesus.

2
Teapot (clay) by Nikki Wilson, 1987. Nikki's work displays the same curves and patterns as the Ephesus stonework. The teapot design is characteristic of modern Turkey too.

3
Nikki has experience of handling delicate pieces of soft clay, which can easily become misshapen and messy.

4
The Video Paintbox operator holds an electronic pen to select and 'redraw' items from the menu. The selected image can be treated in a number of ways – for instance a 'hole' could be made and filled with some other pictures or certain colours could be changed, depending on the size and sophistication of the machinery.

5
Computer art from a student at Middlesex Polytechnic.

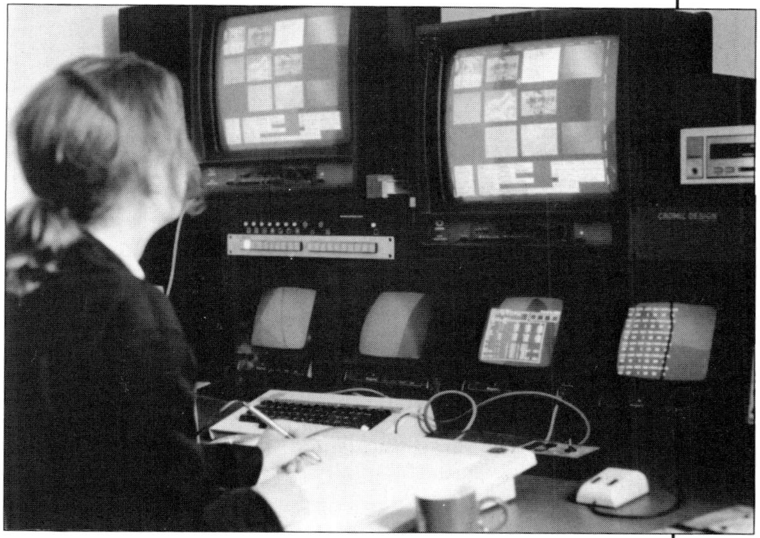

4

5▽

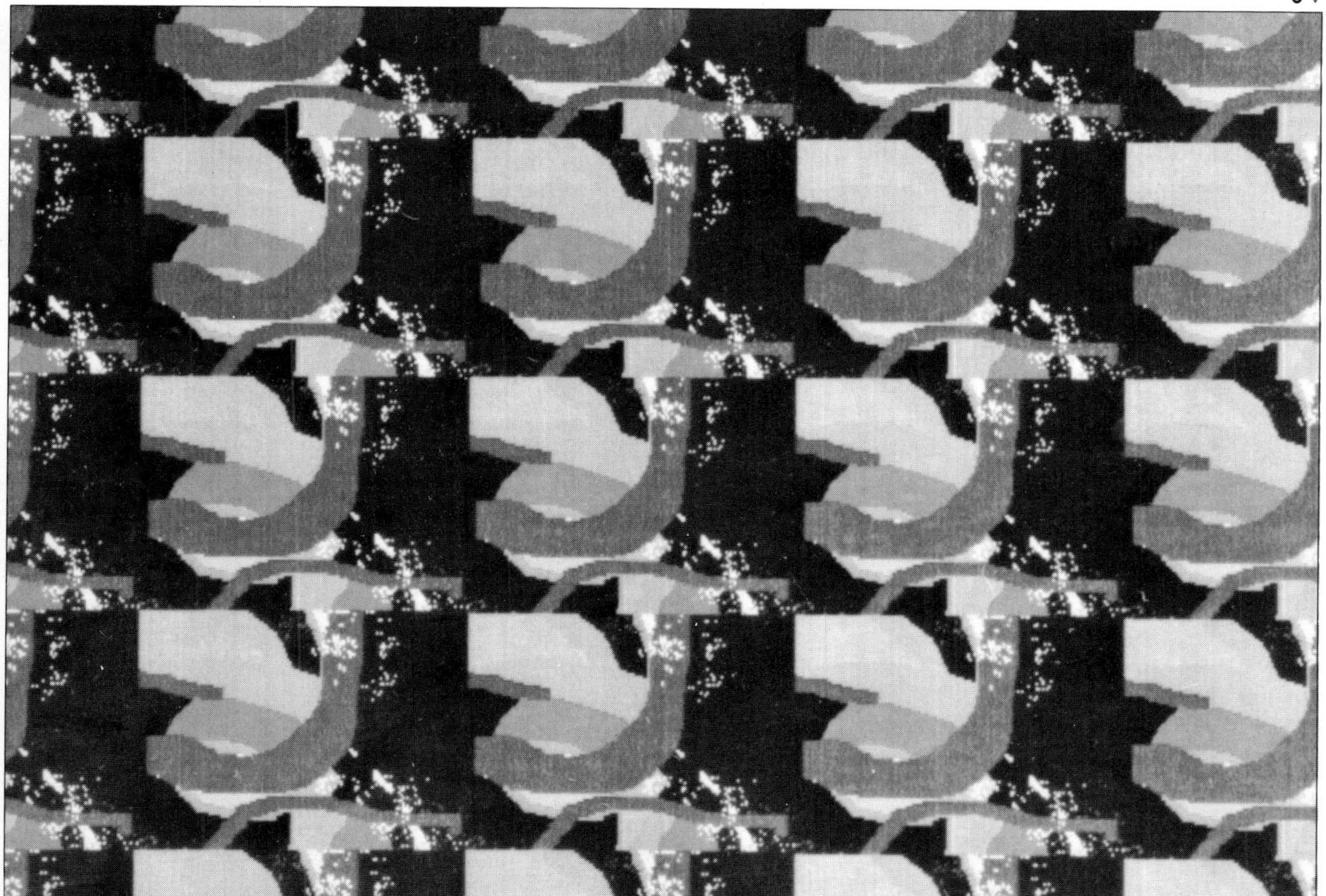

A Painter at Work

Anthony Green is a successful painter, one of the few in Britain who can make a living entirely from their art. The subject of his pictures is almost entirely himself, although he doesn't paint straightforward self-portraits. Usually they are about his wife, his children and his mother. Anthony Green was brought up in Highgate, North London, and he still lives in the same flat there. He went to art school in London, and apart from short periods away he has lived surrounded by the same, familiar things. This environment is very important to him as a painter. It includes not just his family and the family home, but his part of London and the atmosphere and people there.

Like anyone else with their eyes open he absorbed the colours, shapes and patterns surrounding him, especially the art he knew best which he found in the paintings and sculptures in London galleries and other public buildings. All these influences crop up in his work, as well as ideas and things unique to him as an individual. He has always been keen on racing cars and racing bikes. He also enjoys food, especially French food, which isn't a surprise when you discover that his mother's family are French and that his mother's father worked as a chef in a big London hotel. In many ways all these parts of his life have shaped him and the pictures he paints.

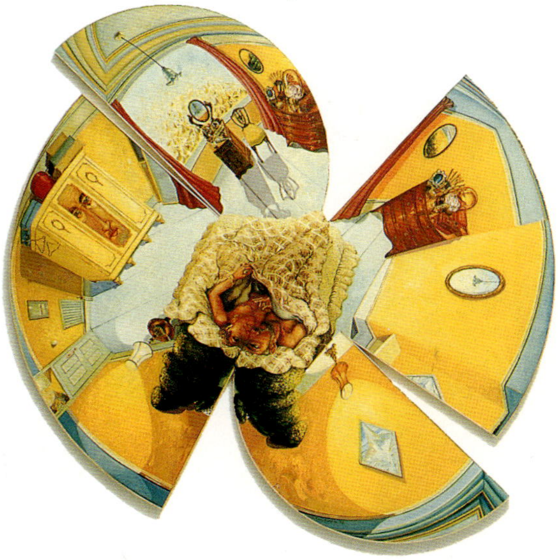

1

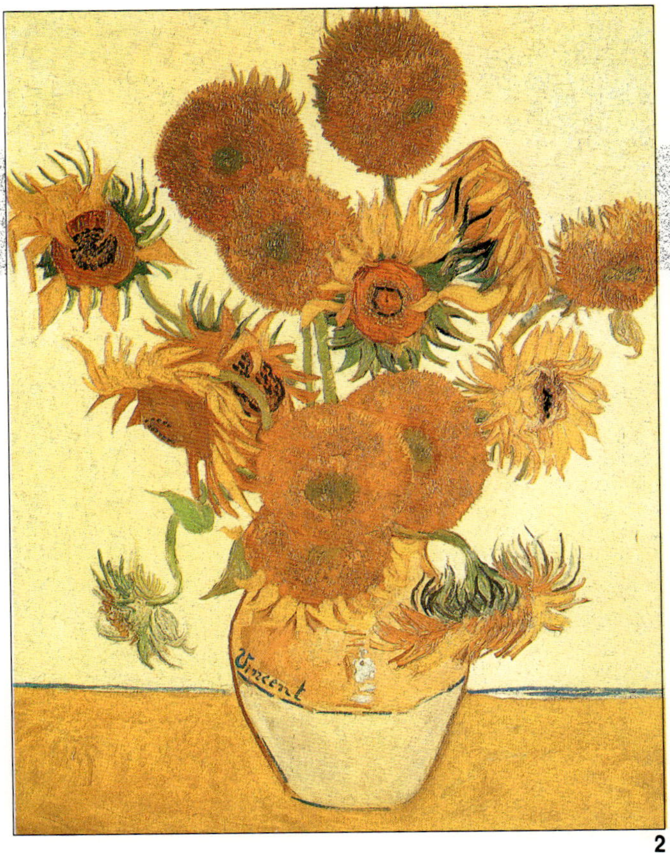

2

1
'Paradise' by Anthony Green, 1988. Anthony Green is in bed with his wife. Many of his paintings have unconventional shapes: 'I've never had a square-shaped thought in my life,' he says.

2
'Sunflowers' by Van Gogh, 1888 (National Gallery, London)
This was one of art student Anthony Green's favourite paintings. He is still very fond of painting flowers, and of using the golden tones and thick brush strokes of Van Gogh.

3
Anthony Green at work. He describes his work as 'a million tiny decisions', relating each mark to all the others and constantly reviewing the total effect.

4
'La France au 14 Lissenden Mansions 1944–5' by Anthony Green. Almost all Green's work concerns his own life, centred on the London block of flats where he grew up and still lives. French relatives stayed here during the Second World War, and he still treasures the officer's kepi, belonging to the brother of an uncle, shown here. This work shows his love of bright colours and patterns, and story telling.

5–6
An artist's visual ideas can come from many different places. Anthony Green shares his studio with many objects, including this Indian carving and this nineteenth-century European clock. Can you see how they are echoed in his work?

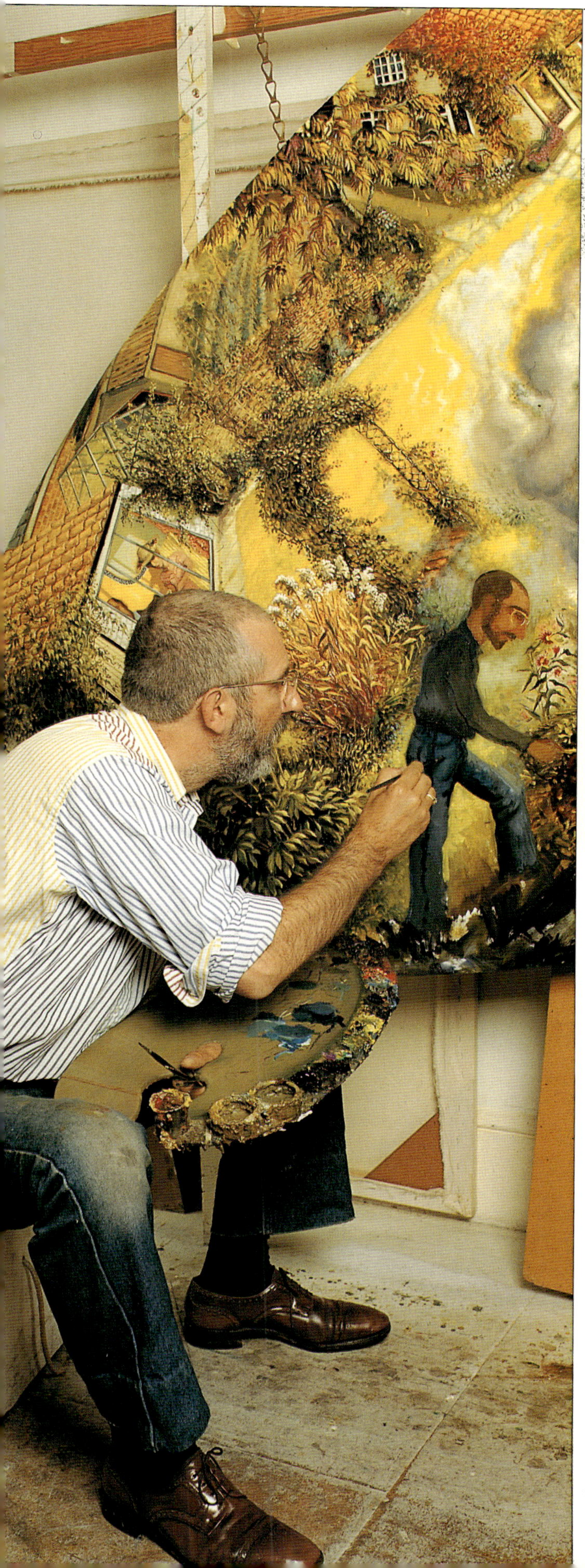

◁3

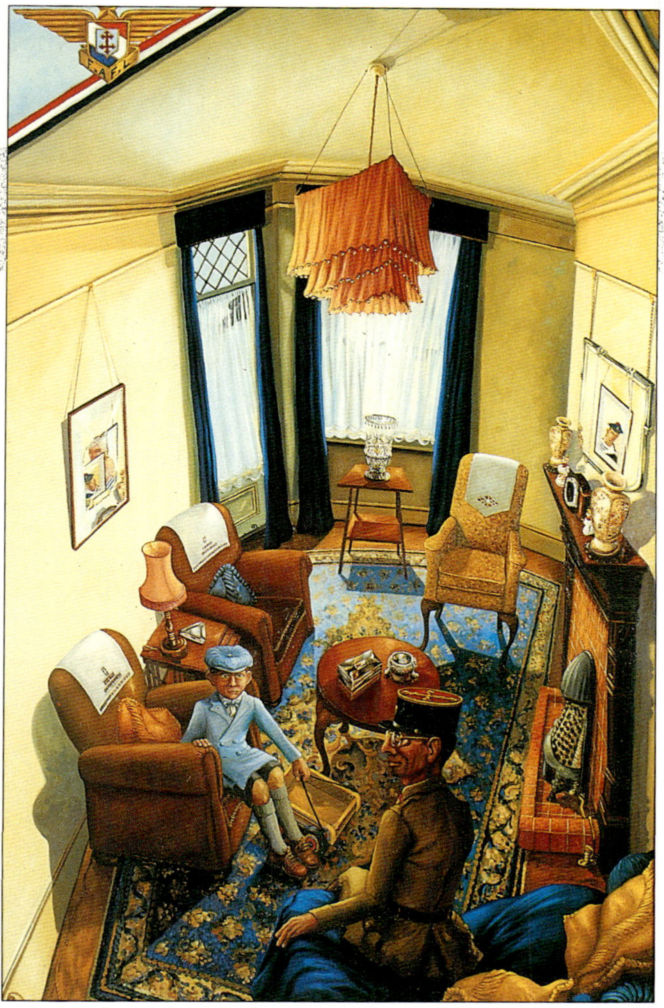

4

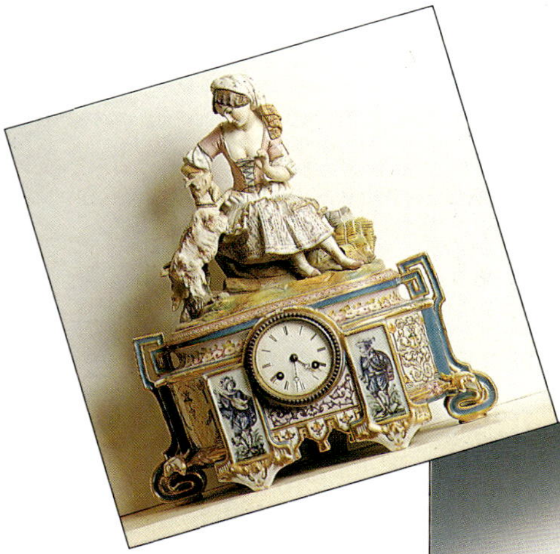

5-6

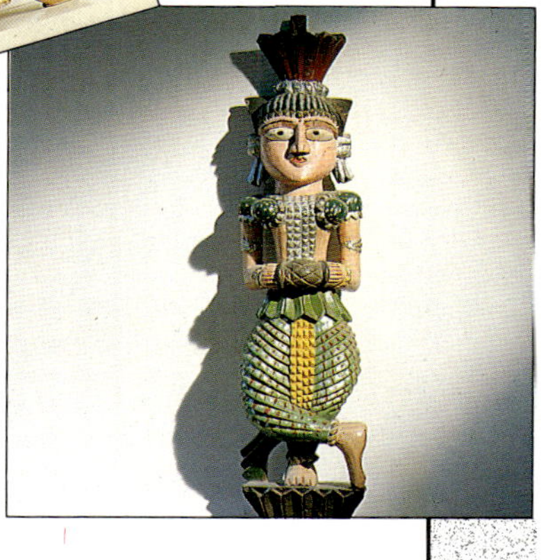

SEEING AND BELIEVING

Things to Do

The practice of art is about two things. First, it's being aware of everything you see, thinking about its appearance and making your own judgements about it. It's about going out with the intention of looking hard and trying to work out why things look as they do. Of course, some of the most interesting things for your eyes to feed on will be officially classed as 'art' or 'design', but many won't and they musn't be overlooked.

Second, the practice of art is about your own work, thinking about your own ideas and how they fit into what you have seen and then making something which as far as you can make it comes close to expressing what you think and feel. If you take your art seriously you are almost certain to create original and powerful work.

Here are some things to do reflecting the way artists approach their work.

1 Produce a 'family tree' of portraits of your friends and relatives. Portray them in their most characteristic clothes and backgrounds. Use any medium you like.

2 Make a display of drawings, paintings, diagrams, models or sculpture of influential objects, people, streets, shops, buildings, colours or patterns in your life at the moment. The display is almost as important as the choice of objects and the ways you use to depict them.

3 Imagine you are making titles for a book or a TV programme, or that you're making a publicity display promoting yourself, your school, a friend, a hobby or your town. Design the items or make a storyboard around your ideas.

4 Make a map or model of journeys you make regularly to look like the London Underground map, or in the style of any artist or designer you know.

5 Make your own collection of favourite designed objects. Find a way of displaying their good and bad points.

6 Study a favourite or a new (to you) artist or designer. Make your own piece inspired by them.

7 Study a period in art history, a culture or a type of object (hats, or road vehicles for example). Make an object derived from your study.

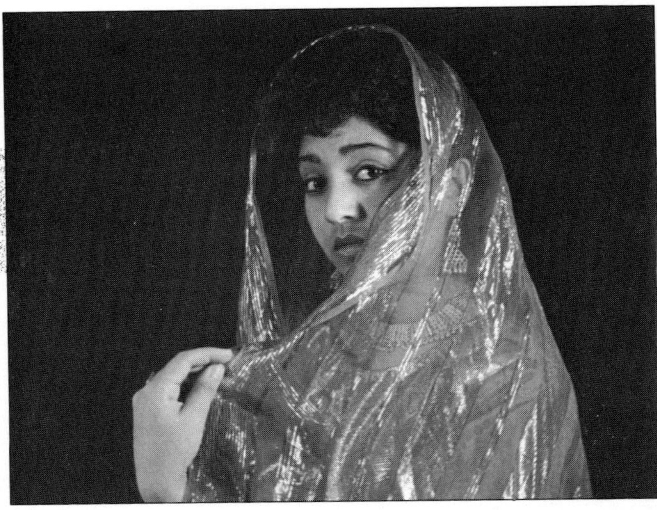

1△ 2▽

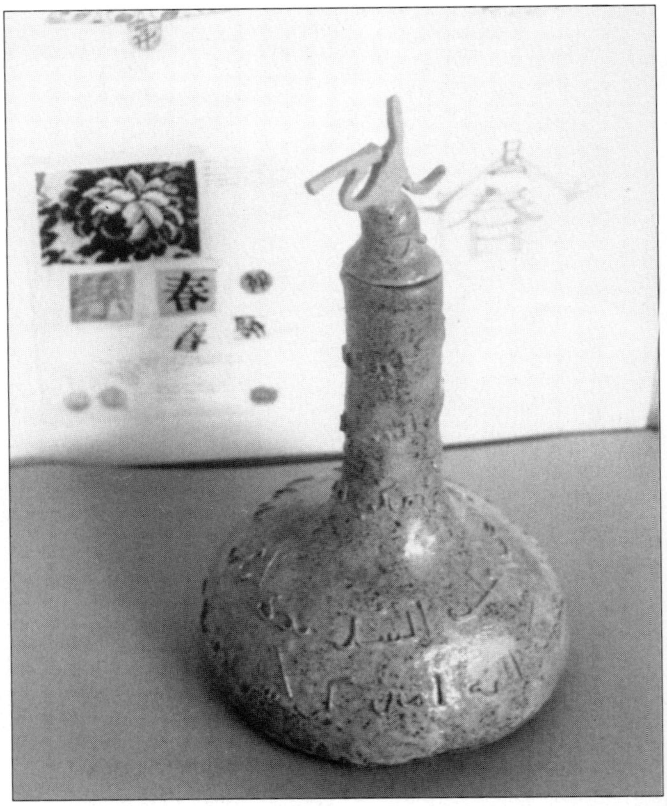

1
Self-portrait by school student, Lancashire.

2
Clay work with some of the artist's sources by a GCSE student from Wigan.

3-4
'Construction' by Michael Brennand-Wood, and 'Yellow Islands' by Jackson Pollock, 1952.

5
Abstract work by a GCSE student from Wigan, inspired by paintings 3 and 4.

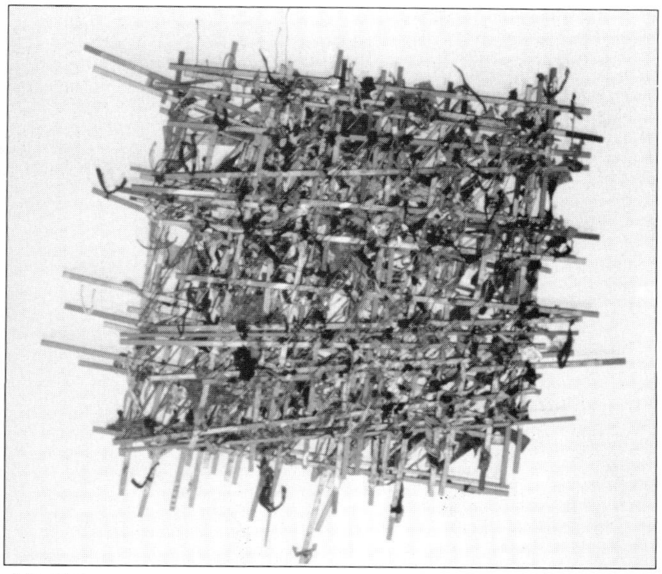

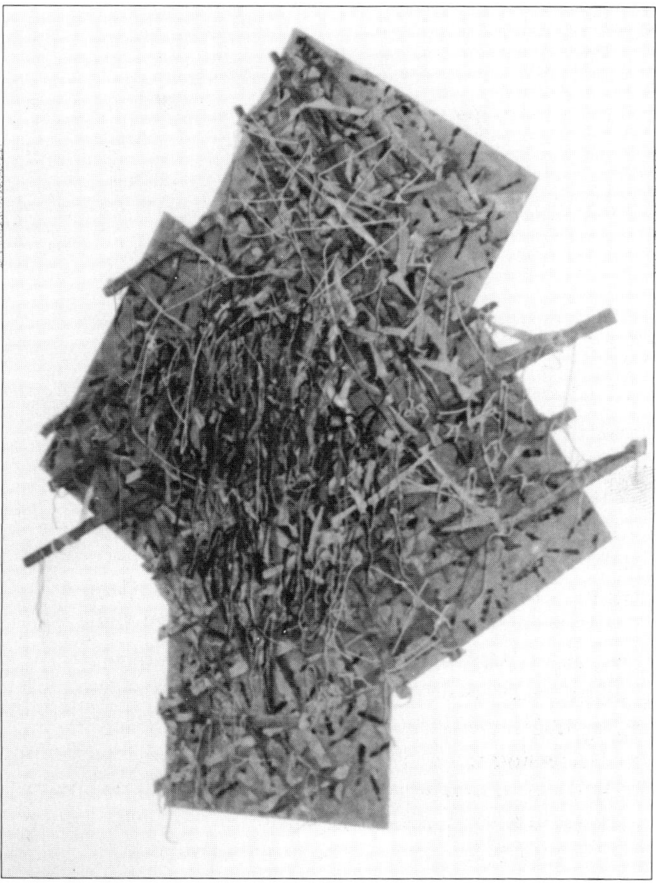

△3-4▽

5△

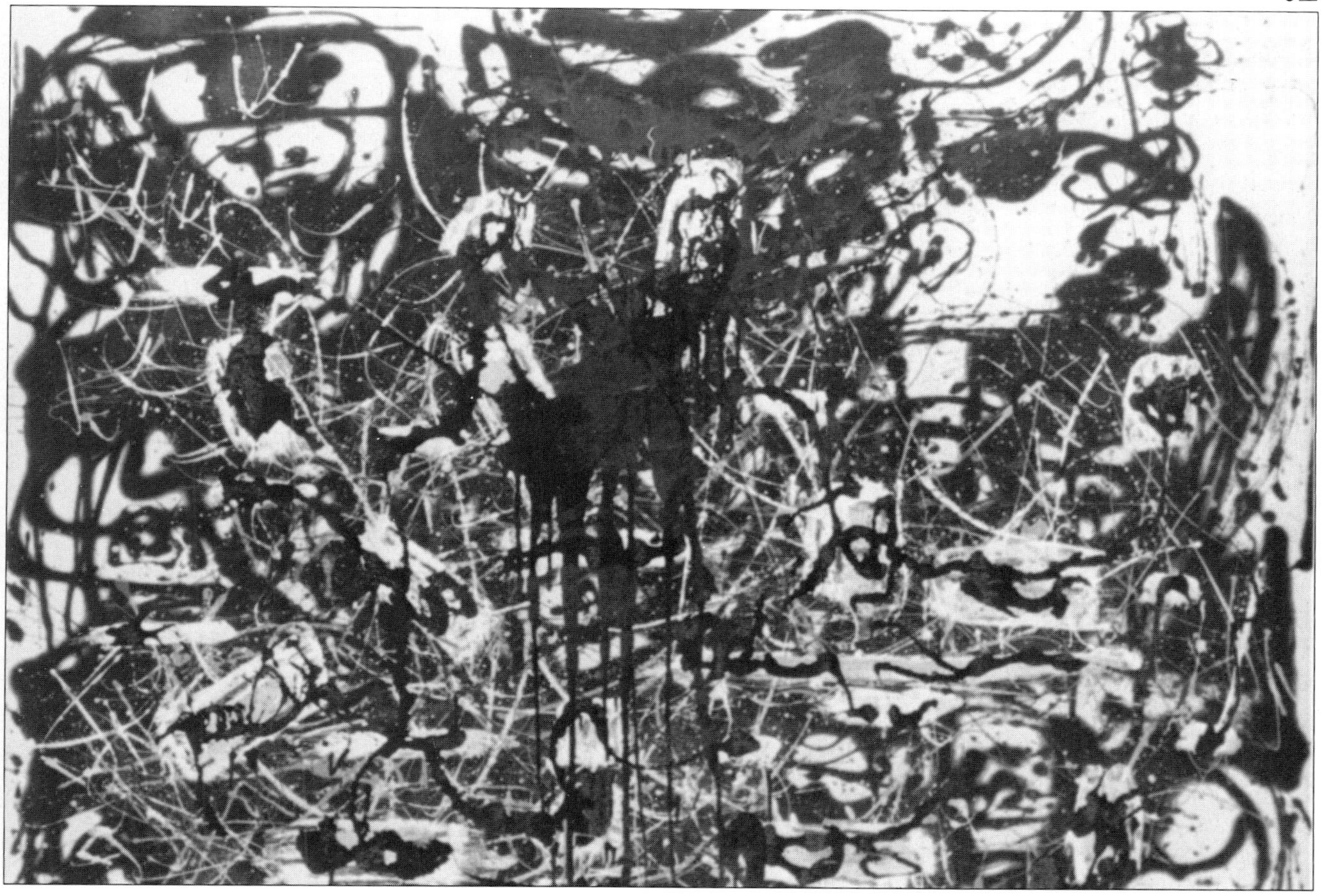

SEEING AND BELIEVING

All Times and Places

When you visit a national or local art gallery, and even those that make their living by selling works of art, you may notice that they tend to display sculpture, paintings and drawings made by artists from Europe, the USA and Australia – places with similar artistic and cultural traditions. All too often the work isn't likely to date from much before the time of the Italian painter Giotto, who was working about 1300. Anyone who wants to improve their work and develop their influences needs to feast their eyes on any art they can find from any time and anywhere in the world. Throughout the history of art artists' eyes have recognised no boundaries and a personal scrapbook or 'gallery' on the wall must contain a wide-ranging collection of ancient and modern art and sculpture that travels far beyond the European scene.

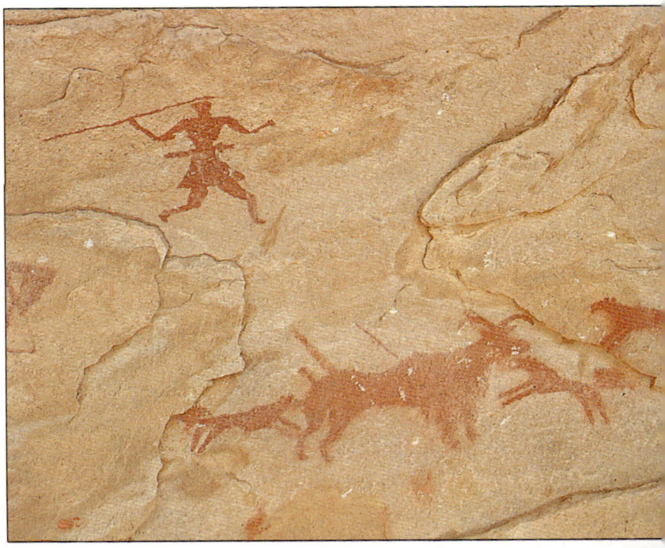

1△

2▽

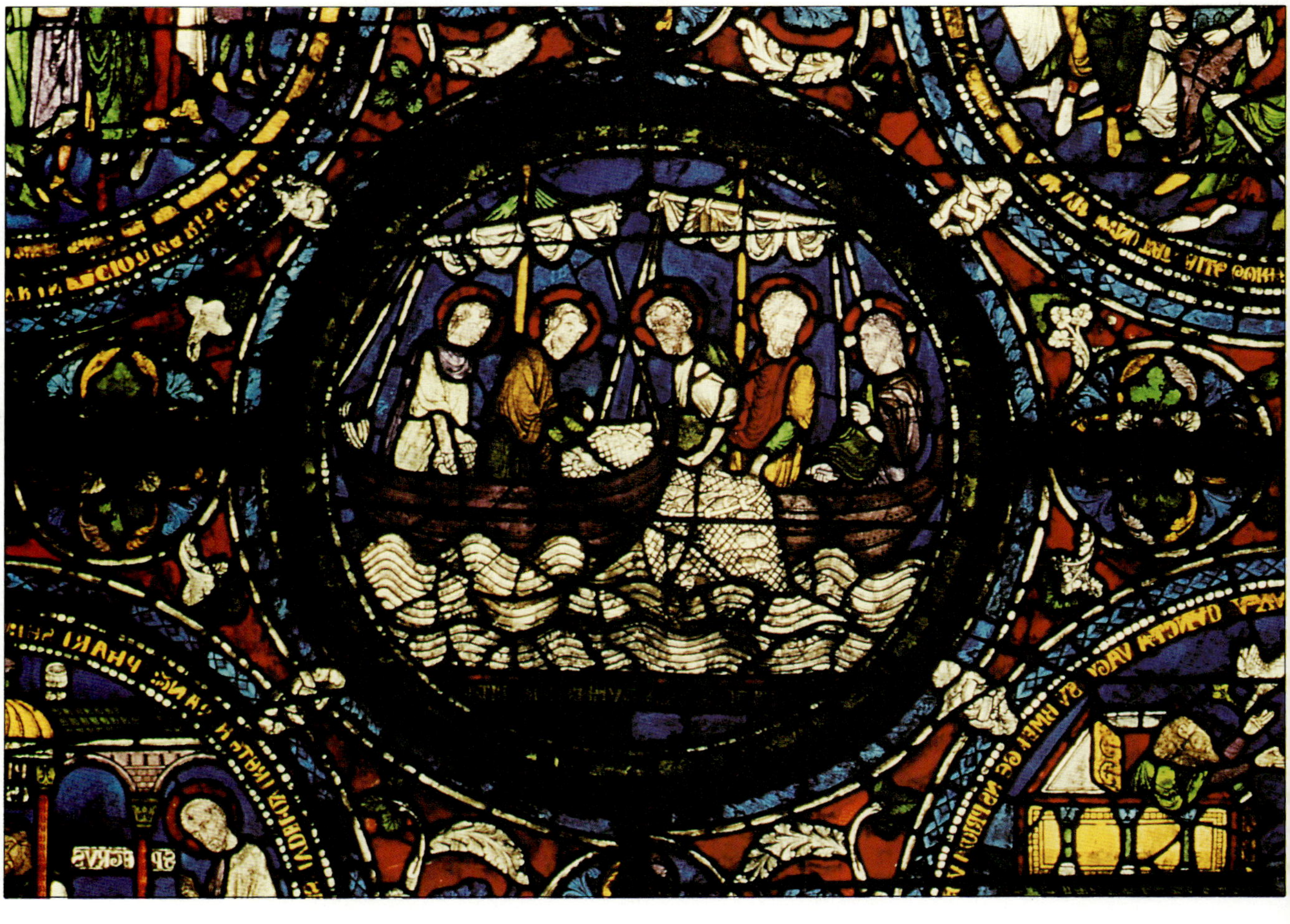

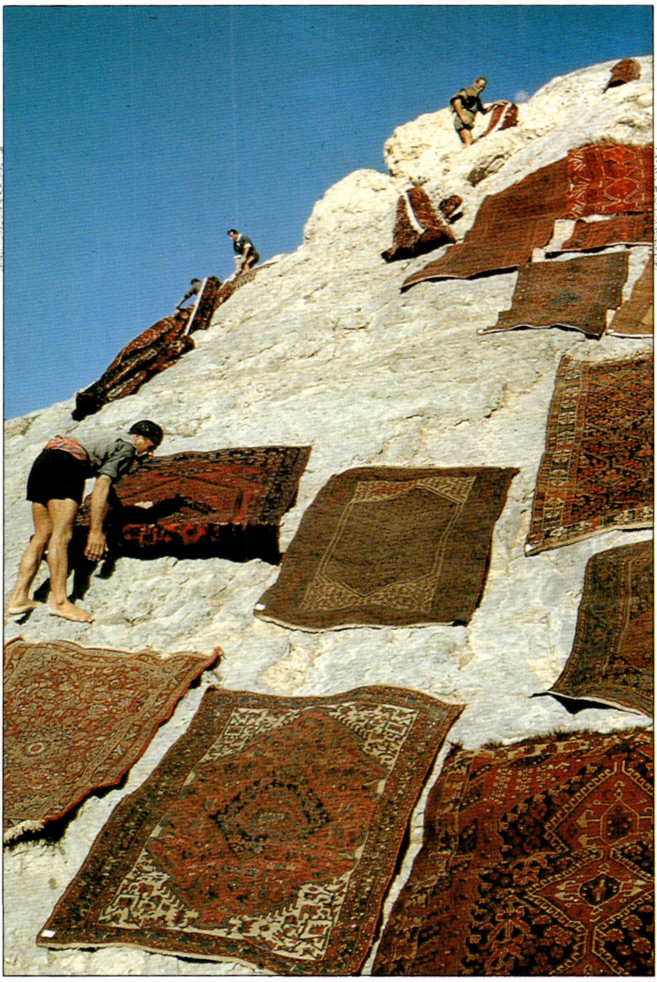

3△

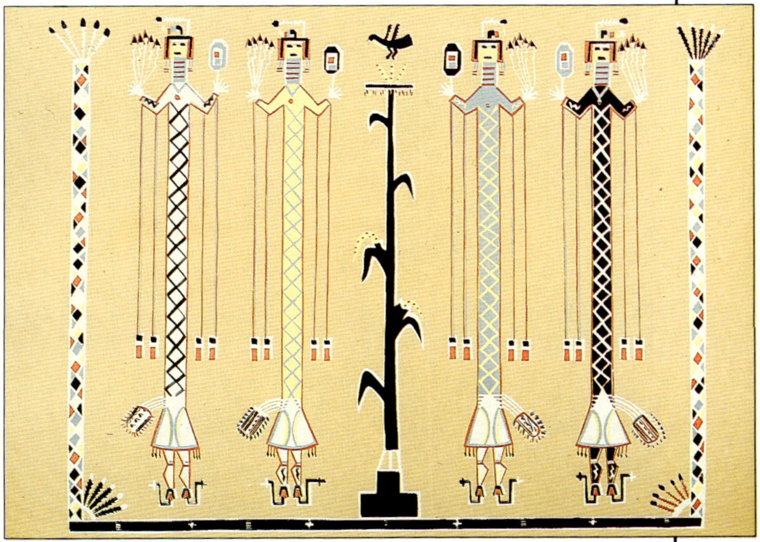

4

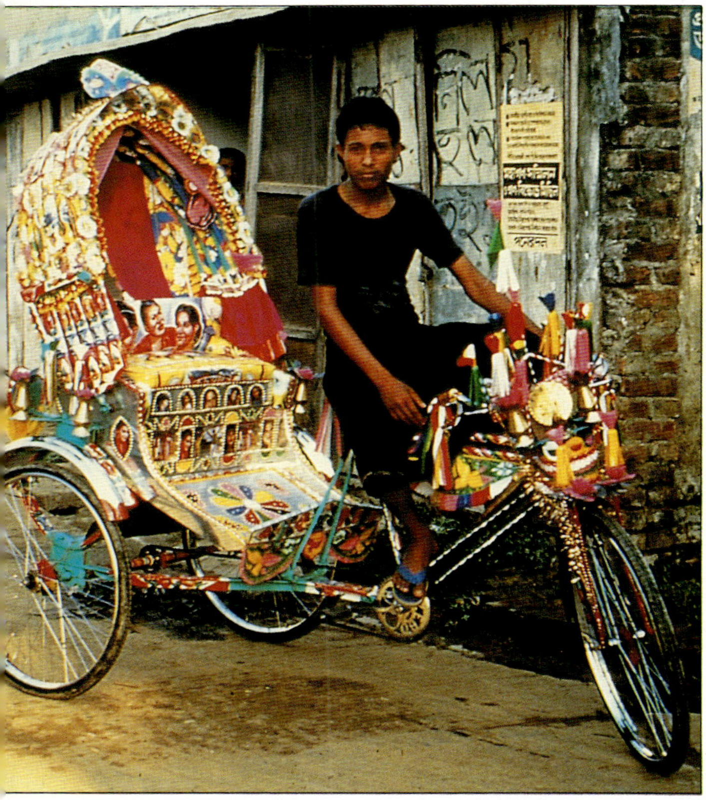

5▽

1
Hunting Scene, Algeria. Painted 10,000 to 20,000 years ago. Cave paintings are full of life and colour.

2
'The Apostles Fishing': Stained Glass from Canterbury Cathedral. Medieval churches were decorated with religious scenes as a visual aid. Worshippers probably knew the stories, but this was a memorable way of keeping them fresh in the mind. Even today the techniques used here are hard to learn.

3
Carpets like this, from the Islamic world, were first produced in one of the most advanced cultures of its time. But that doesn't matter much to the artist or to us. They have wonderful colours and patterns to admire, and that is more important.

4
'The four Thunder People of the south armed themselves to make war on White Thunder of the North.'
This picture was made with coloured sand, a form of religious act for the artist, an Indian of the Navajo tribe of New Mexico, who revere their environment.

5
In Dhaka, Bangladesh, there is more 'serious' art, but a professional artist has worked hard on this decoration nonetheless. Why did the owner commission it?

APPEARANCES

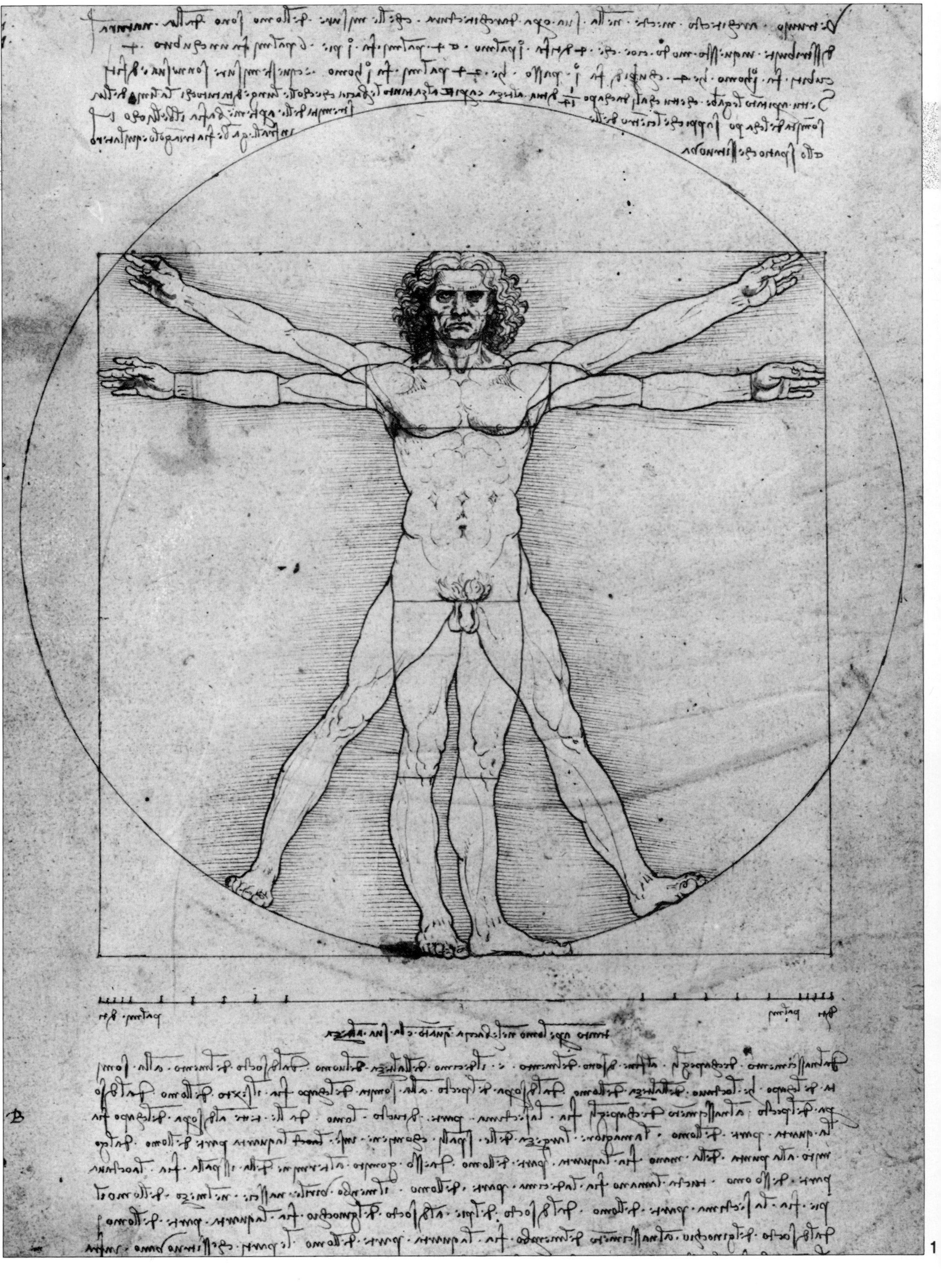

1

Why Portraits?

Artists from the earliest times and in most cultures have drawn, painted and carved images of humanity. When they have been forbidden there have been strong reasons, which themselves throw light on mankind's urge to create in its own image. For instance, Jews and Muslims are not permitted to depict humans in case mankind learns to admire itself too much.

Why make pictures of people? One reason is that it's an attempt to understand someone – to discover the personality and feelings of the subject. The motive for this may be mere curiosity or it may be to find out what gives people their particular talents and strengths. Images of powerful gods and leaders have been used as a reminder of their authority, but the same is true of more ordinary people. We often keep photographs of people we care for, not because we have forgotten what they look like but as a focus for our feelings towards them.

Self-portraiture turns these motives in upon ourselves. When an artist makes an honest self-portrait it is a voyage of discovery mapping the strengths and weaknesses of the character which lie behind the surface appearance. That is why a good self-portrait is full of life and often disturbing or surprising for the viewer.

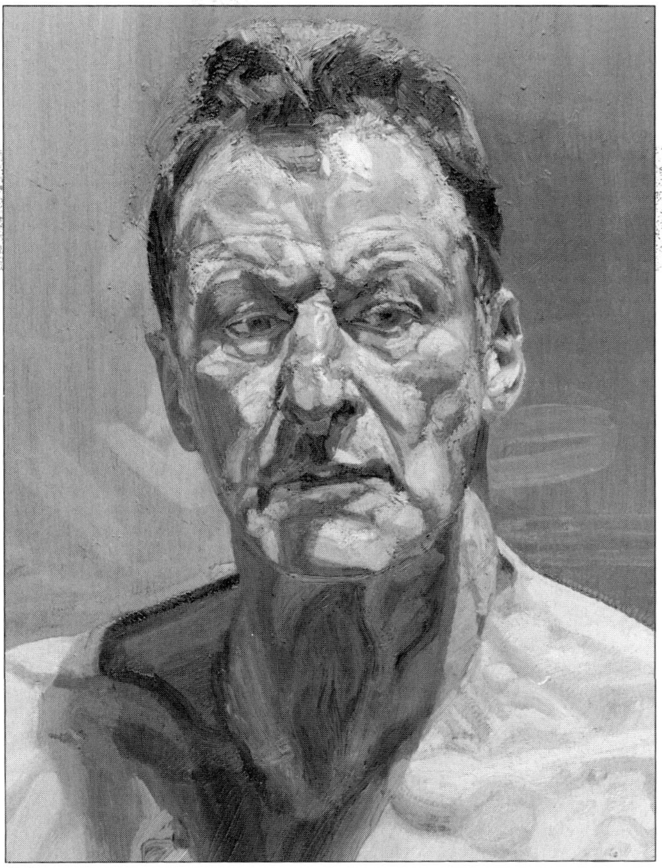

2△

3▽

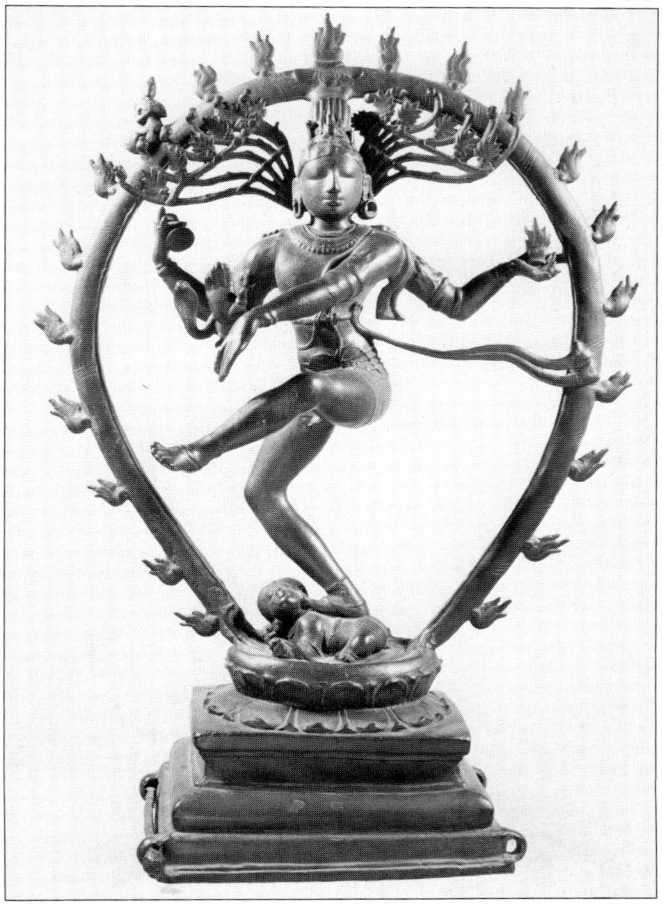

1
Vitruvius, the Roman writer on architecture, saw similarities between the proportions of the human body and the square and the circle, the shapes on which all others were based. Writers and artists in the Renaissance, a thousand years later, often took that to mean that there was something mystical and godlike about the human shape.

2
Lucien Freud achieved this riveting self-portrait with ruthless observation and daring brushwork. Look at the individual brushstrokes. They are surprising until you see how they go to make the whole picture.

3
In Hinduism, Shiva is often shown dancing within a circle – the circle of life.

APPEARANCES

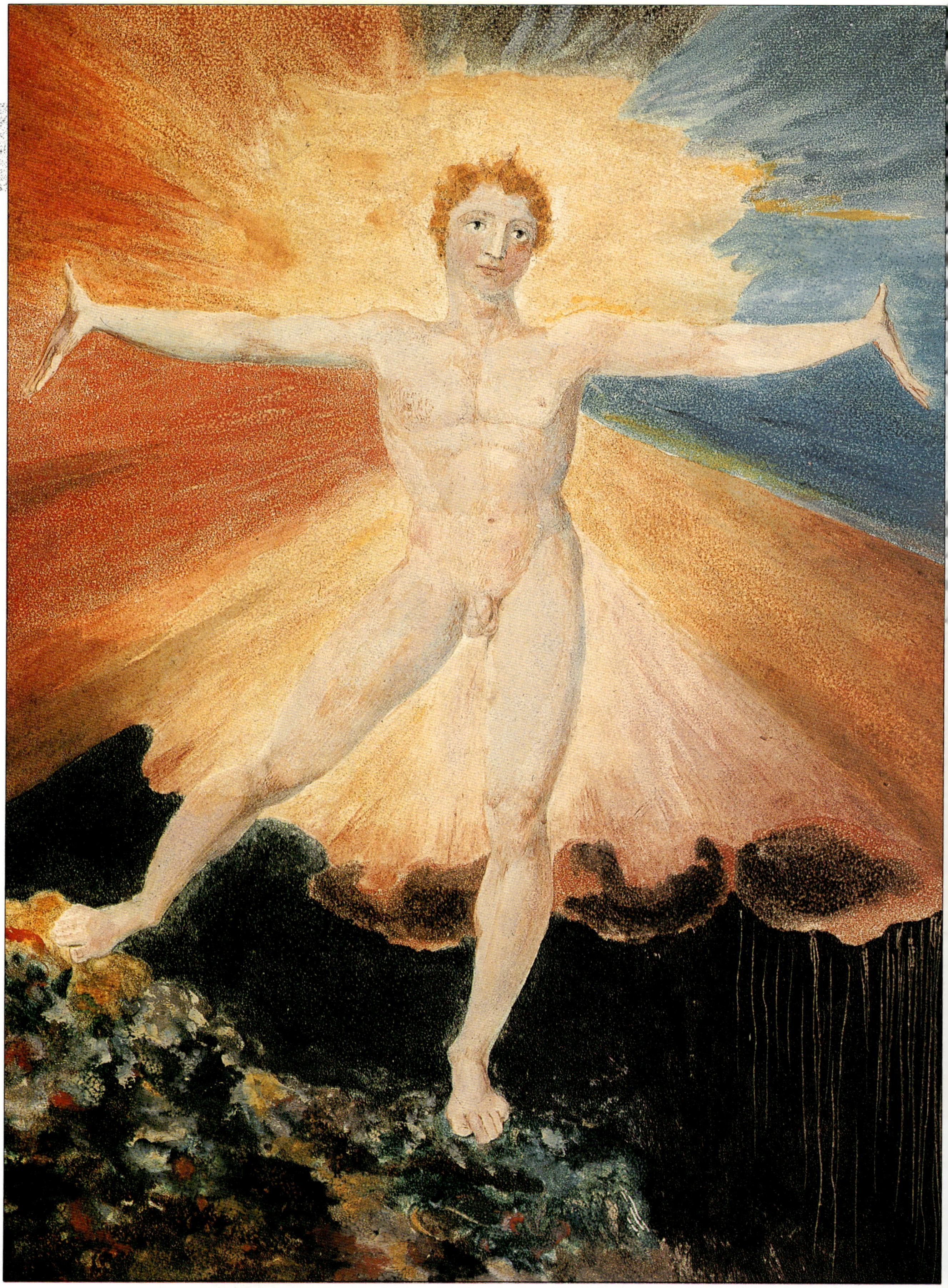

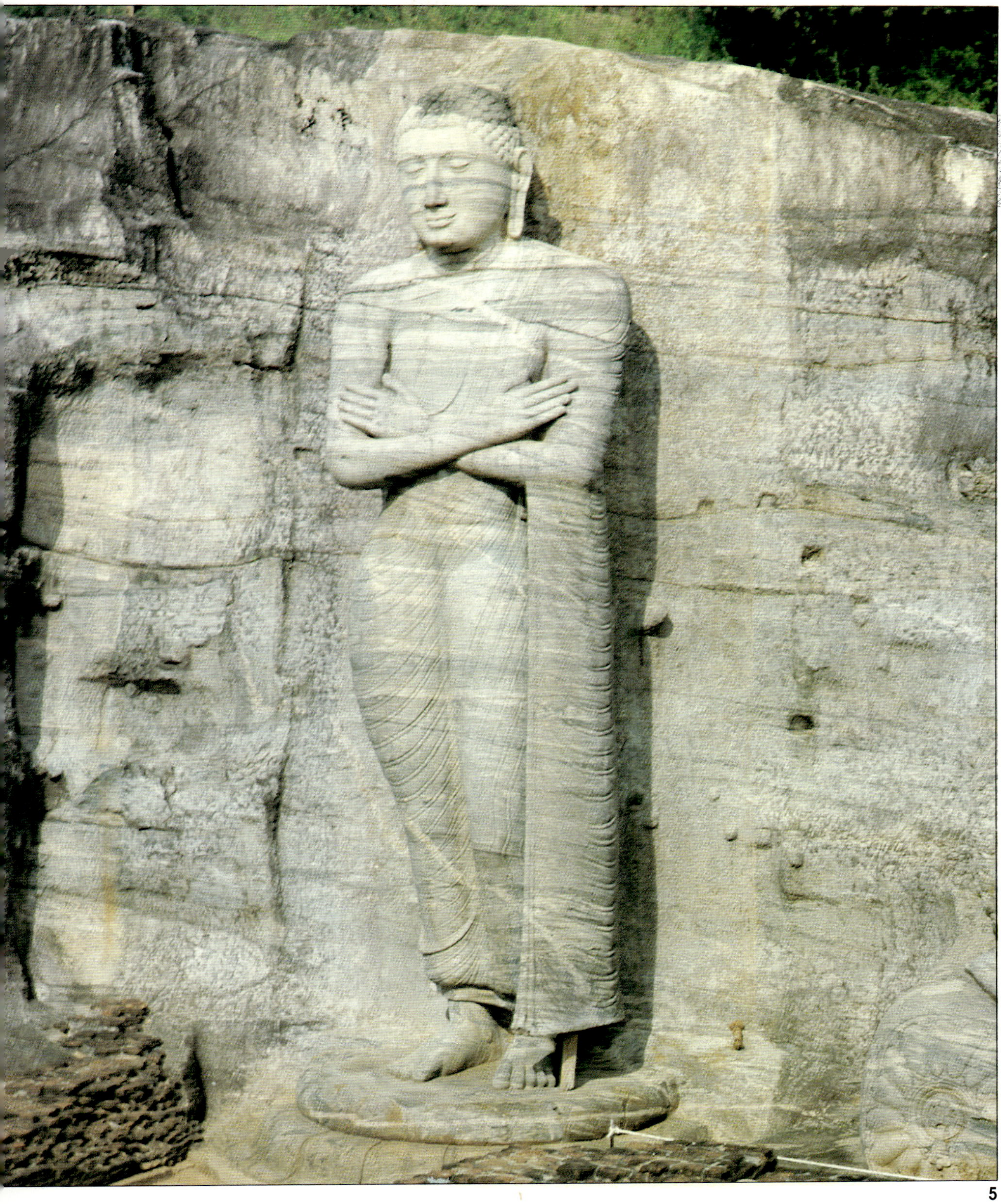

5

4
The English poet and artist William Blake took the Vitruvian figure and gave it another shade of meaning. For him the figure represented Albion, the spirit of a Britain freed from poverty and oppression.

5
Buddha has given his name to a form of religion. He was not a god in the true sense, but a man who achieved the greatest degree of spiritual enlightenment. His example was followed by many, and early on his statue, whether standing, sitting or lying, became a focus for meditation and a symbol of the philosophy of Buddhism.

APPEARANCES

What is Appearance?

What goes into making a likeness? There's a lot of looking to begin with, which will provide a list of obvious visual details about your subject – colour of hair, eyes and lips, the shape of the nose and mouth, the distances above, below and between the eyes, the texture of the hair and skin, and so on. But these are only surface details and you have other things to work at which begin with serious thinking. Your subject has a personality, a long-term state of mind and also a mood. It is important to convey how she/he is feeling at the time of the portrait. Think about people you may know who look almost alike, on the surface at least, but whose different character means that in life they cannot be confused. Since art is to do with what can be seen (or touched at least) you will have to find a visual way of expressing what is inside them.

All this will seem very difficult at first, but there are methods by which to achieve a successful portrait. One way is by showing expression and pose. How does the subject stand or sit? Do they smile much or hold their head in a particular way? Have they favourite colours or favourite 'props'? Again, how do they live their lives? Do they have favourite clothes or food? Are they often seen in a particular place, doing a particular thing? Has something unusual happened to them just *now*? Research and thought will help you decide if including any of these real-life accessories will help capture something of their character. Taking this further, remember that in art there is a long tradition of inventing such accessories, of supplying symbols and objects with a concealed message about the subject of the work. A lily can stand for purity, a dog for faithfulness, a skull for death. How would you symbolise a talent for making music, or a quick temper?

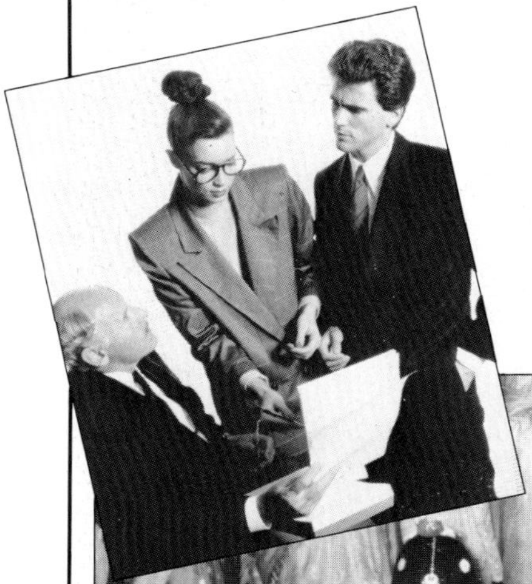

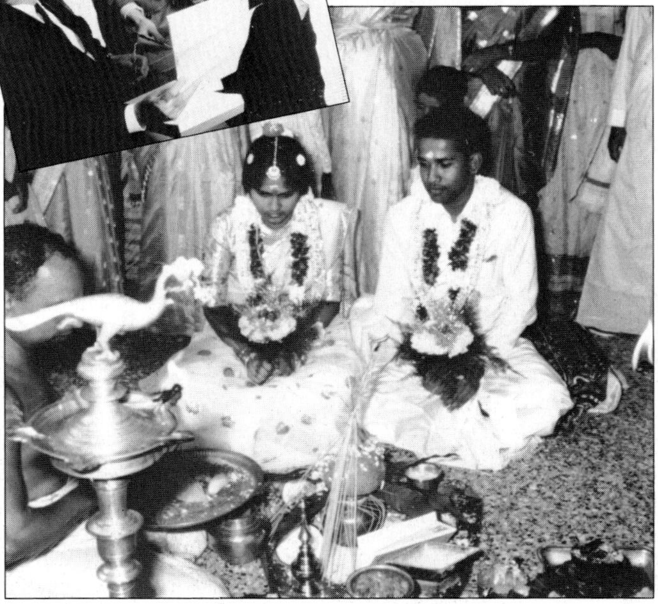

1-2

1-2
Hindu Wedding, India and Office Scene, London. What do these two sets of props say about the occasions, and the personalities of the subjects? Are these photographs as good as paintings?

3
'The Last Supper', 1988. Alison Watt, a young Scots artist, painted this. It's about herself, though not exactly a self-portrait. Try untangling the symbols. What does the painting and its title tell you about her mood and her personality?

4-6
Henry Moore's sculptures have many sources. Here are two: draped figures observed and drawn lying in London tube tunnels, sheltering from Second World War bombs. Next, part of the English landscape. What might have been the connections in his mind? What might they tell us about his attitudes to the human figure? How do they relate to this piece of his sculpture?

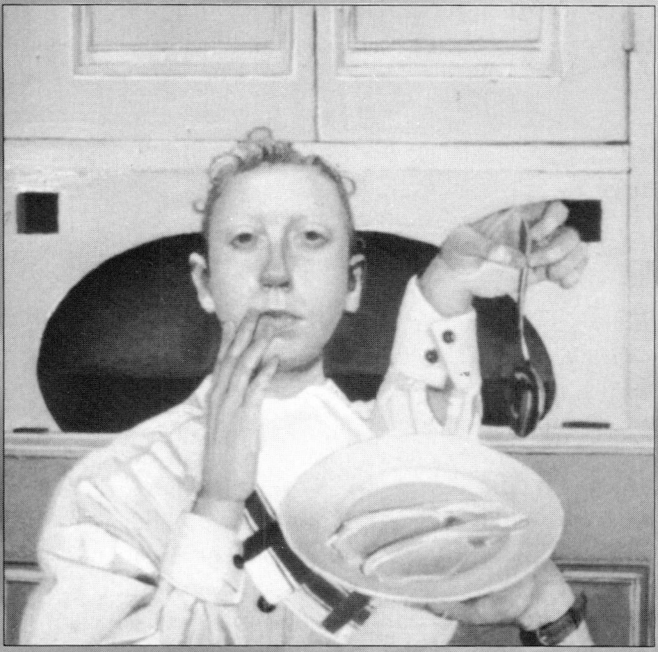

3△

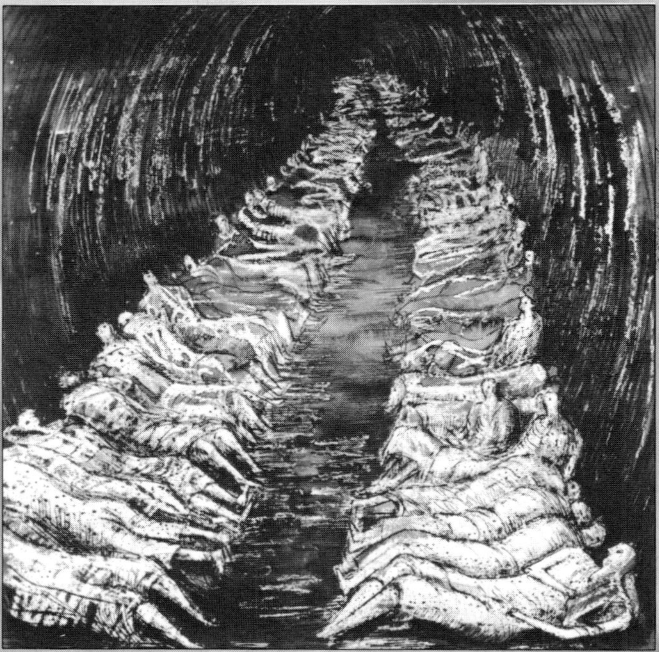

4△

5▽

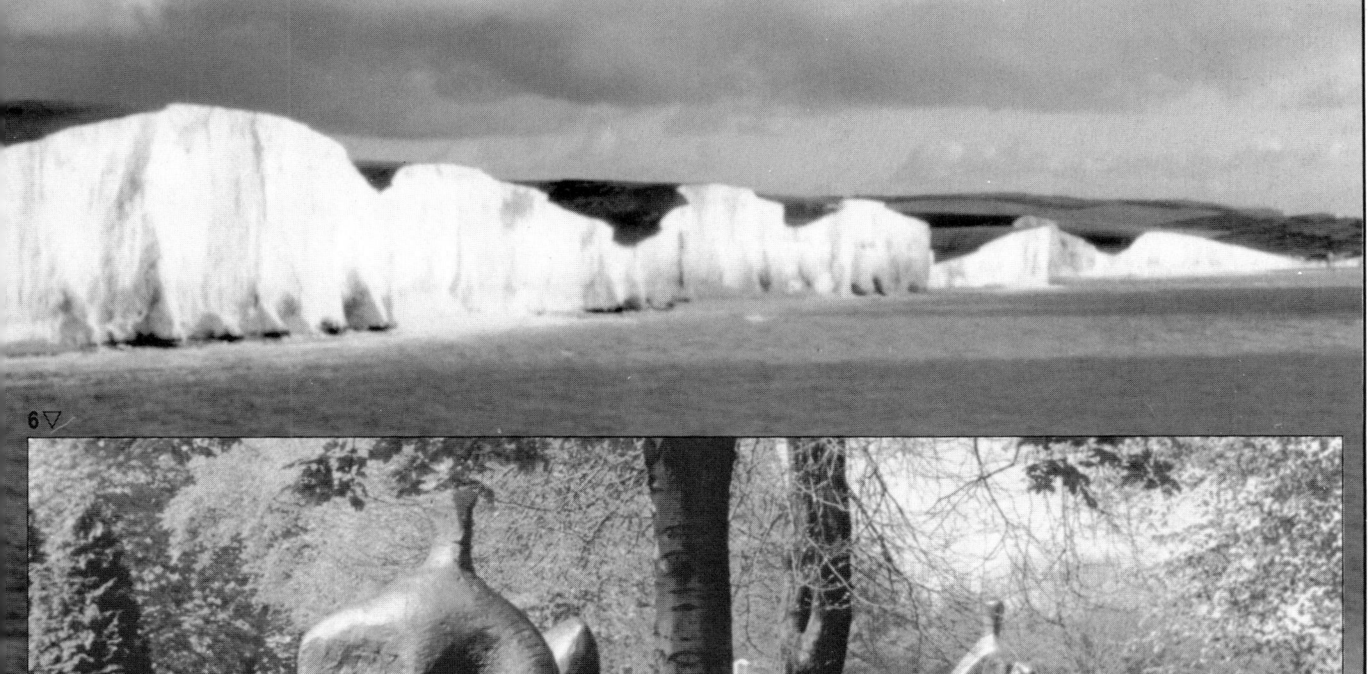

6▽

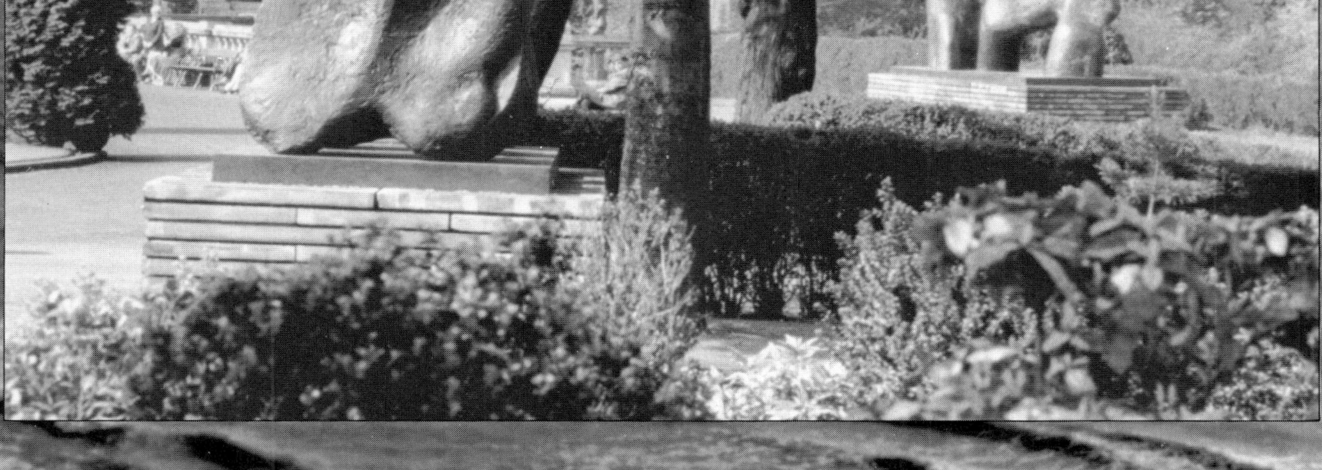

APPEARANCES

A Portrait of Two People

Before you start on your own final work, you will have thought hard, observed and researched. You will probably have done a number of experiments to try out shapes, colours or lighting and props, as well as deciding on the most suitable compositions and style for your portrait. Unconsciously this process will have begun with your choice of subject: you probably couldn't produce anything interesting without feeling something towards him or her. So don't be deceived: a great deal of the portrait (even if it isn't a self-portrait) is about *you*. You've made many choices before the work begins and you've had to come to some conclusions about the personality of the sitter. So the personality you try to show is bound up with your own. For the time you're working together you'll shape each other, as we all do in close relationships.

There also comes a point where your personality will take over. After all, as a person you have your own likes and dislikes. You will tend to choose colours, textures, shapes, patterns and a style you like, just as you chose your subject in the first place. As the portrait progresses you will stamp your personality as an artist on the finished work. You will have your own ideas about what makes a satisfying image, one that will attract an audience as well as interesting it.

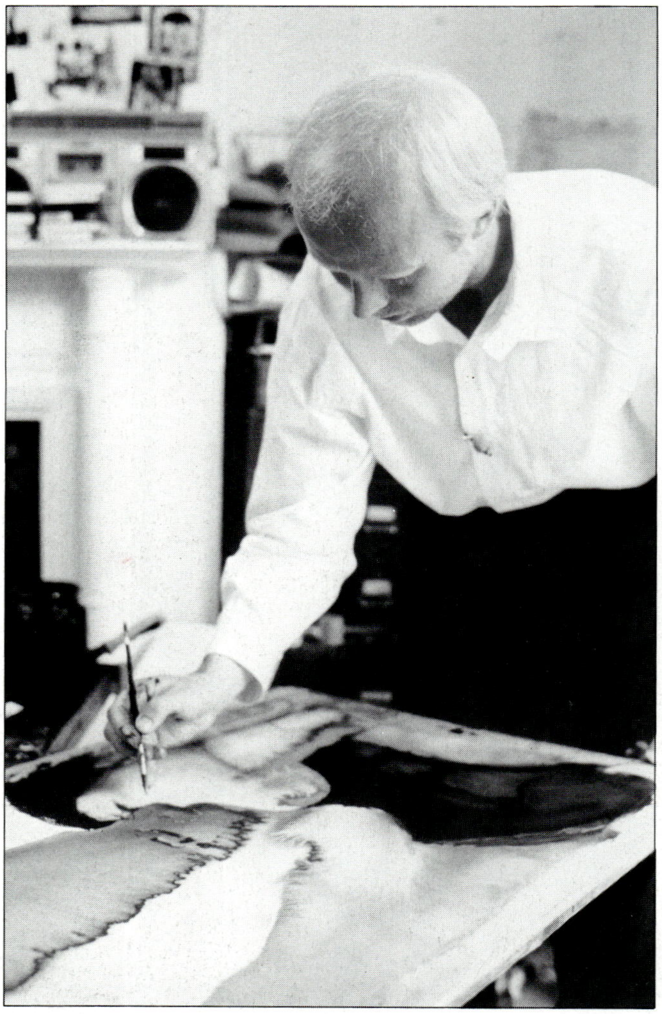

1

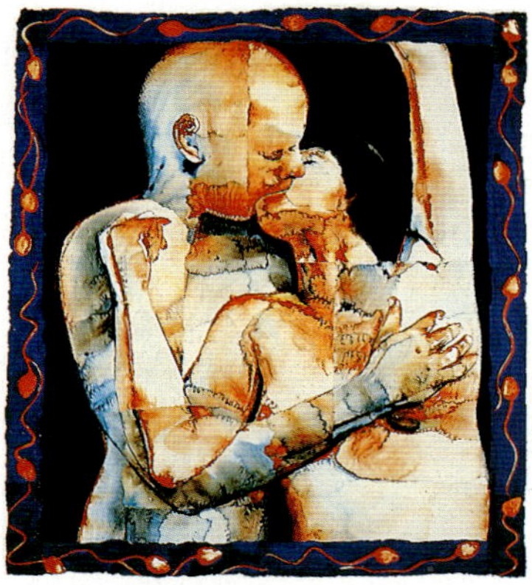

1
Graham Dean produces figure paintings and portraits on dampened absorbent paper in bright water colour. That means that he can control the paint only within limits, and he looks for accidental colour clashes and mixes. He also tears the paper and reassembles his faces and figures to make deliberately startling juxtapositions. His subject matter – mysterious gatherings, intense relationships – are about the disjointed, menacing, emotional qualities of life in the 1980s (see above).

2-3
'Las Meninas' by Velasquez, 1656 and 'In the studio, I' by Leon Kossoff, c. 1962. Sometimes portraitists include themselves in their work. What makes each of these works distinctive? What do they tell you about the artist and his relationship to his sitter?

4
Why did the sculptor of the Mount Rushmore faces choose such a place (the Rockies) and such a scale? Who are the subjects?

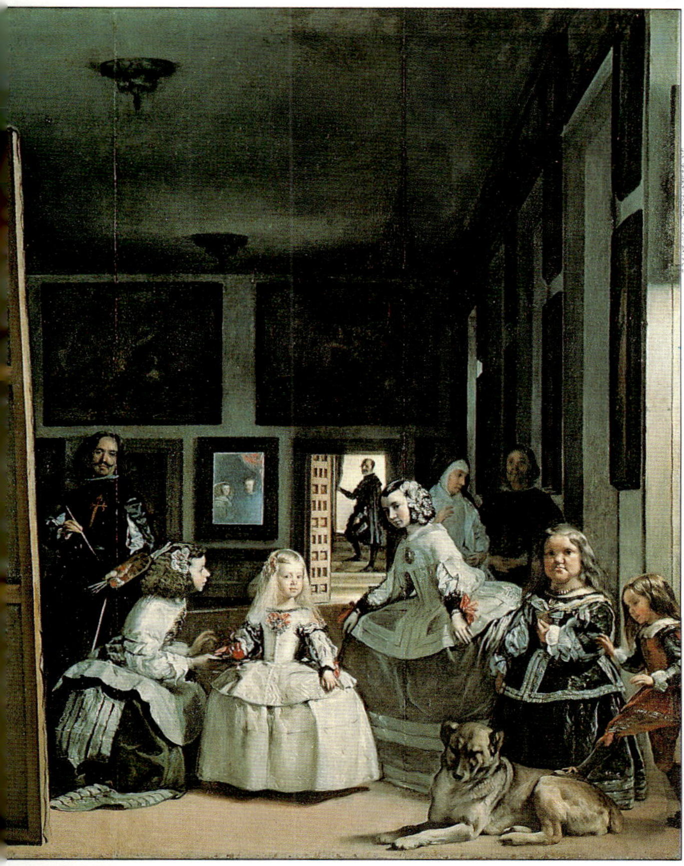

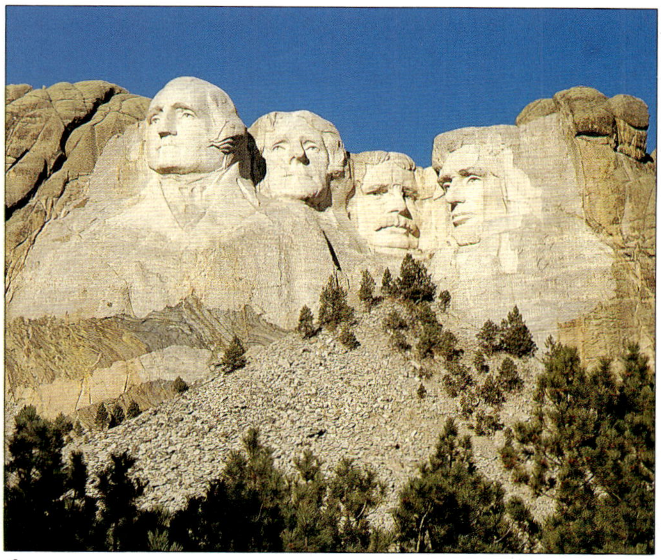

△2-3▽

4

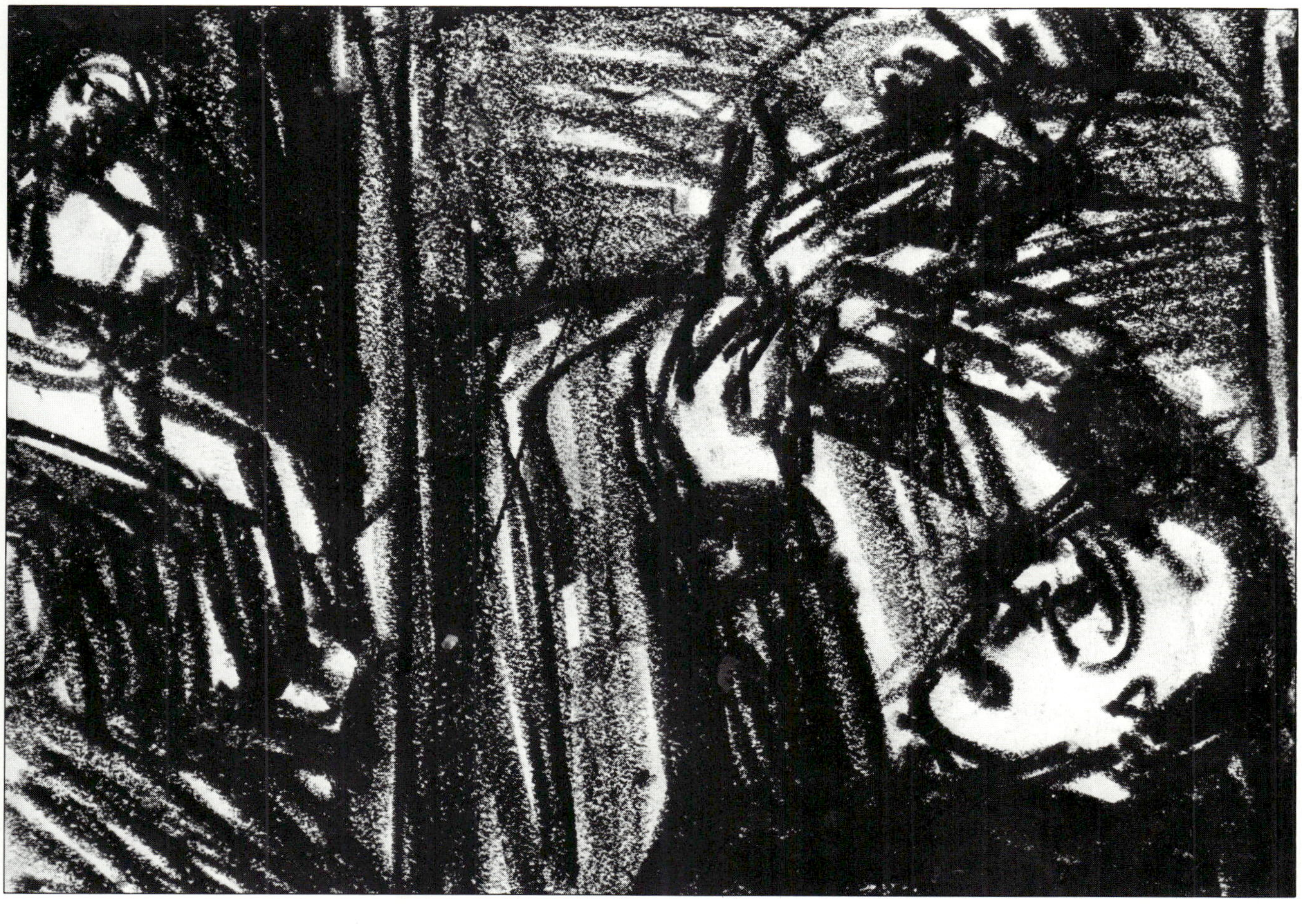

APPEARANCES

Image

We've already talked about the purpose of portraiture: for the subject it's possibly a flattering chance of fame. For the artist it's a way of demonstrating skill and inviting attention. These motives are also present when we think about our own appearance. Usually we're keen that people will think the best of us when they see us. But what does 'the best' mean? We may want to impress on others that we're brave or good looking or powerful or worth knowing, or on the other hand that we don't wish to be picked out in a crowd. We might want to be identified with a group – the army, say, or a particular style of pop music – or we may want to show that we think for ourselves, that we don't want to copy anyone else because we see ourselves as highly original individuals.

Appearance gives off signals, whether we work at it or not. Try looking at people around you and, without hurting the feelings of anyone, see if you can read those signals. Often they will back up the general impression you have of a person, but sometimes you may become confused. Why is that boy wearing old people's clothes that look as if they were bought in a secondhand shop? Why is that girl's hair bright green? Why does one pop star wear a jumble of jewellery and 'tarty' clothes and another is decked out like a nineteenth-century prince in court uniform? There is usually a reason for the apparent confusion. But what about simply making the best of our looks? Some people really shouldn't wear bright checks when dark colours and vertical stripes would help them look more elegant. The colour green goes well with red hair rather than clashing. Too many patterns (or too much of the same one) worn together are hard on the eye. Of course you can break these 'rules' if you want to – but think out the consequences first!

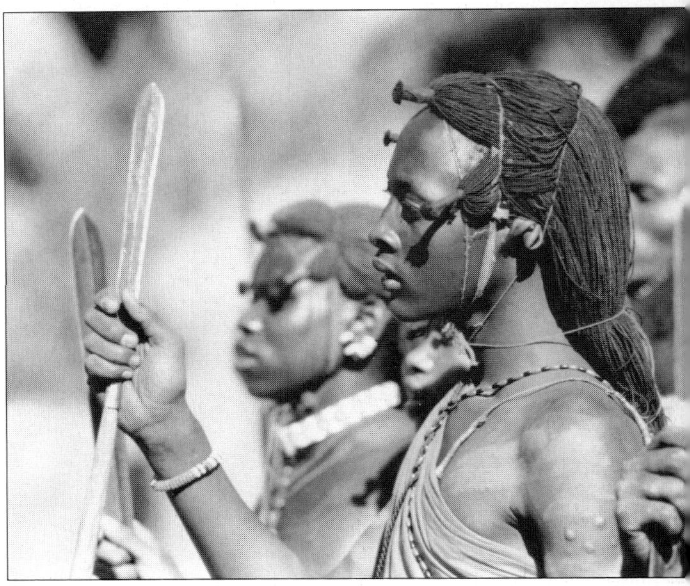

1

1
The ornaments and grooming of these Masai warriors are different, but together they look part of one group, and you could never fail to recognise them.

2-3
Michael Jackson and lookalikes. A pop star's appearance is part of his or her image – which will be a total package taking in music, the style of the act, all products on sale and publicity as well. By dressing like them, the fans aren't just showing admiration – they actually become part of the promotion.

4
Lee Bowery is making a career out of creative dressing, which often satirises fashion. He is a piece of art, created by himself. What signals is he giving off in this outfit?

5-6
Clive Smith graduated from Kingston Art School in 1988. He now works for an international fashion designer in New York. This sketch shows the detailed work involved in producing a garment. His main influences are from the 1950s, and the USA, but the clothes aren't mere copies. How are these designs similar, and different, from those worn by the real 1950s man? You may have to do more research yourself to answer this. Be careful to record it if you do.

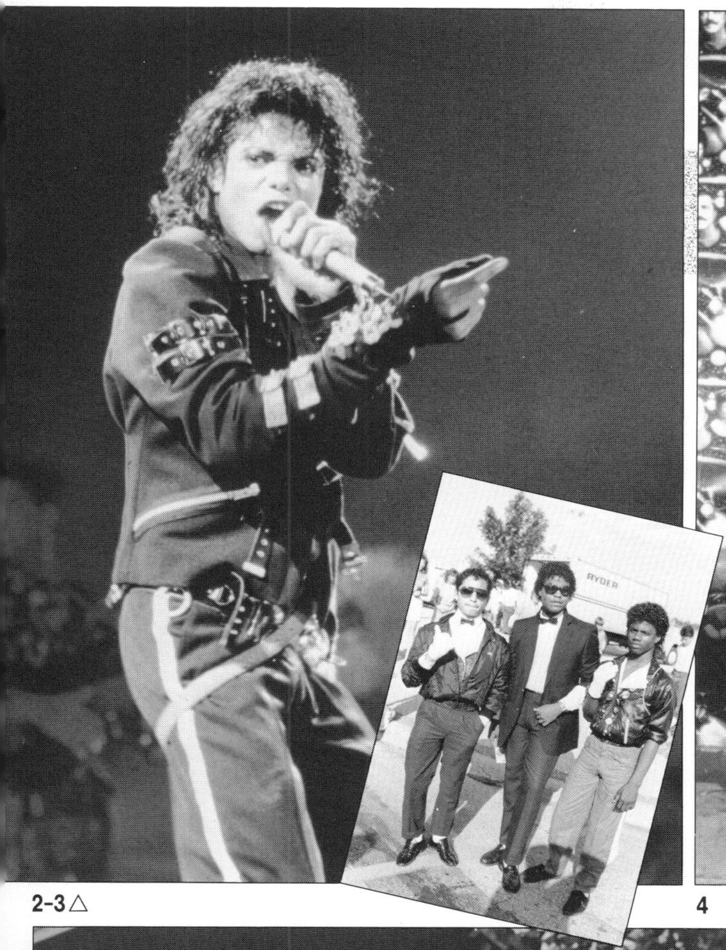

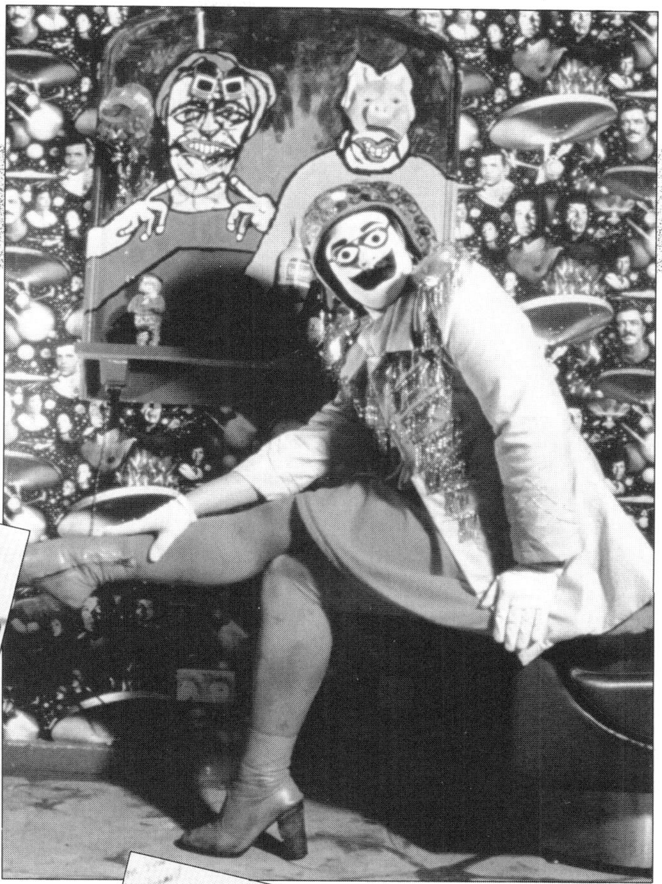

2-3△

4

5-6▽

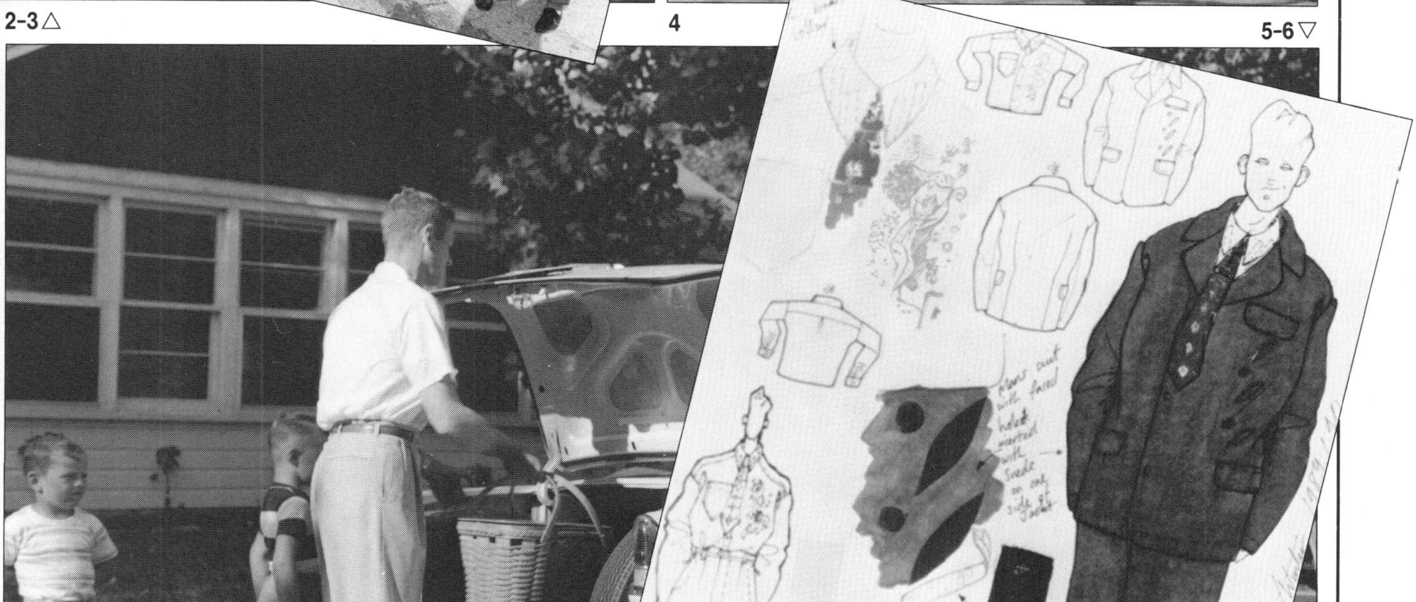

APPEARANCES

Ideas for You

You may have already had a go at a portrait or self-portrait. If you have you probably worked through the different stages from thinking and research, to experiment and towards the final piece of art. It's important that you don't throw away any of the evidence you've gathered along the way! Presented attractively it will provide much more information, a sort of third dimension to what you've ended up with. But there are many more things you can do with the ideas of appearance and personality. Here are some examples to set you thinking.

Pictures 1, 2 and *3* are three very different pictures of the same person: Sir Isaac Newton on a bank-note from the 1970s; on a print by William Blake from the 1790s; and on a Japanese print from the 1860s. Why are they like they are? Think of someone famous (or take yourself) and show them in three different ways. Try to use a different medium for each portrayal. Take another *single* subject and make studies of her/him in different moods. Photography or even video if that is available to you would be a good medium for this exercise.

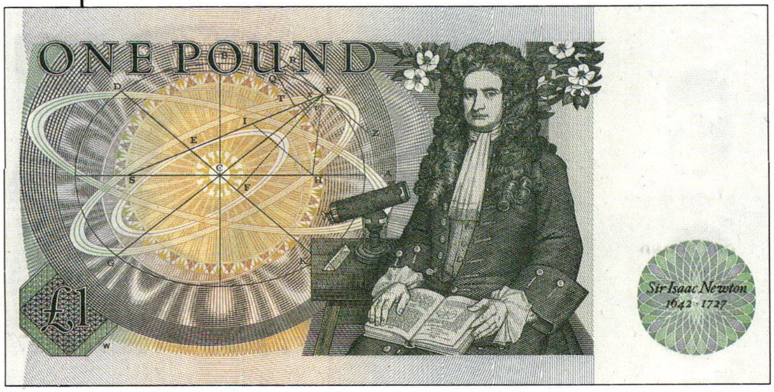

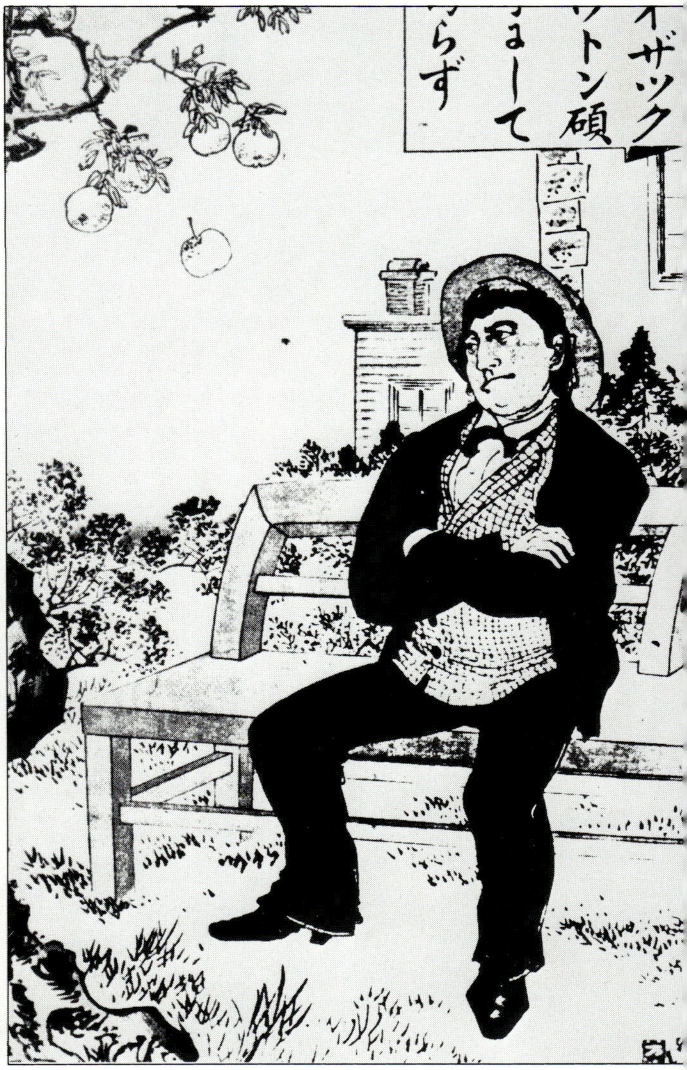

1-3

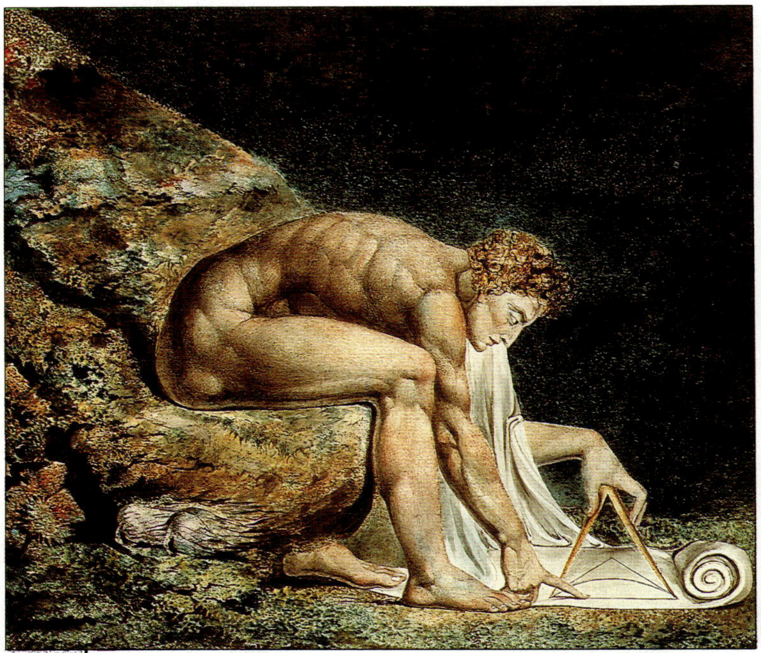

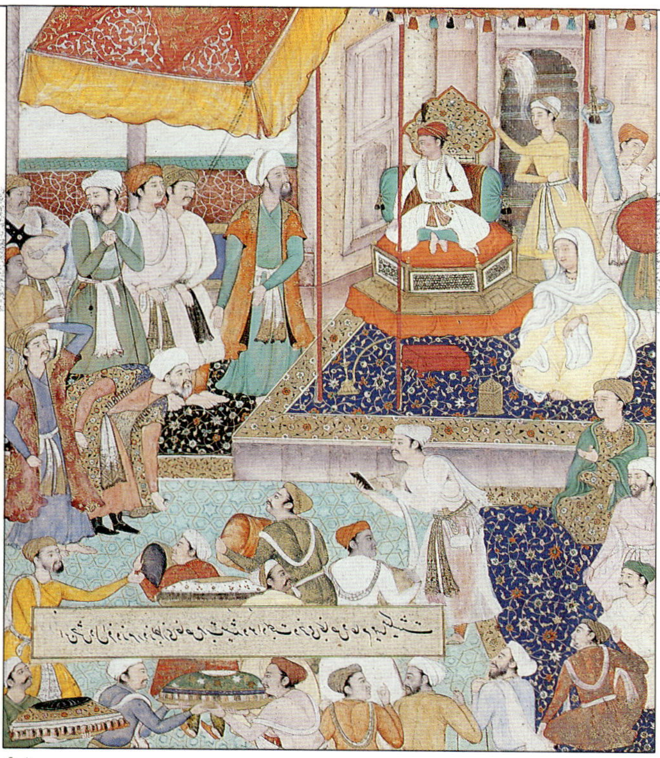

4△

Picture 4 shows an Indian prince about 400 years ago, with all the signs of his wealth and power. If you were rich, powerful or famous today, what would you display to signal your position? Produce a painting of yourself in the Mughal style, surrounded by symbols or elements of yourself.

Picture 5 is William Hogarth's 'Servants', painted around 1750. These are fine portraits showing much about each servant's character and mood. Write a character sketch for each one, or a story or drama about life below stairs in the Hogarth household.

5▽

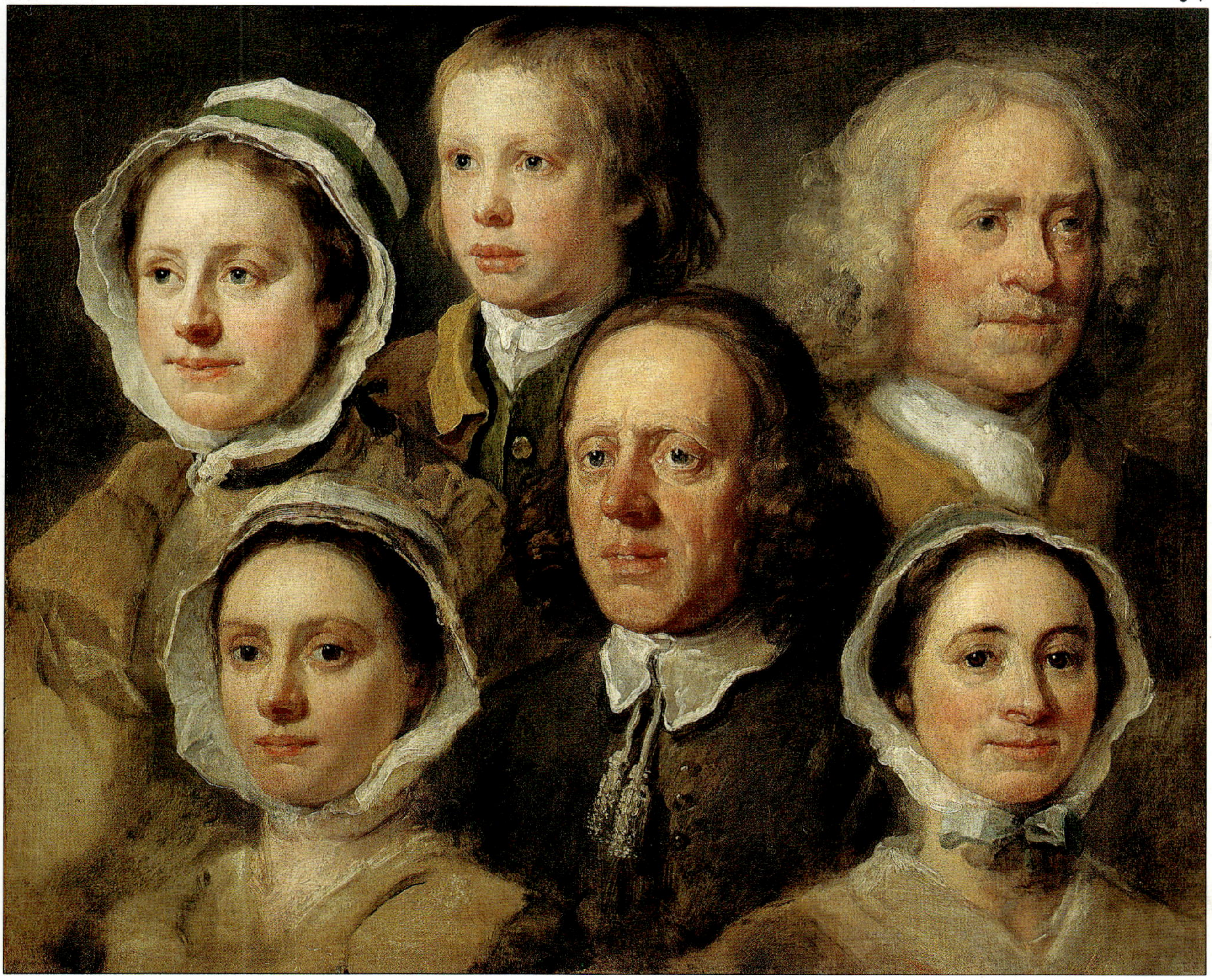

APPEARANCES

Just for Laughs

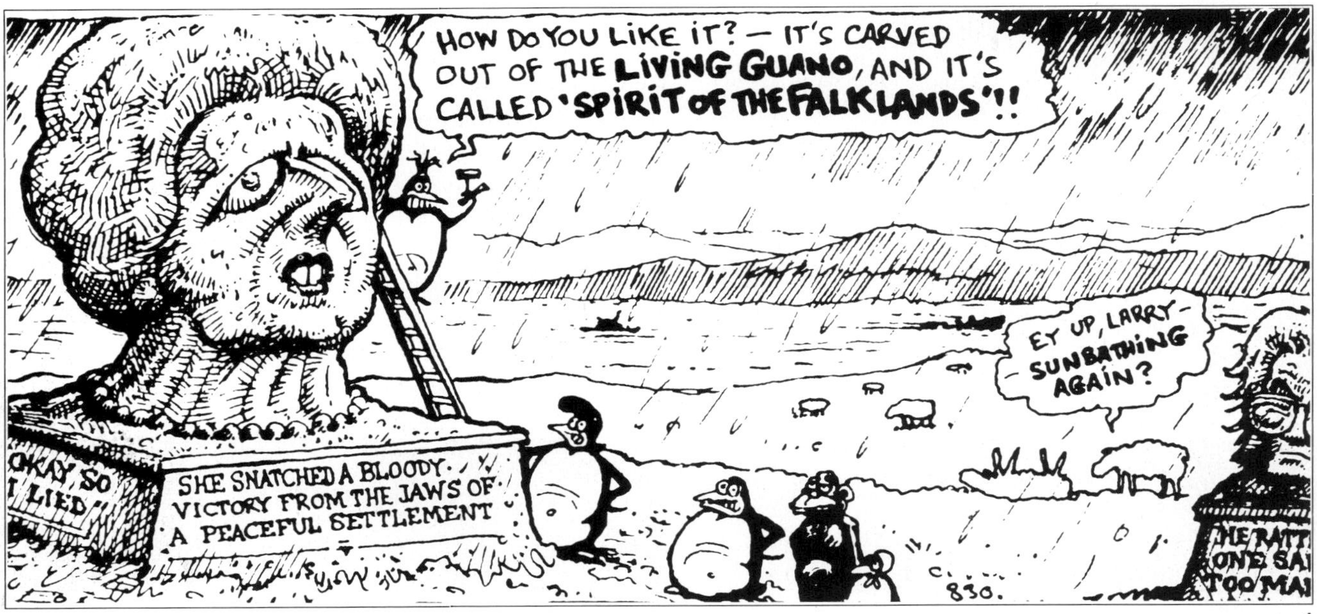

1

We've now looked at many serious examples of portraiture, but one of the ways artists have used them is to make us laugh, and often to make us think hard as well.

Strip cartoons aren't all that old as an idea, but the tradition of telling a story in pictures is a firm favourite, especially when it's funny. Try to design one for yourself, and tell a real-life or imaginary story about yourself or your friends along the way. Remember, try to let the pictures do most of the work. They have to be funny in themselves and yet work together. Limit yourself to a maximum of eight frames. Look at the subjects for the caricatures and decide on the most important features or props to exaggerate. You will probably have to experiment to get them right. If you have the resources and time, you could try an animation too.

Of course, cartoon strips are often saying something very serious. Ex-art teacher Steve Bell is one of the sharpest and funniest cartoonists in Britain today. Look at this example in *Picture 1* and try to do something similar about school events or issues, or something in your community. Once again, work on the caricatures as much as the story.

Have you noticed how often something looks like something else that is in fact completely different? The Italian painter Archimboldo thought that too, as you can see in *Picture 2*. But could he also have been thinking about the idea 'you are what you eat'? Try to create an Archimboldo head or figure, and make it from any type of object (the stranger the better).

You can do something similar showing how an idea has developed. Try starting with one object and then in five or six pictures change it into something else. If there is an amusing link between the beginning and end so much the better. The example in *Picture 3* shows the dim and dozy French king Louis Philippe (who reigned 1830–48), drawn by one of his subjects.

Puppet art has a long history. Puppets can reveal to the audience all the dash and glitter of the theatre for a fraction of the production costs. In Britain, during times of state censorship, puppets performing censored plays did so much more freely than actors could. Puppetry and puppet performance would make an excellent research project, ending with the work of Fluck and Law (*Picture 4*).

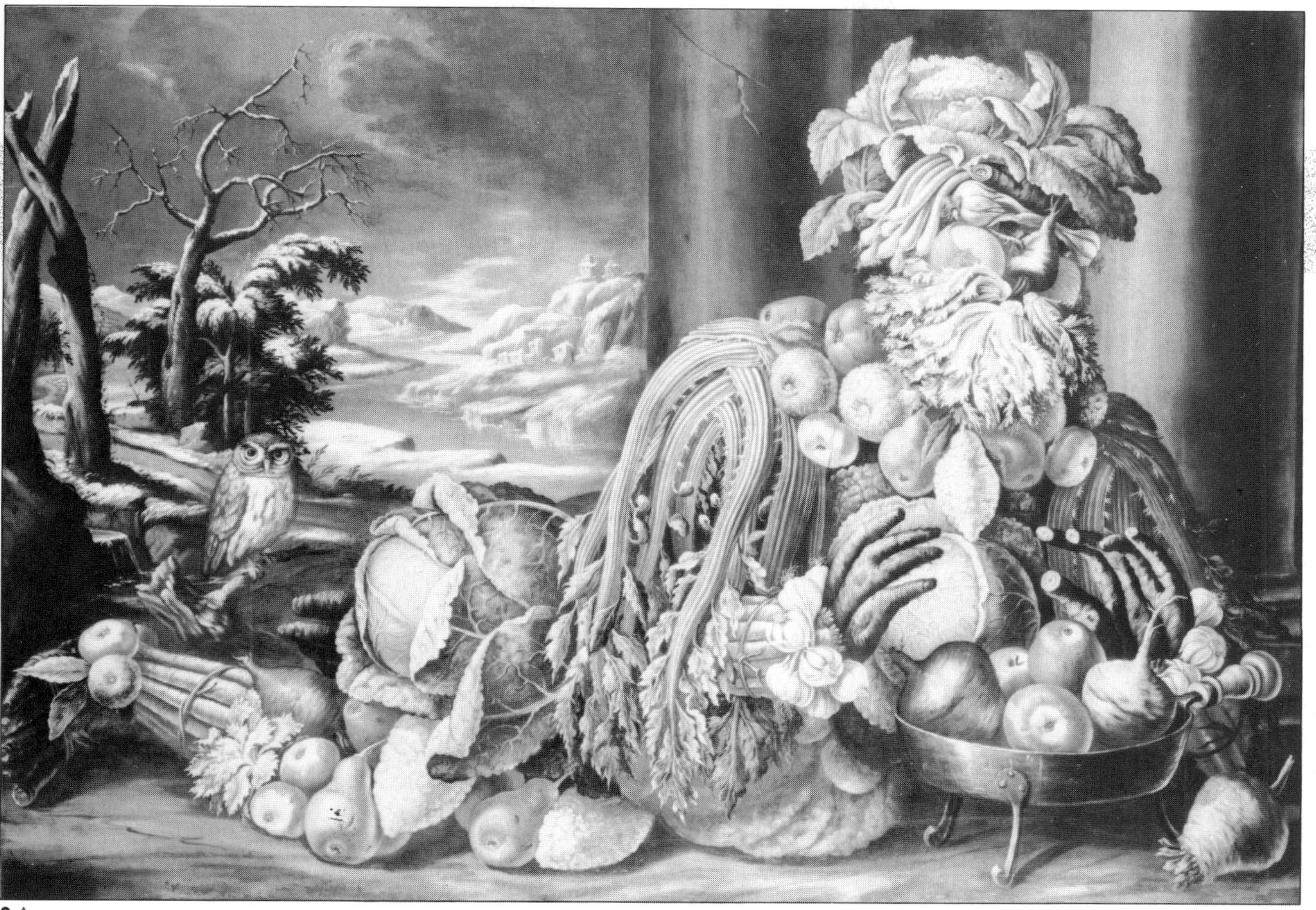

2△

3▽

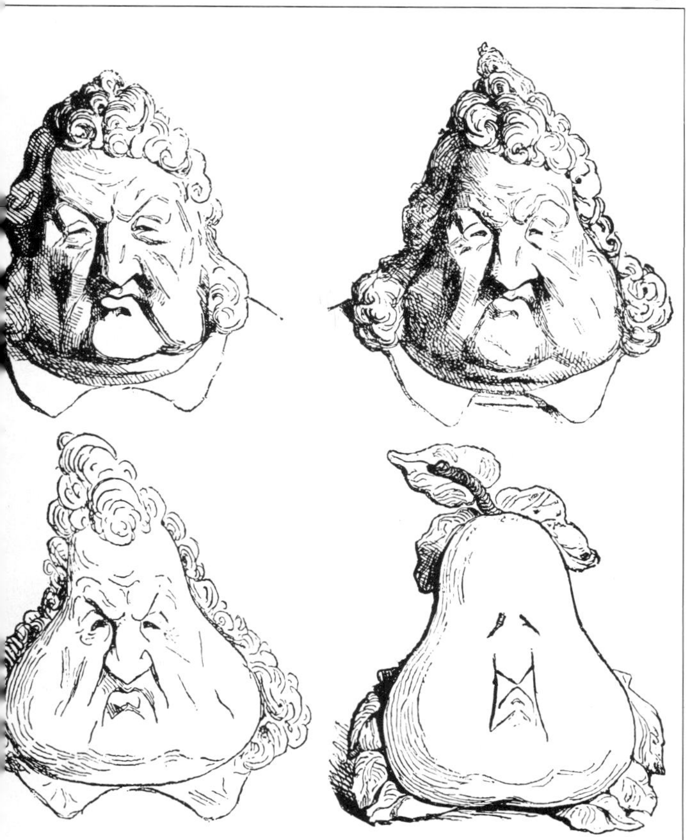

4

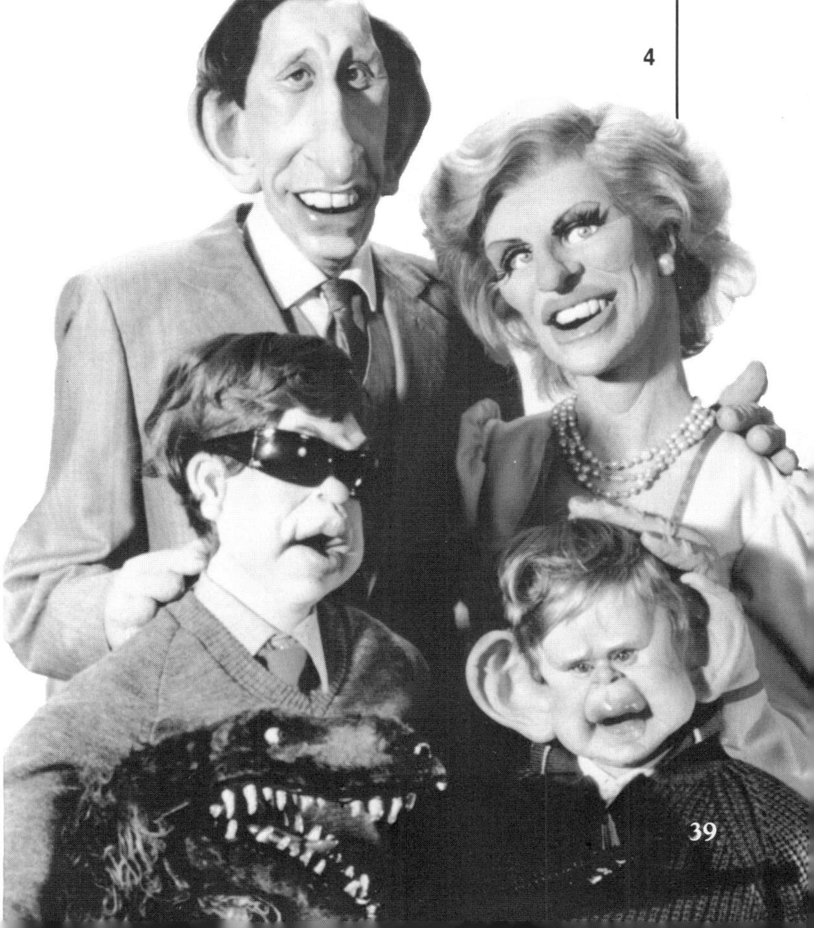

STYLE FOR LIVING

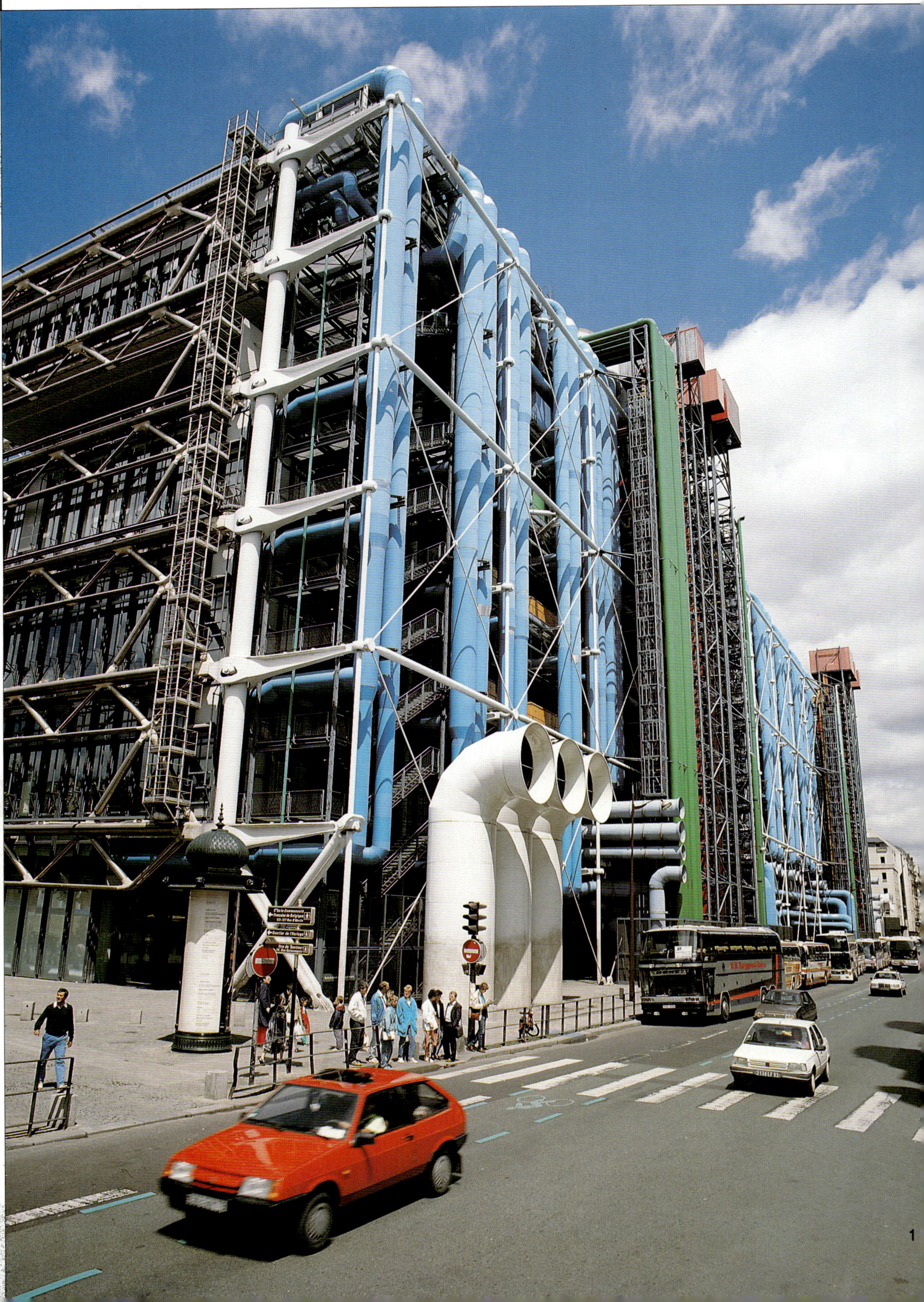

What is Design?

Designers have the same things in mind as artists. Indeed, in most places in the world, and in Europe in the past, artists and designers were seen as one group. Designers set out to make something easy and efficient to use, and also to make it *look* easy and efficient too. If it feels and looks right as well, the user will be happier and more relaxed and it's also more likely to sell. But that isn't the whole story. Designers have to take the user's past experience into account, how similar objects have been used in the past and how people expect them to look. That's why early cars looked like horse-drawn carriages with engines. It is also important to bear in mind that certain 'looks' are fashionable at certain periods. The familiar London Underground map, first re-designed to look as it does in the late 1920s, is not only clearer than what it replaced but also has a similar appearance to some of the paintings of the time.

Since everyone uses designed objects all the time, we're constantly looking at them and filing them away in our minds with other things we have seen. Their appearance affects how we see, and since they are more likely to catch the eye than most objects they are quite important in affecting our taste and that of other artists as well. In the same way artists are users like the rest of us and are more likely to notice something which is eye catching. So it isn't surprising that art is affected by design, just as design is affected by art.

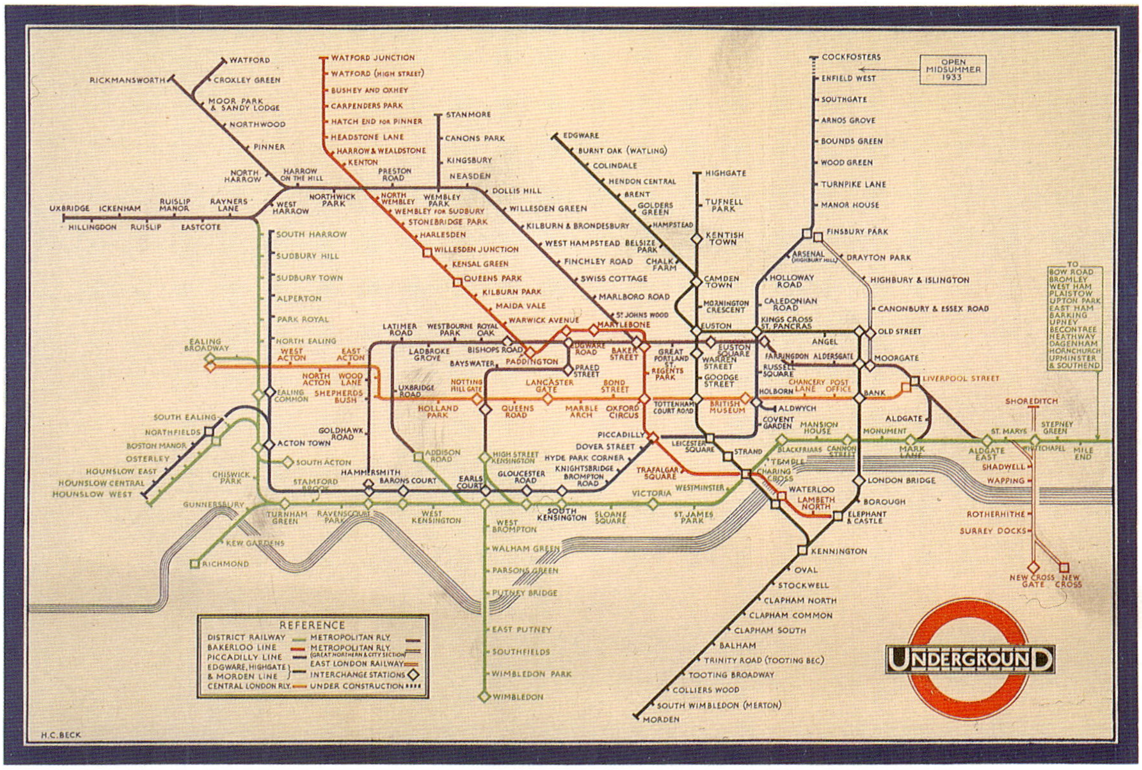

2

1
Pompidou Centre, Paris, designed by Richard Rogers, 1977. Why does this important building have all its 'innards' outside?

2
London Underground map, 1933. The underground system is extremely complicated. With the help of a London street map, work out how the designers came up with the new map. How different is it from 'reality'? Find paintings and sculpture with a similar look.

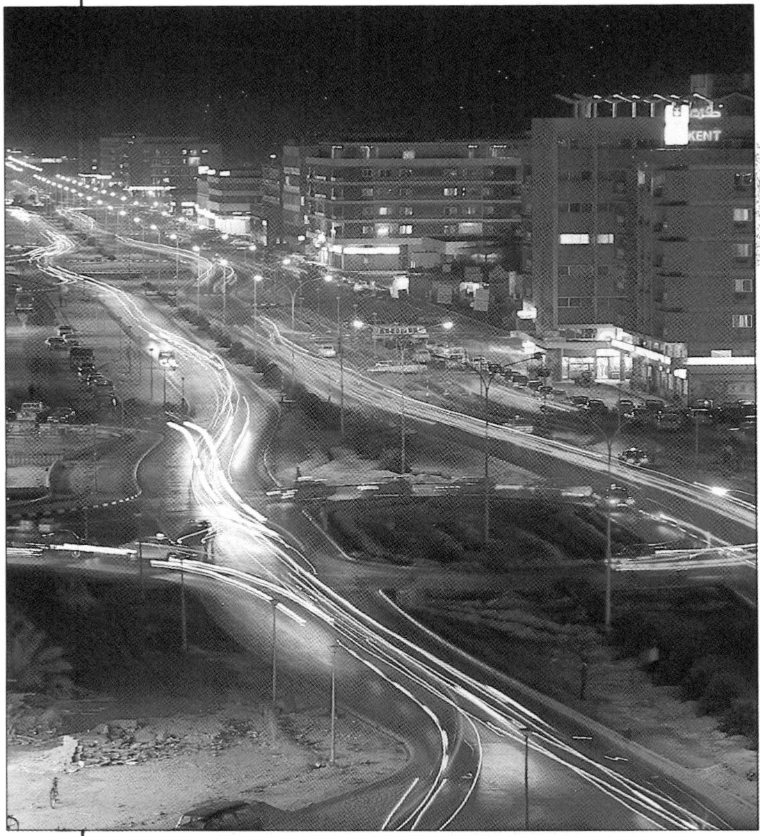

3

3
A night scene, Abu Dhabi. Bright lighting and neon signs have transformed our view of cities at night and with comparatively slow photographic film this has become a standard image of sophistication and excitement. Compare the appearance of this photograph with illustrations 1, 3 and 4.

4
A Bugatti type 35 racing car, 1935. A shape that spells speed and adventure. And even under the bonnet, fine engineering *looks* as if it does its job well. The favourite car of artist Anthony Green.

5-8
Shaker chair (USA) c. 1860.
Victorian chair.
'Modern' chair (UK) 1930s.
Comfortable chair by Fred Baier, 1984.
What does a chair do? How does the way it looks affect the user? How would you feel sitting in the chairs illustrated above?

4

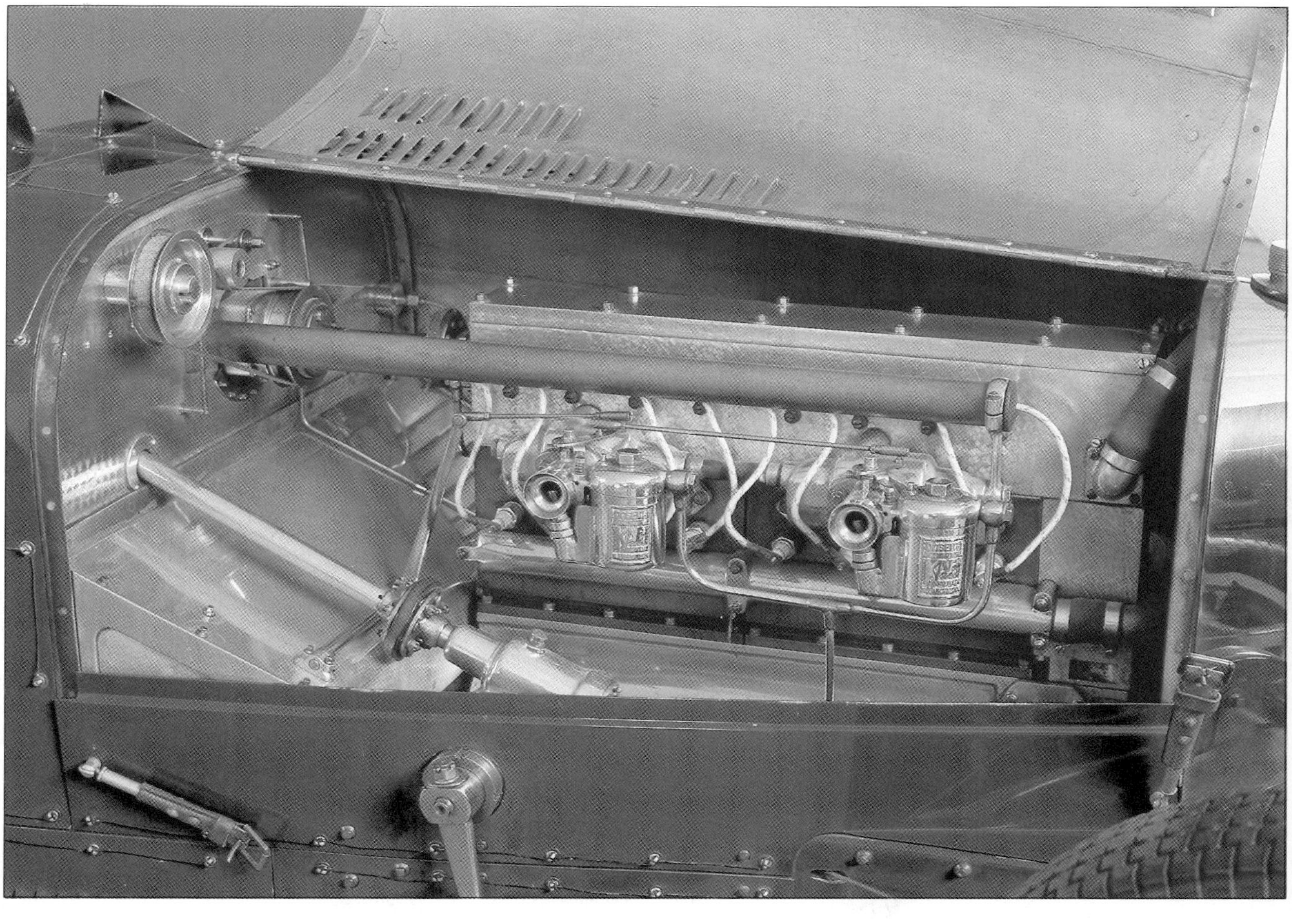

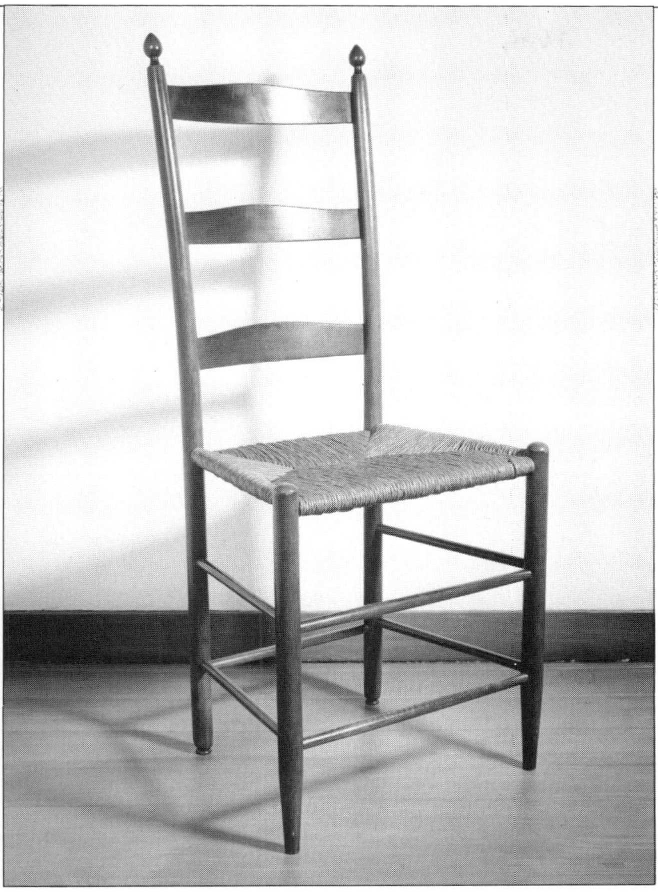

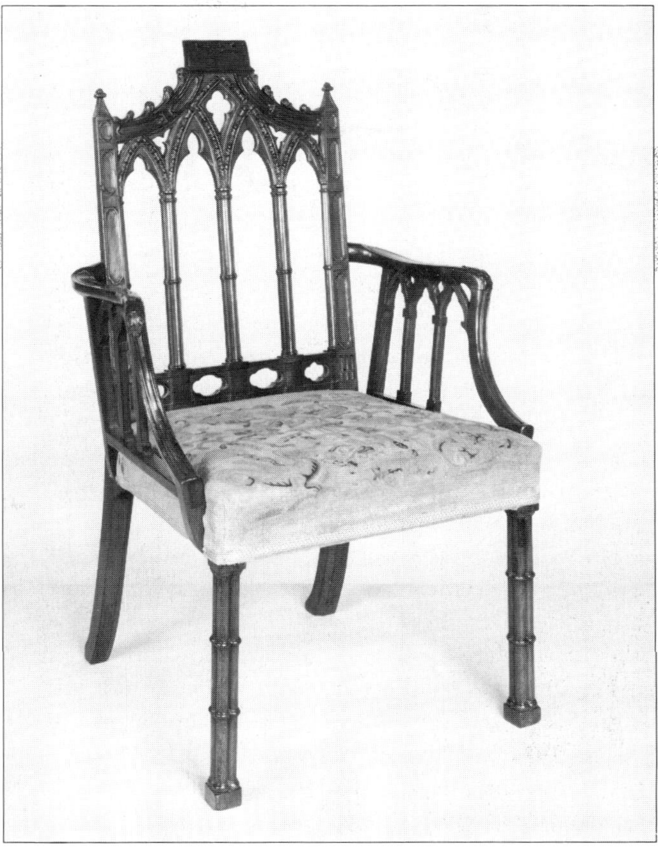

5-8

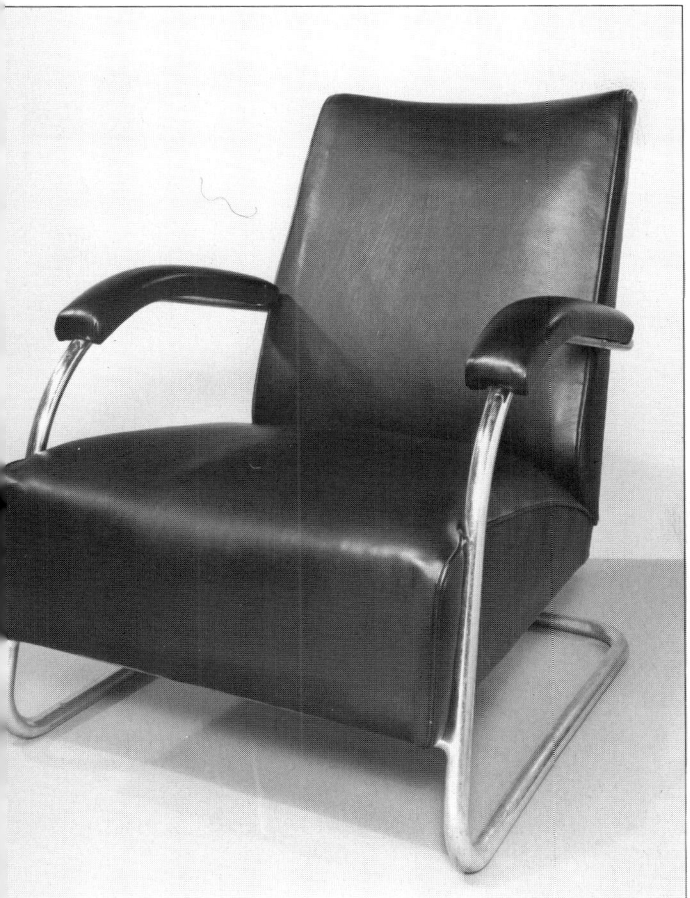

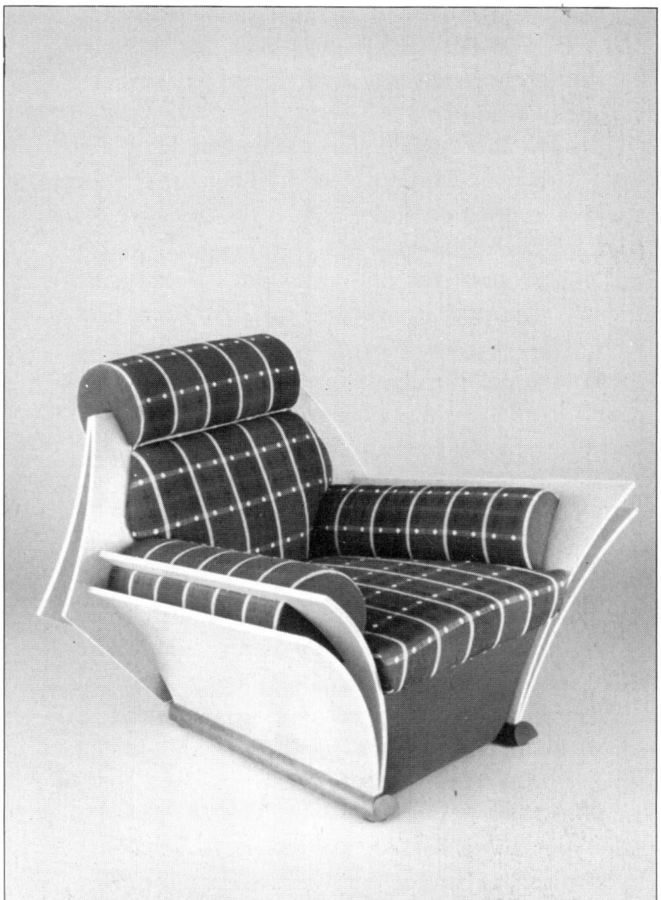

Two Styles, Same Method

'Design' is the art of making objects easier and more enjoyable to use – 'user friendly', as they say. There have always been designers, but nowadays we know far more about what they do because their importance has been recognised. In a world where there is a wealth of choice, how well a thing works and how good it looks will helps sales tremendously. A good design can keep down the costs of materials and manufacturing too. Designers today work on most objects which are made for use, and up and down any high street almost every shop has been *designed*, not just built, inside and out. We have chosen one aspect of design – the interiors of buildings – and looked at two contrasting designs – a new branch for an upmarket chain of outfitters and a small chapel in a hospital run by nuns in the Lake District. Their designers, Rasshied Din and the partners Gordon Benson and Alan Forsyth, are specialists in their very different fields, but their way of working is surprisingly similar.

The first stage begins with working on a brief with the customer. The brief is a list of things the design must do and the rules the designer must stick to. For an interior of a clothes shop, it is obviously important that customers can see that goods are on sale and that assistants can help them find what they want and pay for it. So the designer has to think about the display and the storage of stock, access to all areas and places for trying goods on and then the wrapping and the collection of money. But that is only the beginning. A clothes shop has to have racks and shelves, counters, tills and changing rooms. It also has to have lighting, heating, safety exits, a security system, a place for the staff to leave their belongings and wash, office space and a stock room with easy retrieval. Everything must be easy to maintain and alter, because of constantly changing displays and the possibility of future changes of 'identity'.

A chapel must contain certain items used in worship, such as places to sit and kneel, read and pray. Light is very important too, as is the right atmosphere of calm and privacy needed for prayer and meditation. On a more commercial front, the interior has to be built at the right price and in the right length of time. It must fit into the space available and not infringe the planning regulations.

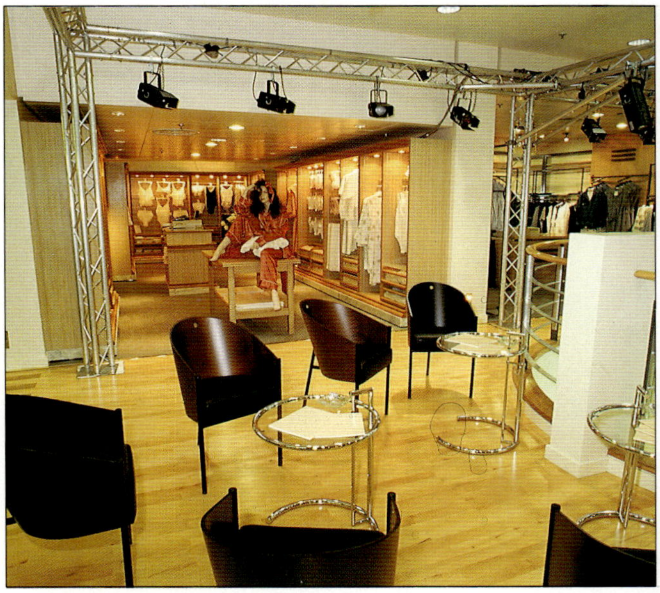

1 1

Interior of 'Next' shop in Kensington High Street, London. Co-ordination doesn't work well unless it is carried right through the design and affects even the smallest detail, but the hardest thing to take into account is customer behaviour: everyone is an individual with individual tastes.

2

Sketches for the Oxford Street design and (inset) the finished shop. Most shops in any high street today have an 'identity' designed specially for them. This will begin with a logo (the shop name or symbol) and be carried through into the interior and exterior design, the fittings, the assistants' clothes, the notices and price tickets and the wrappings. The identity is designed to go with the goods on sale, and to appeal to the taste of a targetted group of prospective customers.

3

Benson and Forsyth's design for a hospital oratory, Grange over Sands, Cumbria. Atmosphere is tricky for designers to calculate. It will depend on colour, the material used, lighting, shapes, textures and also sound.

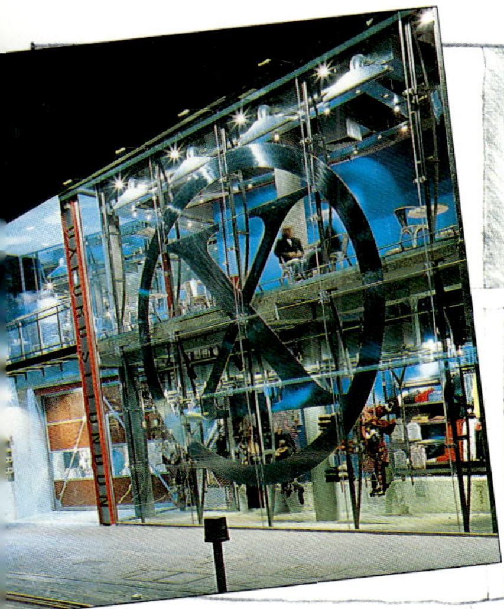

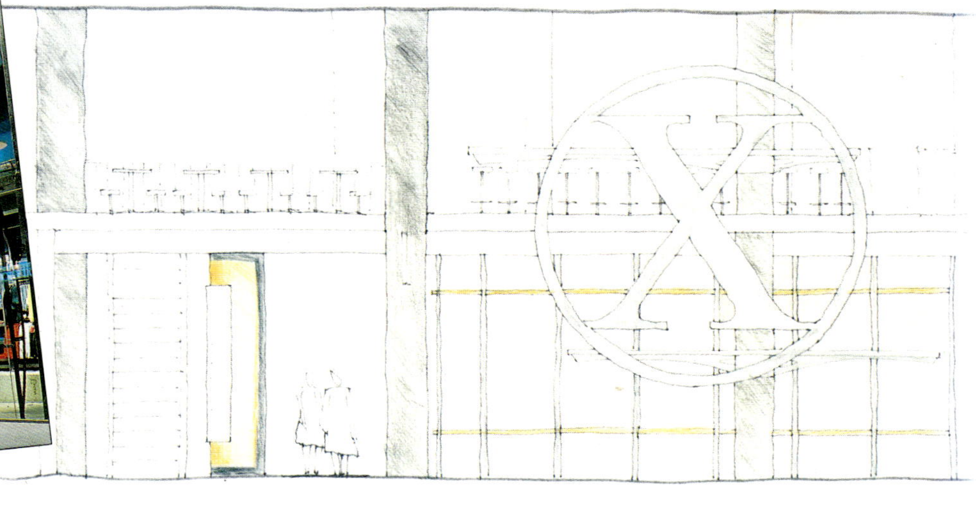

2△

3▽

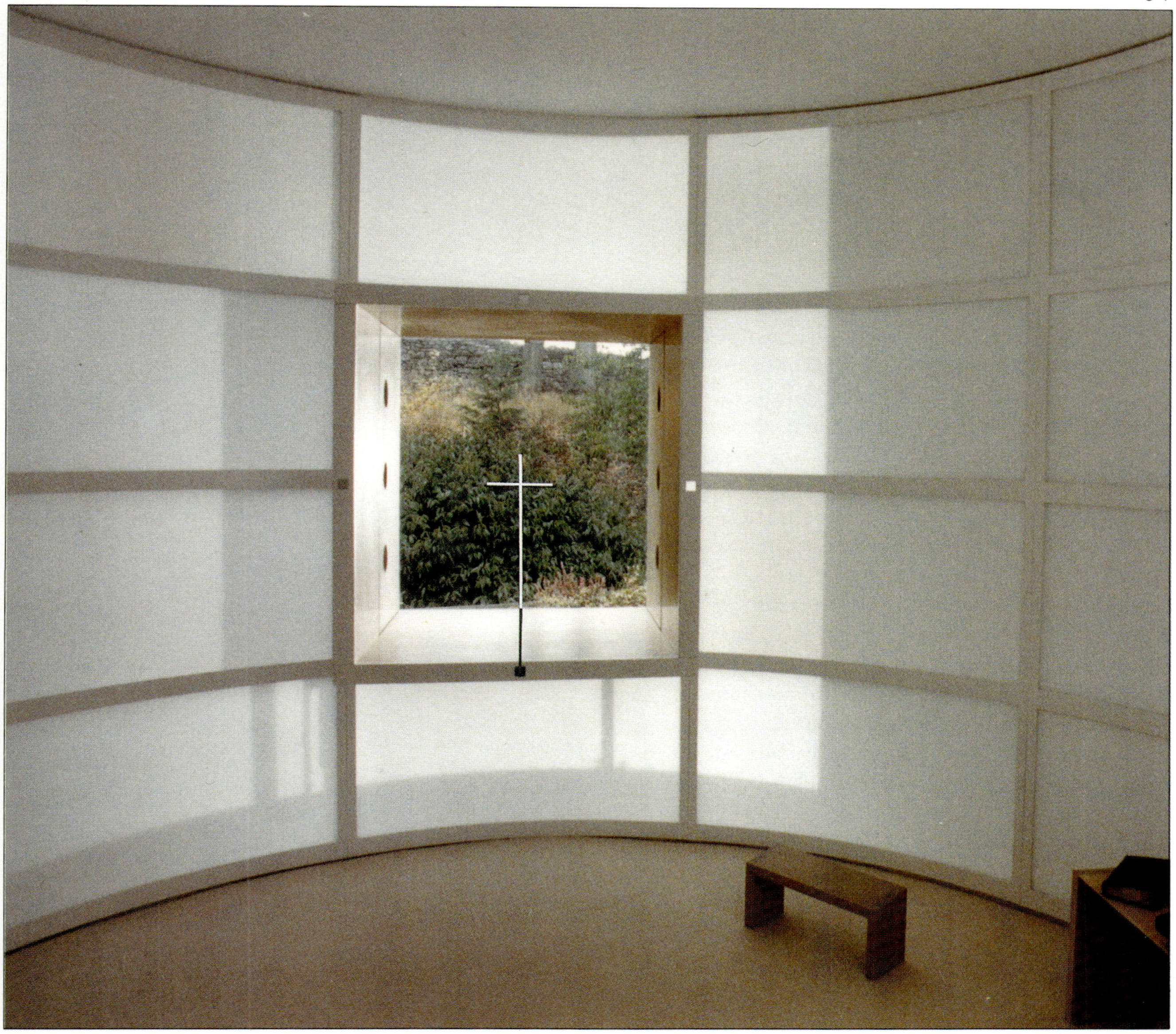

Research

The first working stage of research involves collecting information about the project. For a shop this means thinking about what the shop will sell and who the customers are likely to be. It's often very useful to make a careful survey of the site, to see how it is affected by other buildings, traffic, passing pedestrians, light and noise and so on, and to note any existing features which can be used in the new design. Then the designer has to begin thinking about possible starting points, and that means drawing on experience. Rasshied Din's experience working on other 'Next' shops told him what was likely to work best, and the identity loyal customers recognised and felt comfortable with. But he was keen to produce something new and eye-catching without completely discarding that familiar look, and the brief asked for a design which would appeal to a new group of less sophisticated customers. His eye had been caught by a computerised stock handling system in the 'Next' warehouse in Leicester. It wasn't just what the machinery did but its appearance which fascinated him. This would provide the keynote for the new shop, but he still had to bear in mind the qualities found in earlier shops – the combination of pale wood and matt black metal fittings, the elegant typeface of the logo and the other graphics, the overall air of cool, quiet, unfussy stylishness a little similar to the interior of a traditional Japanese house.

For Benson and Forsyth the traditions of the Christian church provided the key to their designs. The circle is an ancient symbol of perfection, and of God. There are a number of traditional round churches, and the two designers looked to them for inspiration. There were also practical advantages. A circular chapel would fit the available square space in a corridor and it would also be a very satisfying and interesting shape.

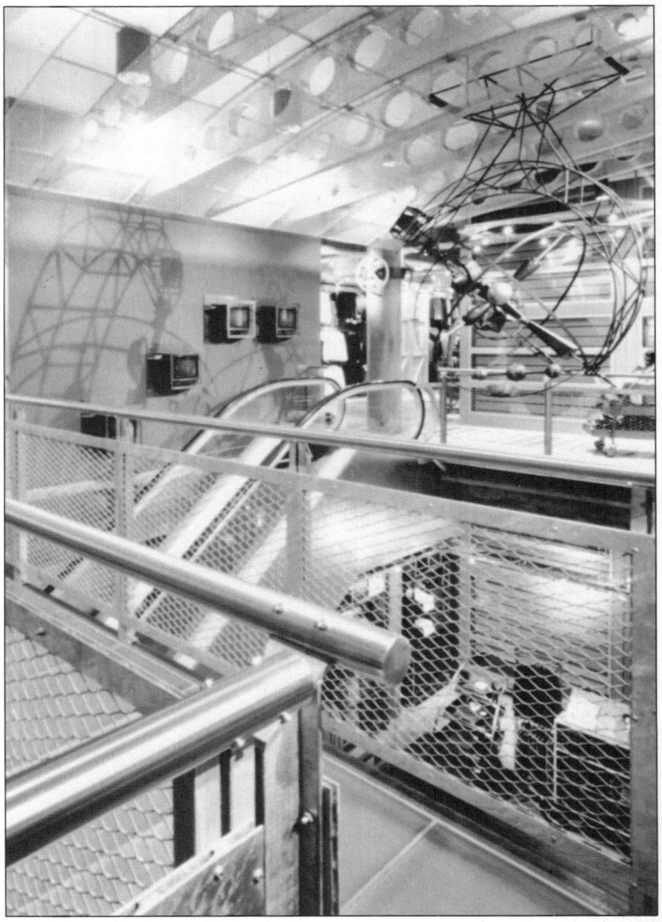

1△

2▽

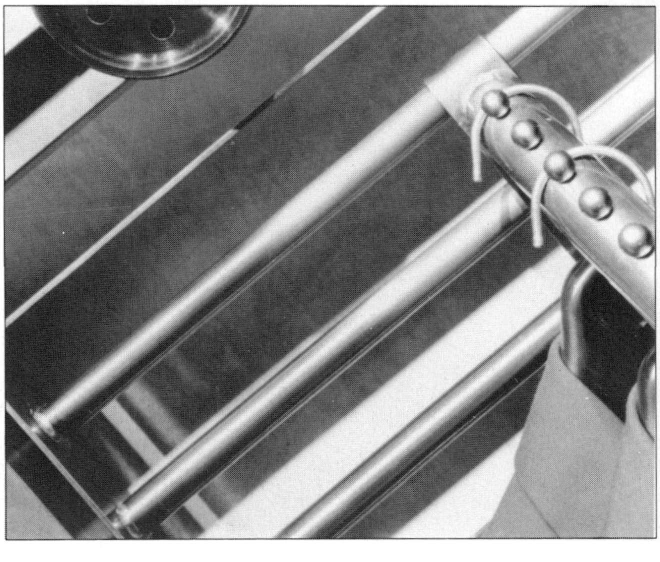

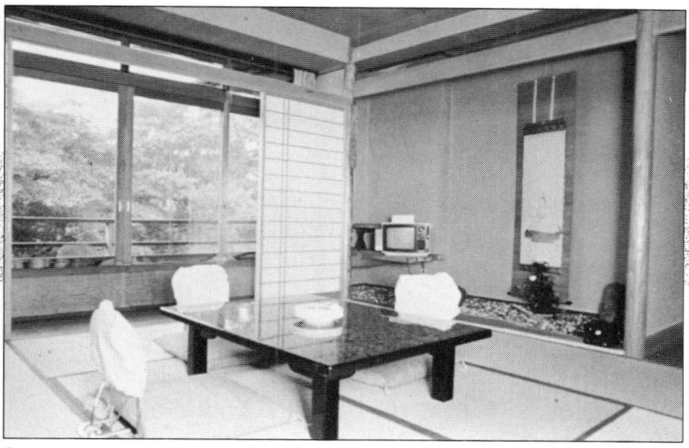

3△

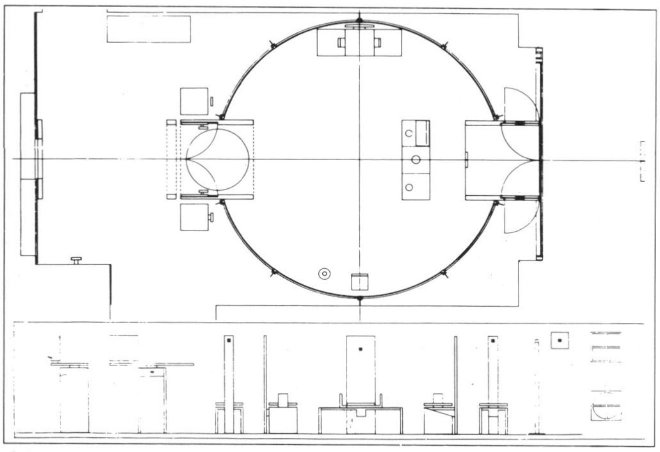

4△

1
An interior view of the 'X' design. Describe the feeling it gives you, and guess at some of the visual sources.

2
A close-up of detailing.

3
Interior of a Japanese house.

4
Benson and Forsyth's plan for the round chapel. The axis lines are used to arrange features in a logical way.

5
An Italian church relying on the square and the circle for its plan, from the Renaissance period (1524).

5▽

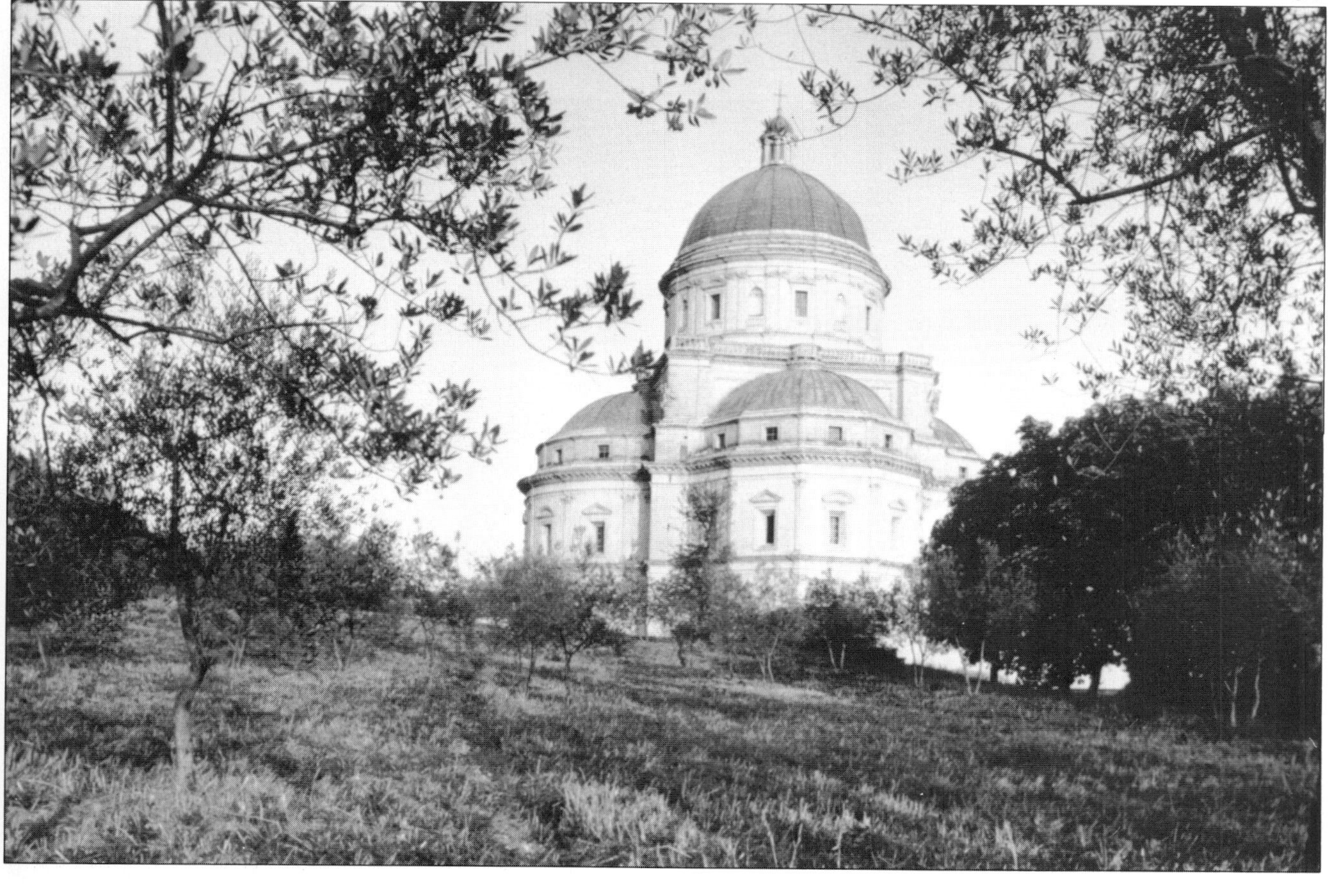

Experiment: The Practical Problems

Do the ideas and discoveries that come from research actually work? For the designers their choice of materials was crucial. There were few ready-made answers and each team had to take down catalogues and visit warehouses looking for items which would do the practical jobs required of them, look right and come within the price laid down in the brief.

The biggest problem for Benson and Forsyth was finding a material for the circular 'walls' of the chapel. They had to be solid enough to stand upright without buckling, but at the same time it would be an advantage if they let in light. This was because lighting from above would be harsh and directional and meant that a fussy array of fixtures would be visible. By lighting through the walls from outside there would be no lights to be seen and the effect would be soft and mysterious. Finally after a search they found a suitable material – a light-weight curved glass sheet with a layer of matt white on the inside. This also had the practical advantages of being easy to assemble and keep clean. The other materials were chosen or treated to co-ordinate with this. Woodwork was bleached and left unpolished and the carpet was a soft, oatmeal colour (good for kneeling on, and a useful sound baffle). This neutral background was the perfect foil for a matt black chair and the shining gold of the tabernacle and cross detailed in coloured enamel. Most of all it was perfect for the view through the window of the garden, which in contrast to the soft whites and creams inside seems brilliantly coloured, crisply focused and full of exciting shapes.

The materials chosen by Rasshied reflected his plan to combine the feel of a hi-tech factory and a conventional shop. As he collected them, he was drawing his working ideas on a tear sheet for comparison and experiment. He frequently spends a lot of money building a full-size mock-up of an interior at a warehouse at the 'Next' headquarters to make sure there are not too many surprises. This may seem expensive, but it is worthwhile in the long term.

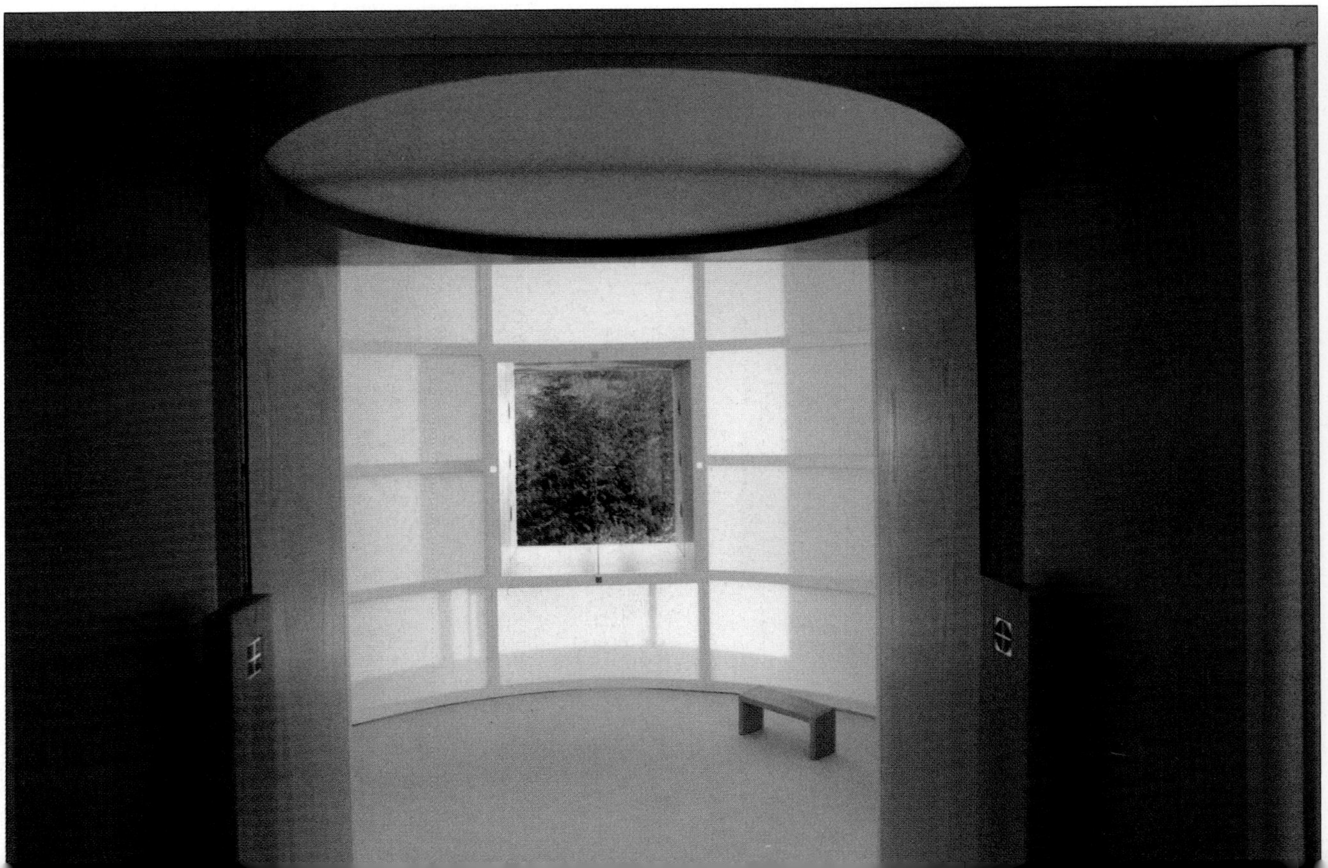

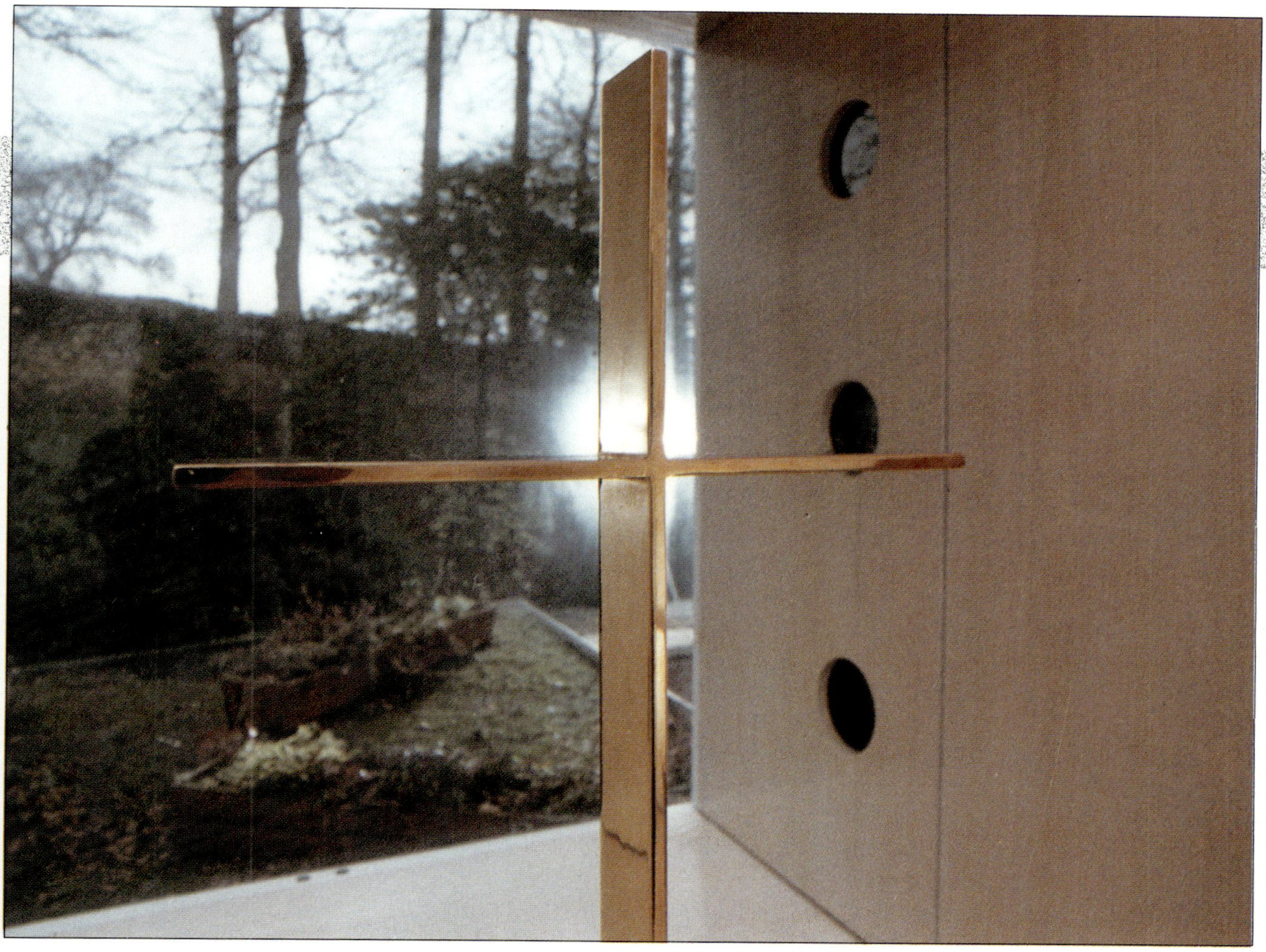

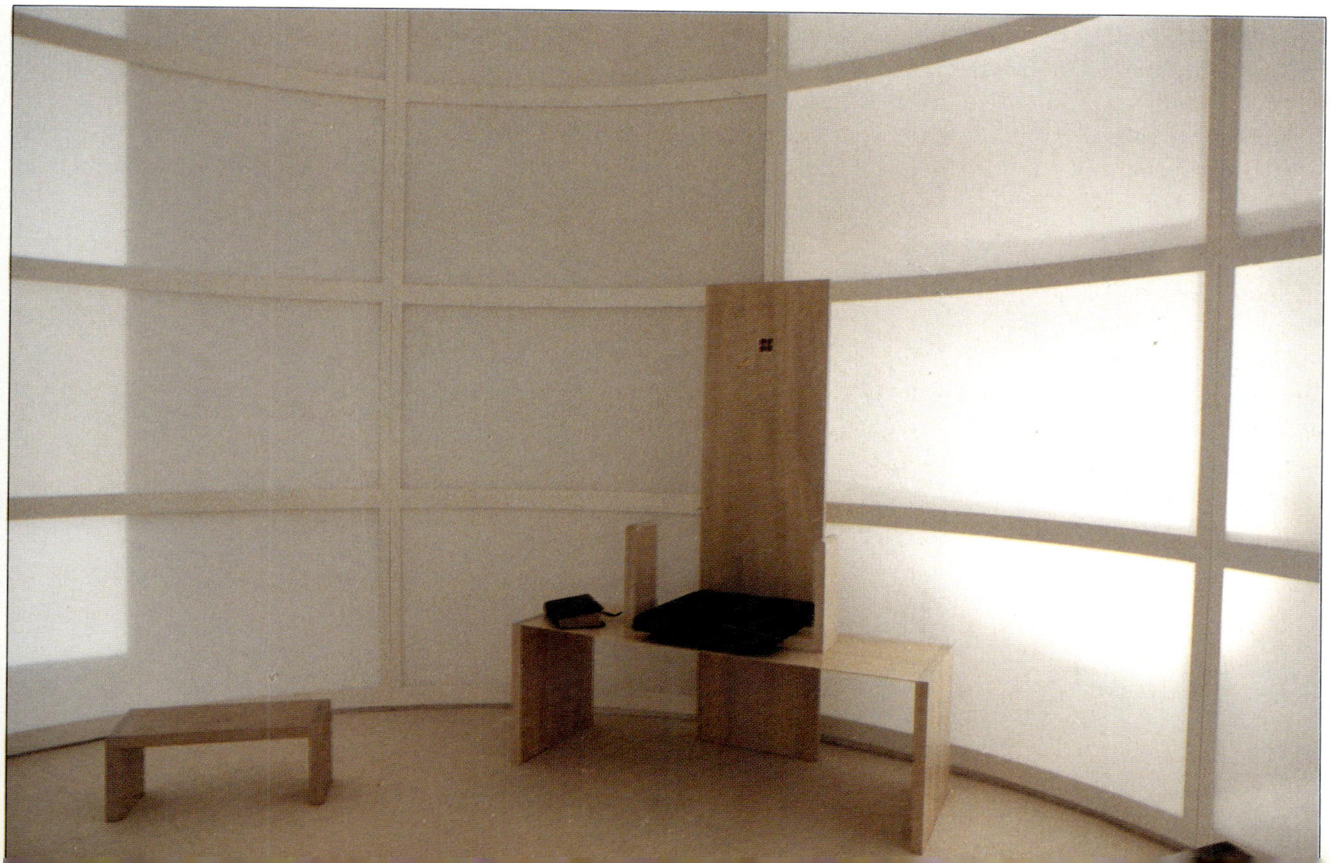

The Customer is Always Right

The two interiors we have examined are now both in use and both clients are satisfied. For the hospital nuns the chapel has become a haven of peace in their busy and sometimes harrowing working lives, a place where it is easy to meditate and pray. It is not only conveniently planned, quiet, private and close to their work, but it has the dreamlike atmosphere intended by the designers, with a few objects to contemplate as a focus for thought and prayer.

Rasshied Din's new shops, one in London and the other in Glasgow, set out to attract a younger, less sophisticated clientele than the usual 'Next' customer. Once again, the satisfaction of the client in the money the shop has made proves that the designer correctly identified the tastes of the target market. The shop's atmosphere has interested them enough to bring them in, and the design works efficiently too in helping them choose and buy painlessly.

It's important for us to understand that only rarely can designers work on something that fits in with their own tastes. But by approaching the problems with an interest in the clients and their needs, and by working methodically to the brief, they can be reasonably sure that a project will work and that it will be popular too.

1-2
The chapel in use.

3
The 'X' facade: much of the stock is visible from the street. The logo letter is still in the 'Next' standard typeface, despite the new 'stronger' look.

4-5
Colours, materials, finishes are partly old, partly new. The tracks of the computerised stock retrieval system are clearly visible.

1-2

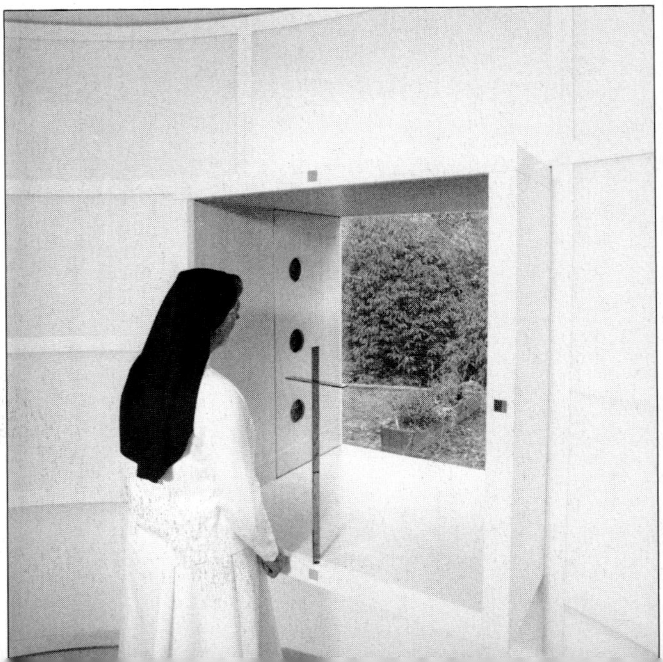

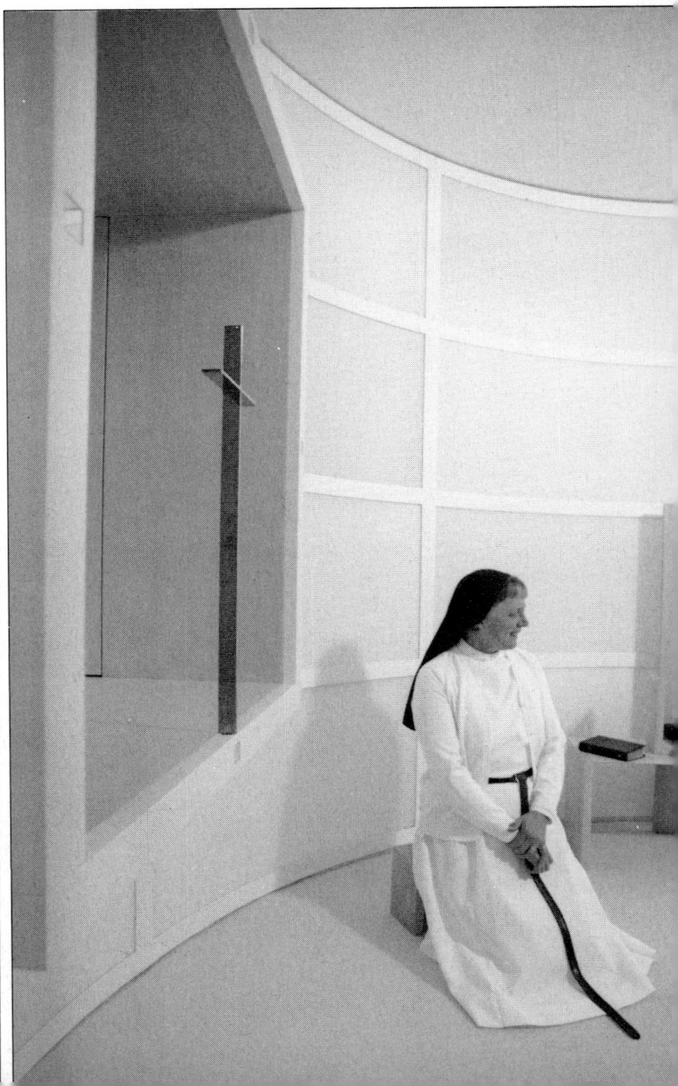

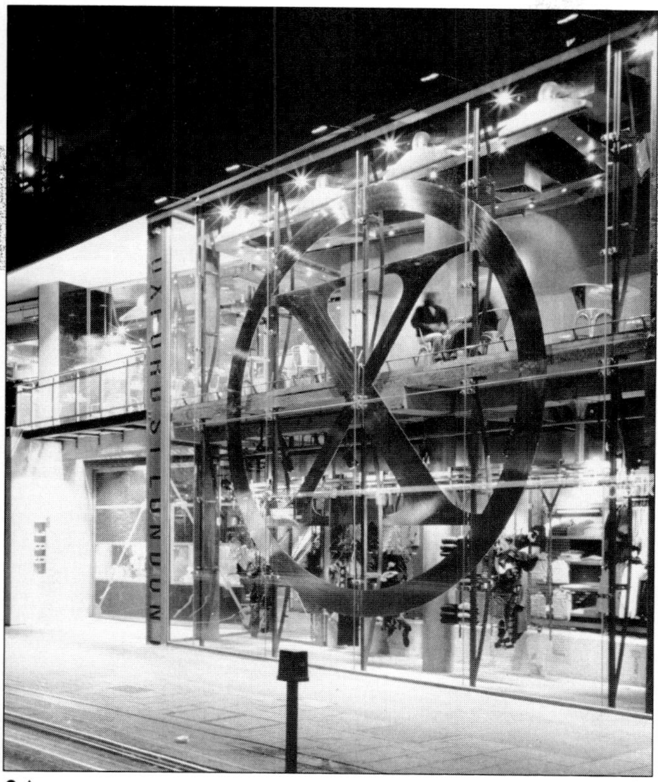

3△

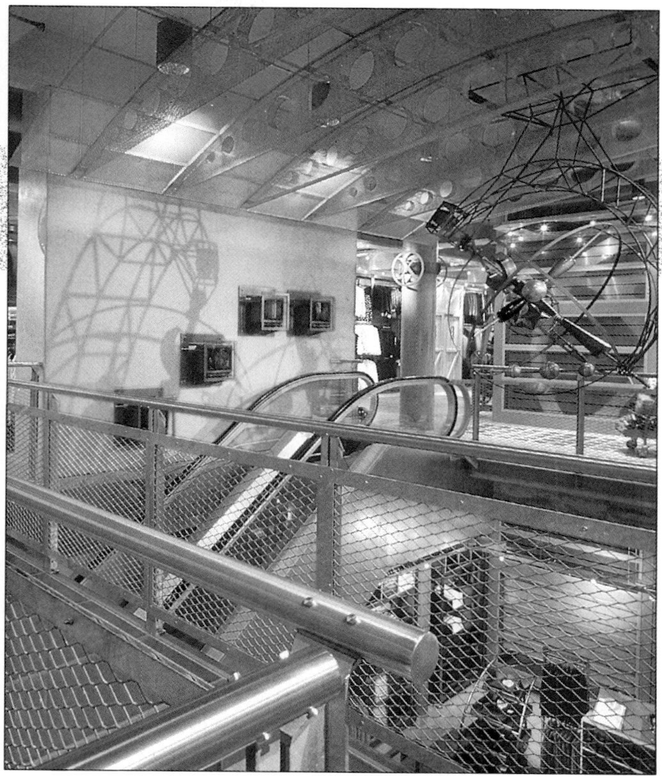

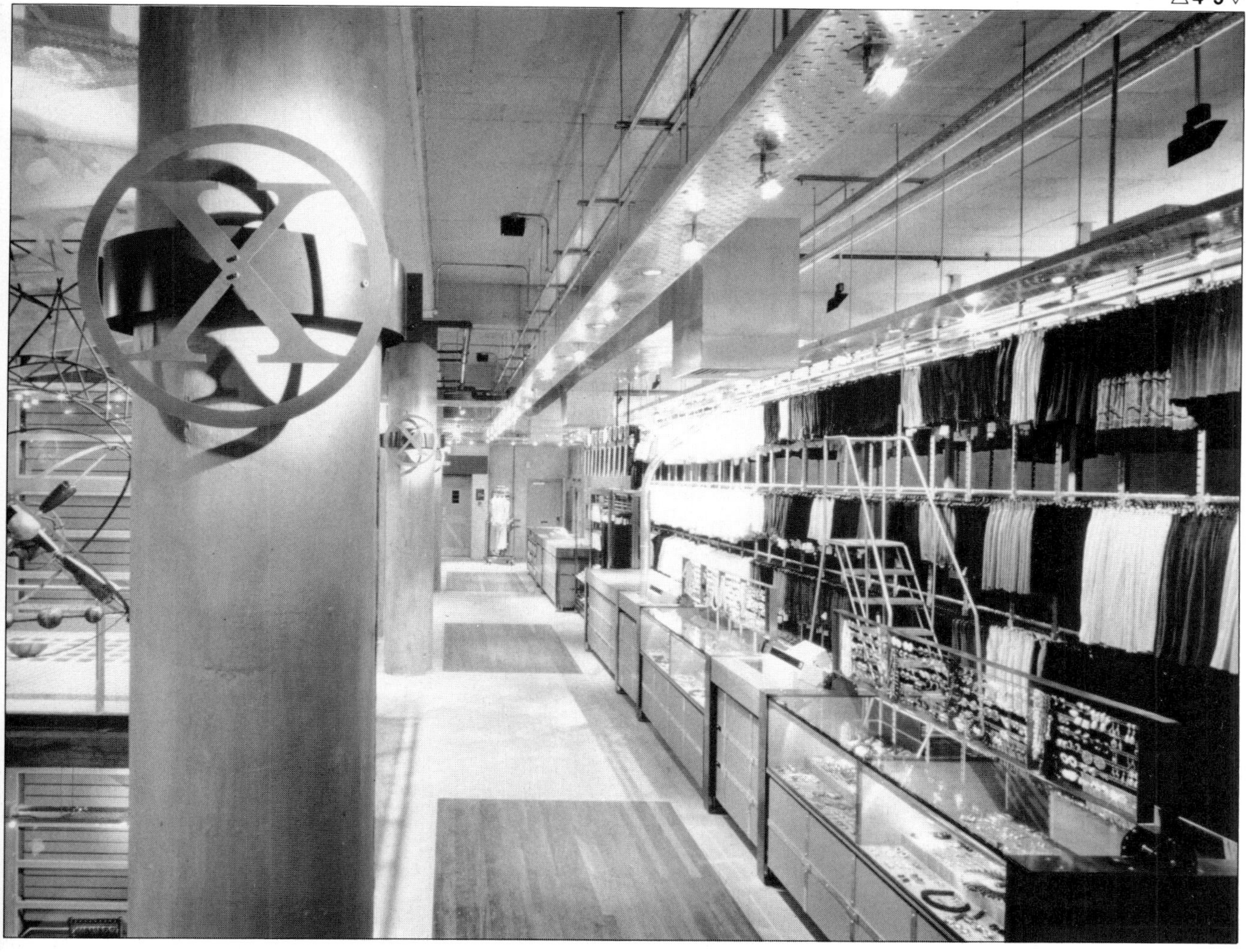

△4-5▽

STYLE FOR LIVING

Ideas for You

A major factor in designing is thinking hard about an object, how it is to be used, by whom, and then what kind of features would please its users. There's no actual artistic talent involved here – just the ability to see matters from someone else's point of view.

When you have chosen your design project you need to begin looking around for the best way of carrying it out. Now we're thinking about interior design, so it would be a good idea to look in magazines, catalogues, price lists and in shops for materials and design ideas that might apply. Then you need to produce scale plans and sketches to show the finished concept – not just the atmosphere and how that is produced, but the practical things too. Make up your own modulor (see *Picture 4*) to find the most efficient and comfortable dimensions for the furniture and fittings. You can make scale templates of different items, and move them about the plans to find the best arrangement. Finally, you might try a model or a full-scale mock-up if you have room. Get volunteers (appropriately dressed) to people the interior, and take photographs. Don't forget items like graphics and co-ordinated colour schemes. To round off the project try costing it with the help of price lists or catalogues.

Here are some more ideas about research and changing tastes:

1 Survey your high street in general and list the best and worst shops with a brief description of their style.

2 Choose one shop and with the permission of the management take photographs and make plans and sketches of the design. If possible interview customers and staff about the good and bad points.

3 Try to find a photo of the high street or individual shops in the past. How has the design changed and why?

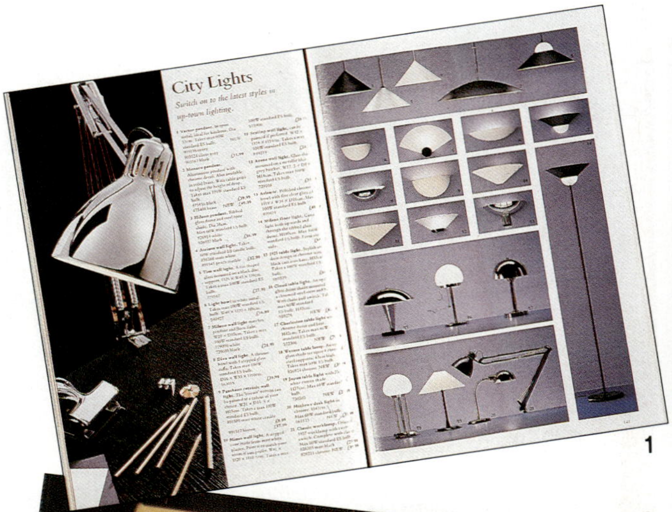

1

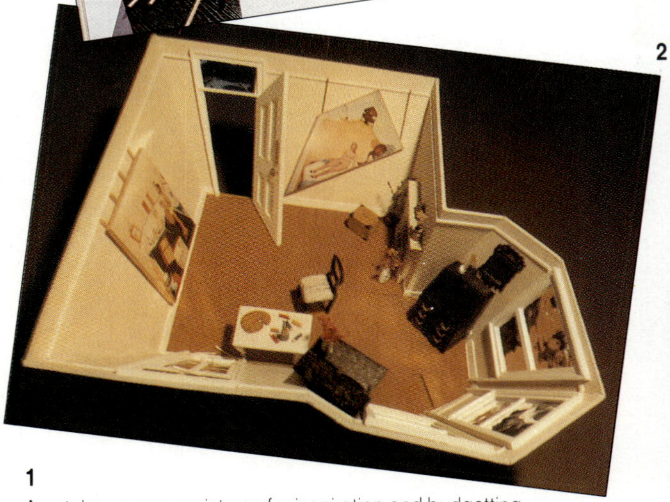

2

1
A catalogue can assist you for inspiration and budgetting.

2
A model of Anthony Green's study, itself treated as a three-dimensional work of art in Anthony Green's style.

3-4
A fantasy restaurant with all the theme details correct. Can you design an interior to get the atmosphere exactly right?

5
A 'modulor' by Le Corbusier, the French architect of the 1920s–1950s.
'Ergonomics' is the modern study of measurements to be used for designing furniture and fittings which will be comfortable and efficient in use. They are based on average body sizes and proportions. Echoes of Vitruvian Man!

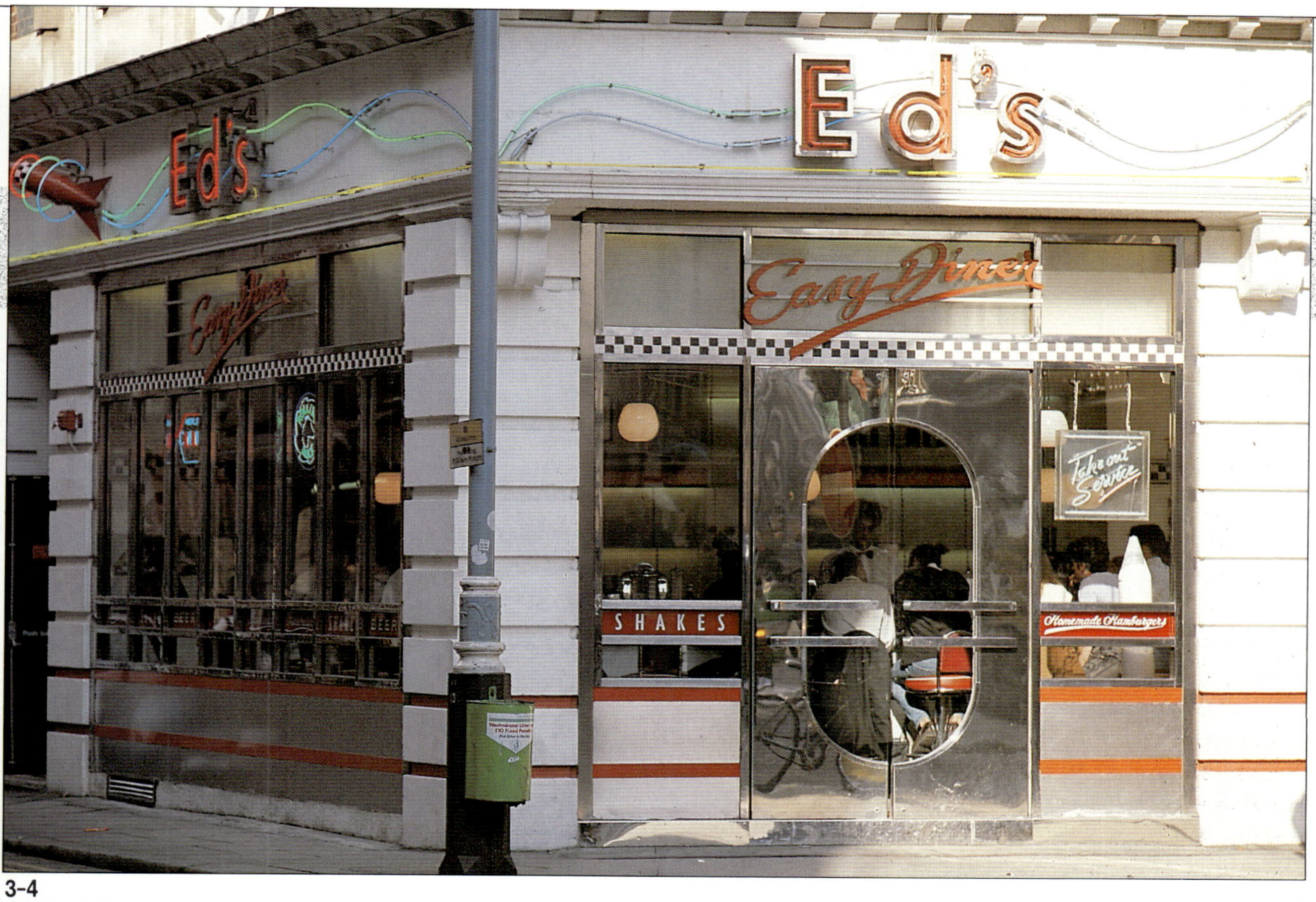
Ed's
Easy Diner
SHAKES
Homemade Hamburgers
Take out Service

3-4

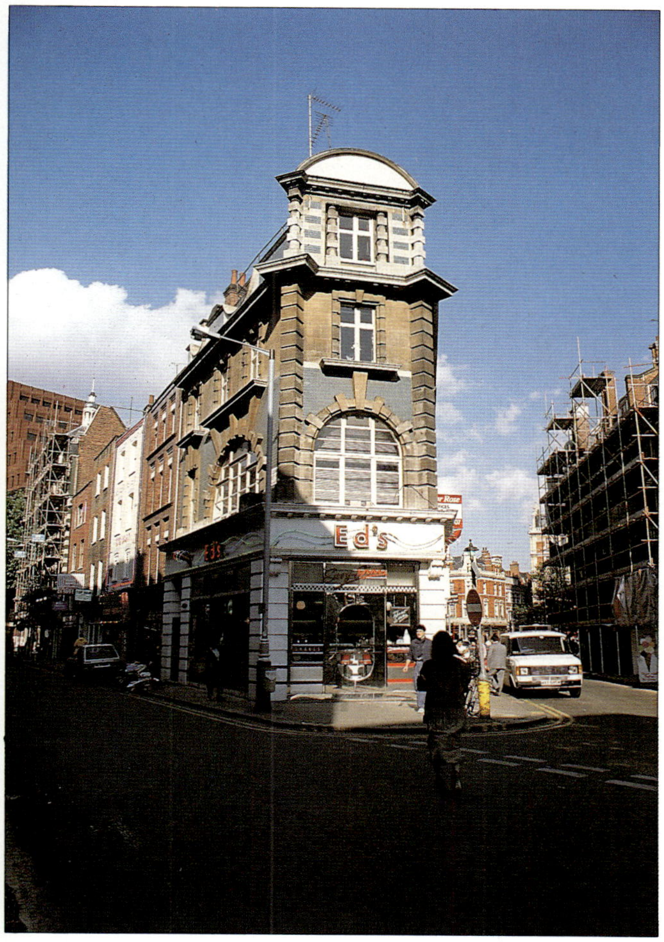

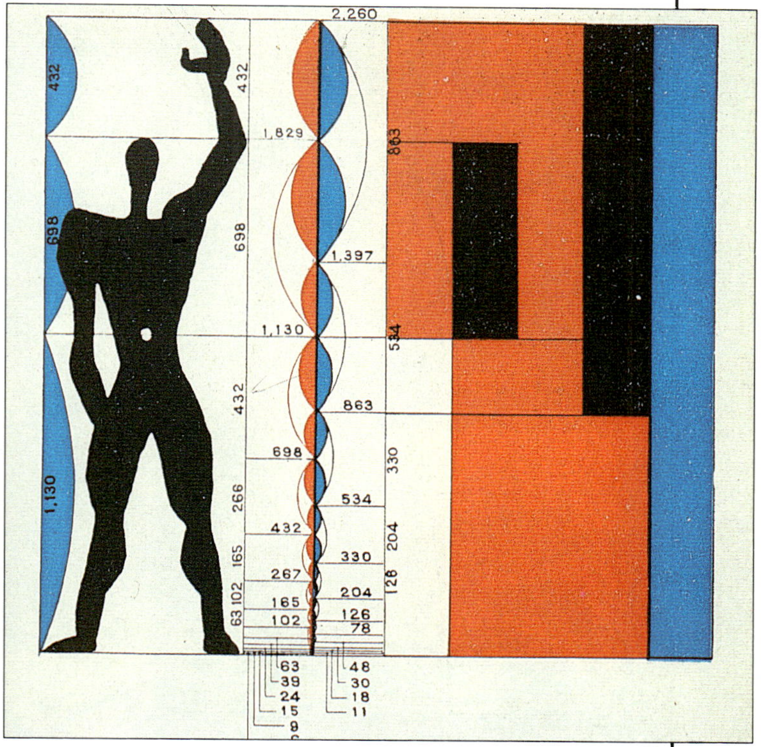
2,260
1,829
1,397
1,130
863
698
534
432
330
267
204
165
126
102
78
63
48
39
30
24
18
15
11
9

5

STYLE FOR LIVING

Take Off Here!

Not everyone has the same ideas about how to approach a design. In many places in the world, and throughout history, people have not worried about co-ordination, but often we outsiders can recognise the time and the place of a particular design despite the jumble of styles they may have used.

1 Look at the interiors and exteriors in the pictures below. First describe them, then try to work out where or from what period of history they come. Why did these particular styles of furnishing and decoration come about?

2 How would you design a shop, a club, a specialist or ethnic restaurant, a theme park or a grand party? Choose a concept which is either 'straight' or something wilder – how about a fishing tackle shop designed to look as if it's under water? Or an Arab restaurant set in a desert tent? Or a party set in the Stone Age? Or a club called 'Surprises'? Or a theme park based on 'Things to Come'?

3 Where we live is important to all of us. Pick a willing friend and ask him or her about their favourite surroundings. Then design a room or flat which you think will be ideal for your friend. Remember to build in co-ordination (or lack of it), colour, shapes, textures, sounds, lighting and gadgetry. Think, research, experiment, plan, build and do them all methodically. Carefully record and keep your findings – doodles, lists, catalogues, material samples, sketches, scale plans and models and photographs of full-scale mock-ups – for a display. How does your 'client' like the design?

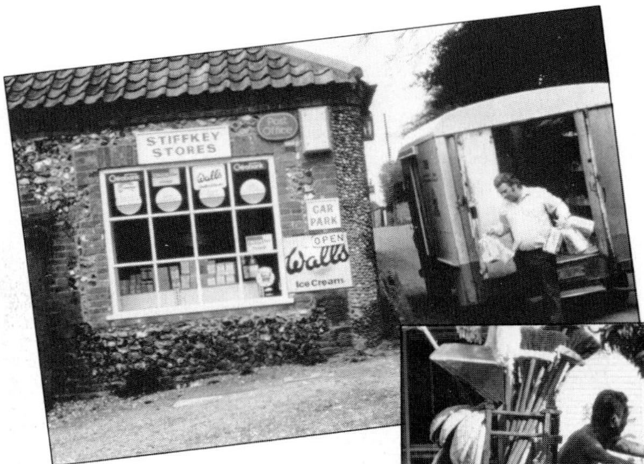

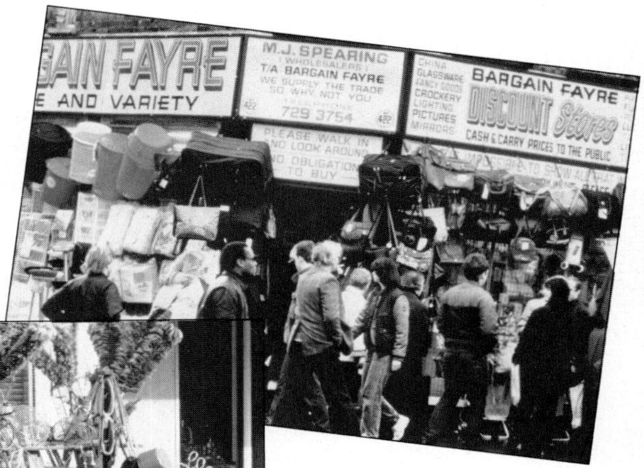

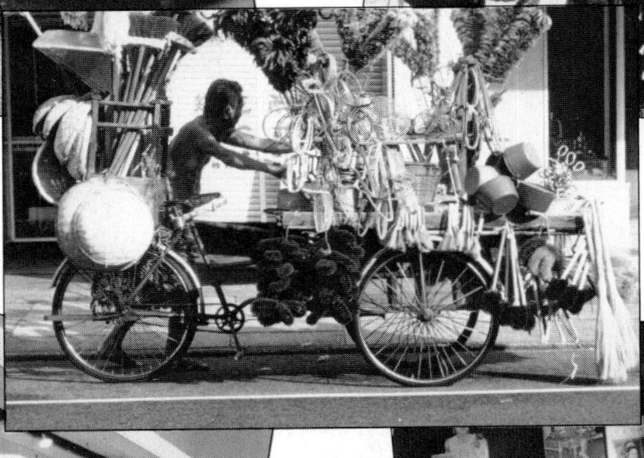

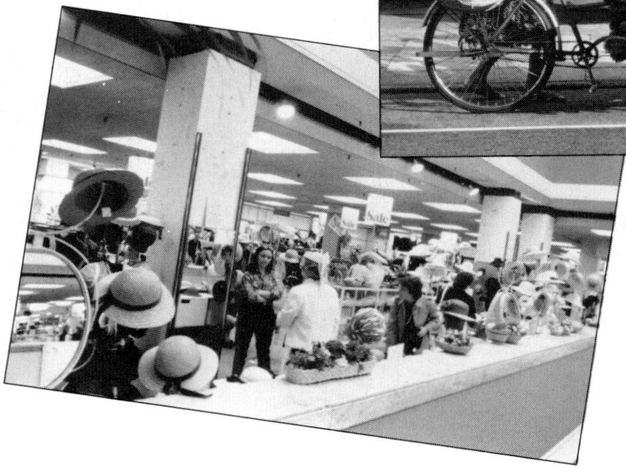

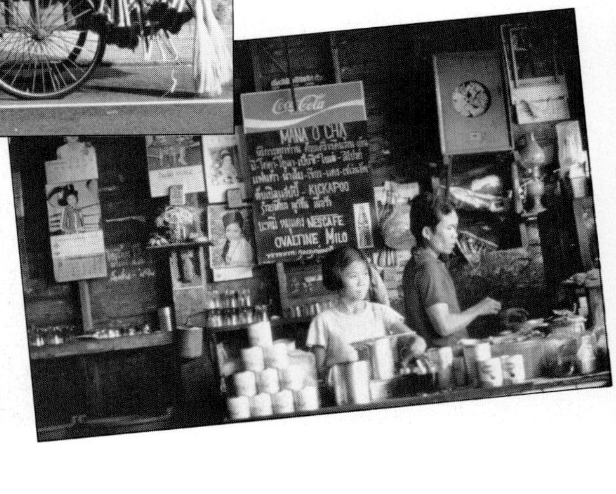

1

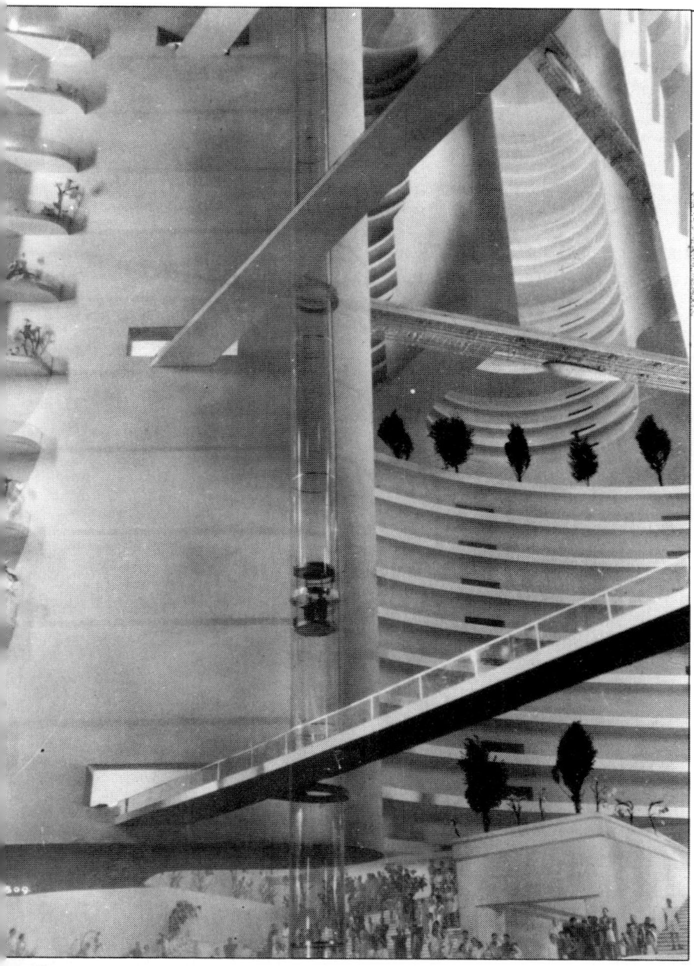

2

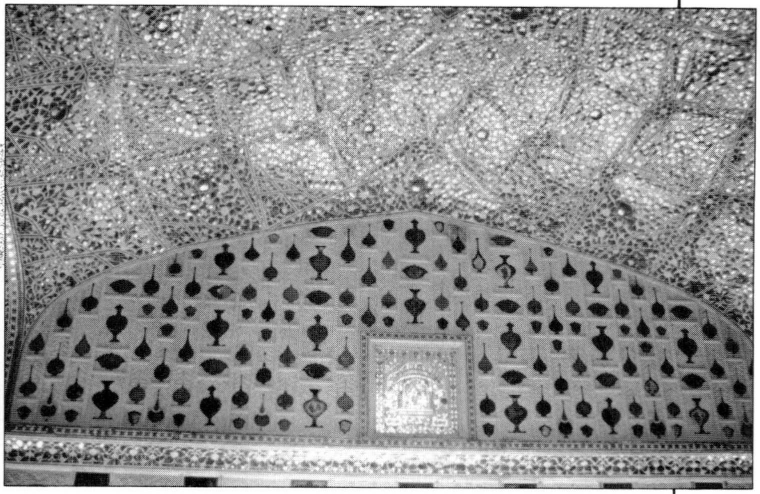

3△

1
Shops and selling pitches from Britain and abroad.

2
Still from the 1940s film *Things to Come*.

3
Mirror Room in the Amber Palace, Jaipur, India.

4
Sixteenth-century doorway, Rome.

5
Flat (designed in 1985) for the manager of a pop singer. There is no reason why lines should be vertical or horizontal or parallel, or why doors, windows and furniture should be made square or rectangular. But think about why most are!

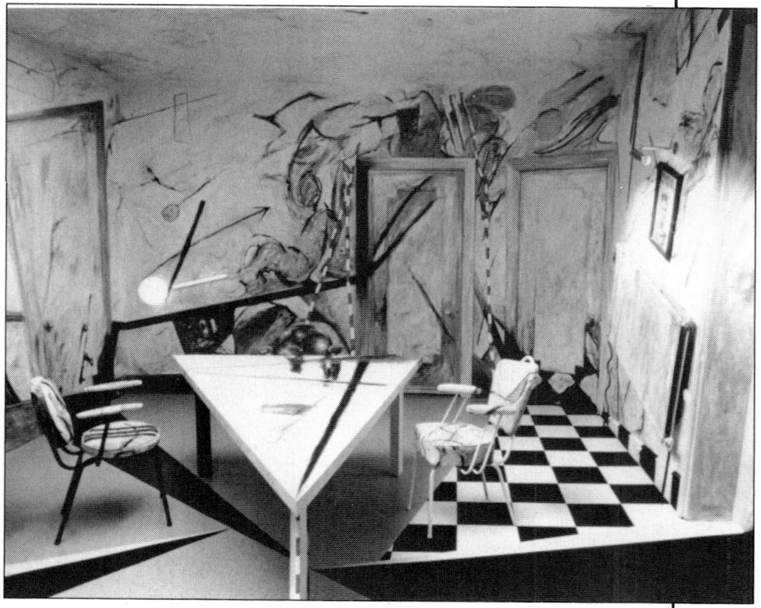

5

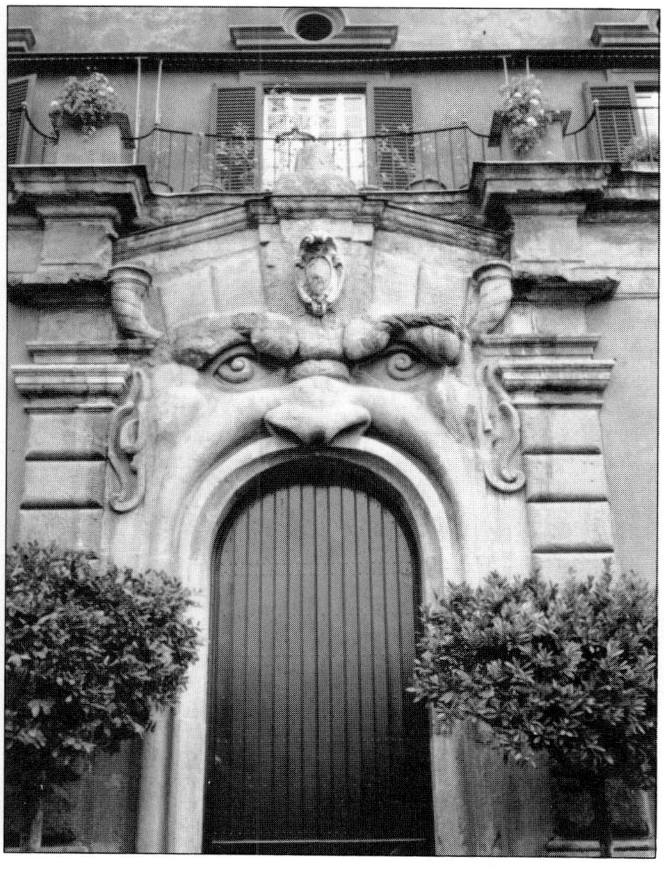

4

POINT OF VIEW

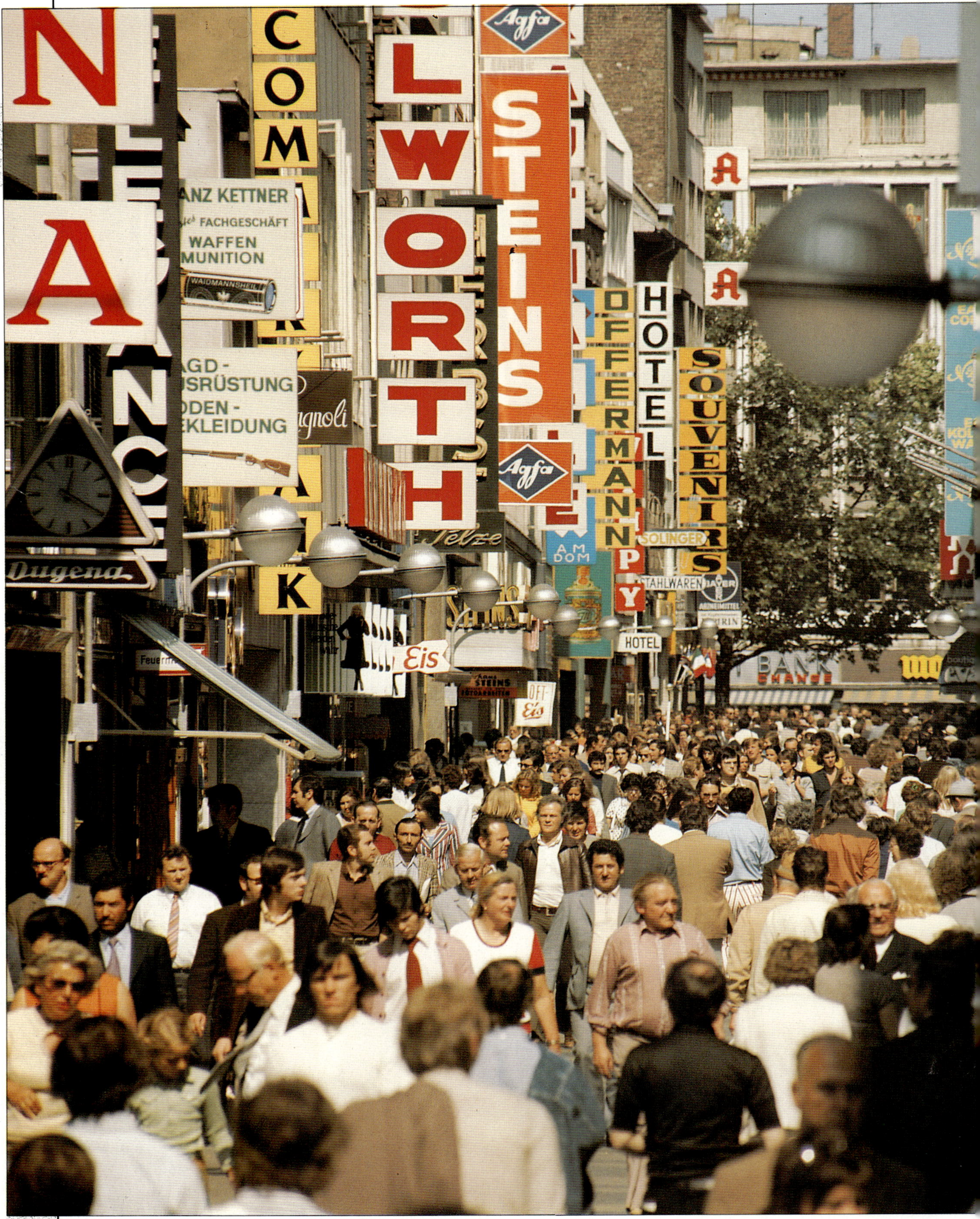

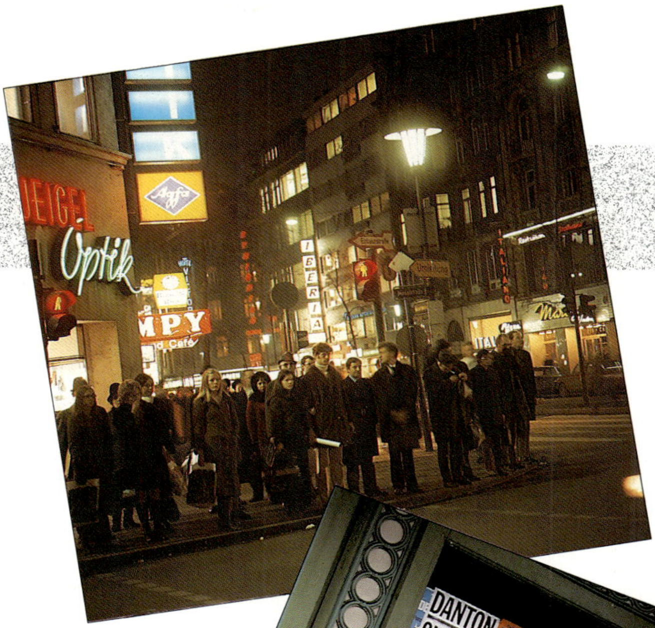

Graphic Design

Writing is a way of putting ideas and messages on paper, or wood, or stone or computer screen, in a code agreed by everyone in a certain culture. Once you understand that code, a door opens and you can learn the wisdom and experience of millions by reading it. As well as that, laws and customs of the culture are made clearer to you and by reading signs you can find your way about. Even if the writing is in another language you can normally read place names, have a rough idea of how to speak the words you read and get a good idea of the message. But imagine what it would be like to go to Japan, where you don't understand the code at all. You don't know what words 'look like' and you wouldn't even recognise your own name.

Most writing began as a set of symbols: the little drawings were pictures of actual objects, but because a new picture for every new idea would have been too much to learn the whole system gradually became simplified. In most languages writing now represents sounds. It isn't as attractive to look at, but it is more flexible and much easier to learn. But increasingly single pictures or symbols for key objects or ideas are again replacing the many letters needed to be written out to express them. It's quicker and easier to recognise them when we're in a hurry.

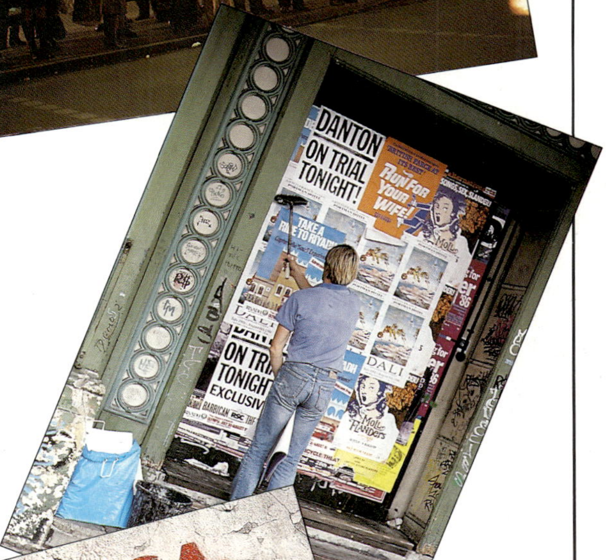

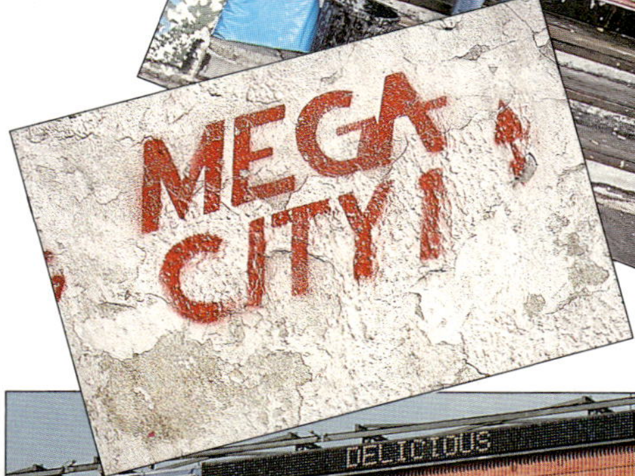

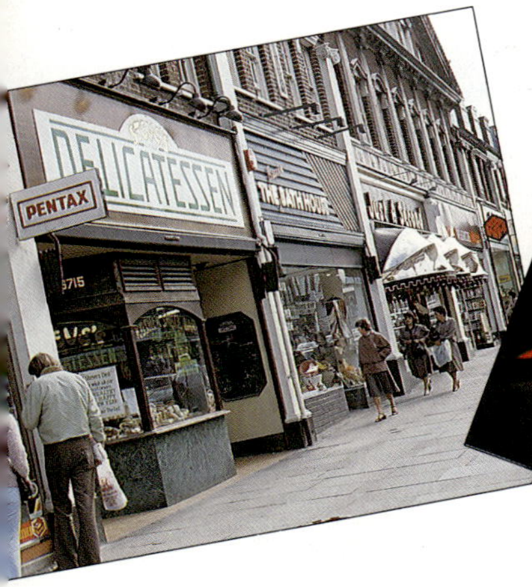

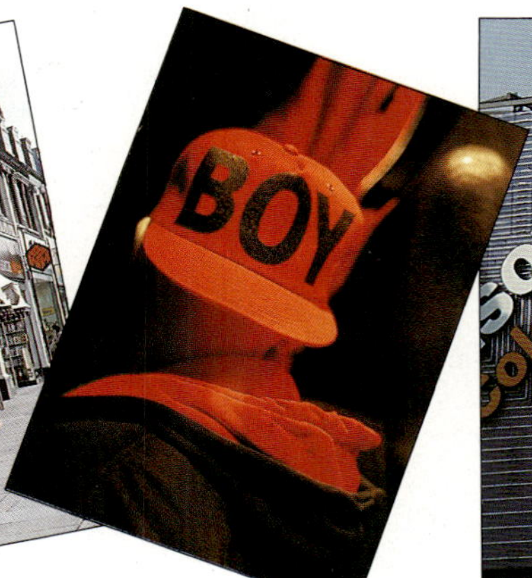

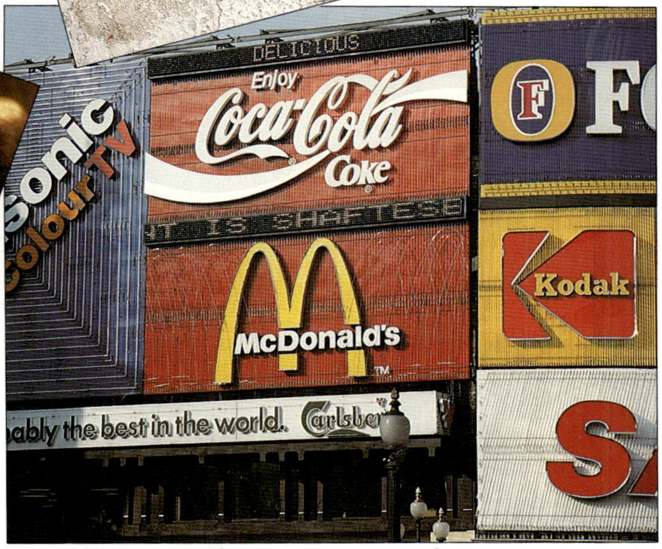

1
A jumble of signs. They are everywhere we look. Why do we need them? In these pictures which are the easiest to see, and why?

POINT OF VIEW

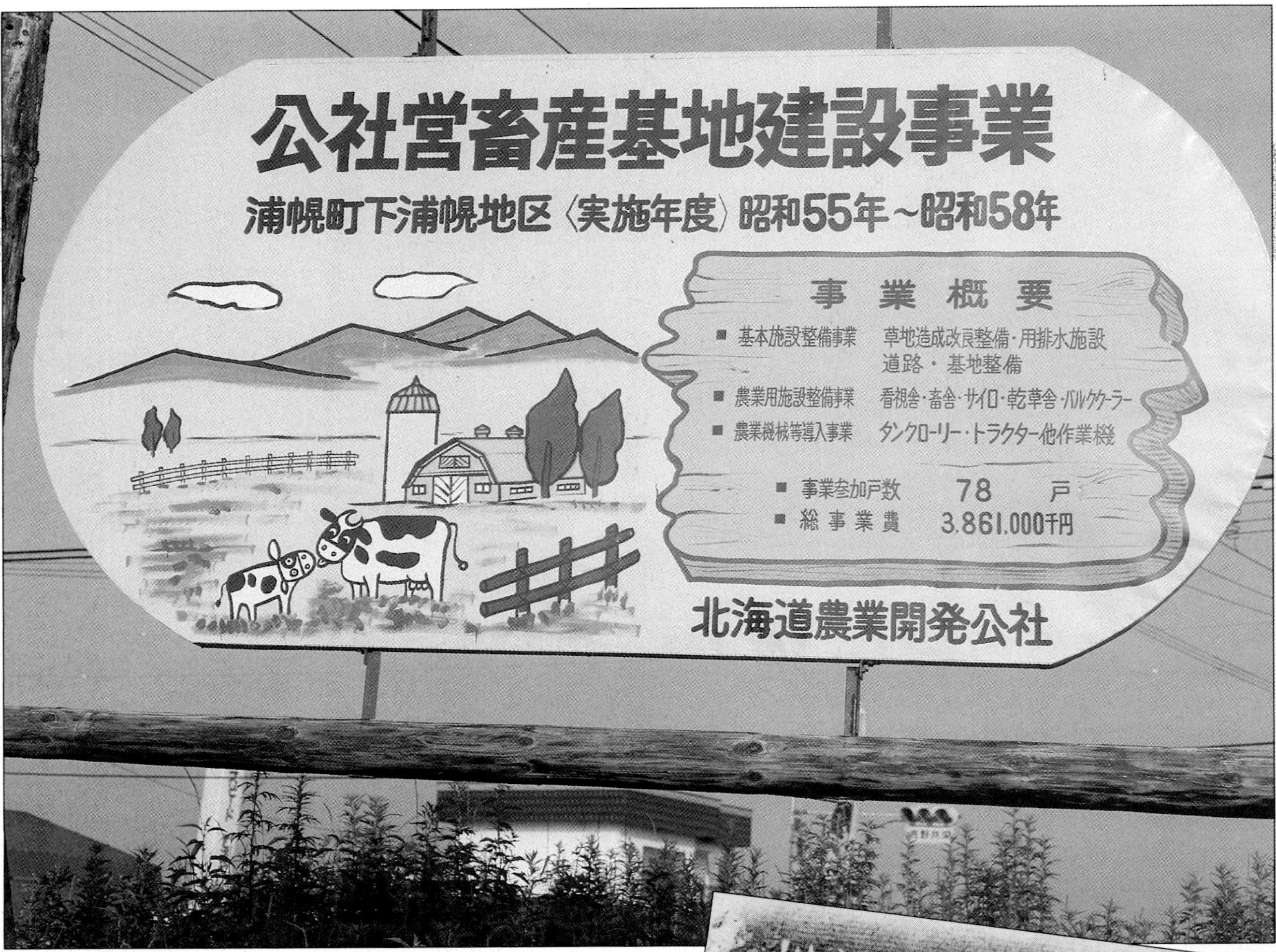

2

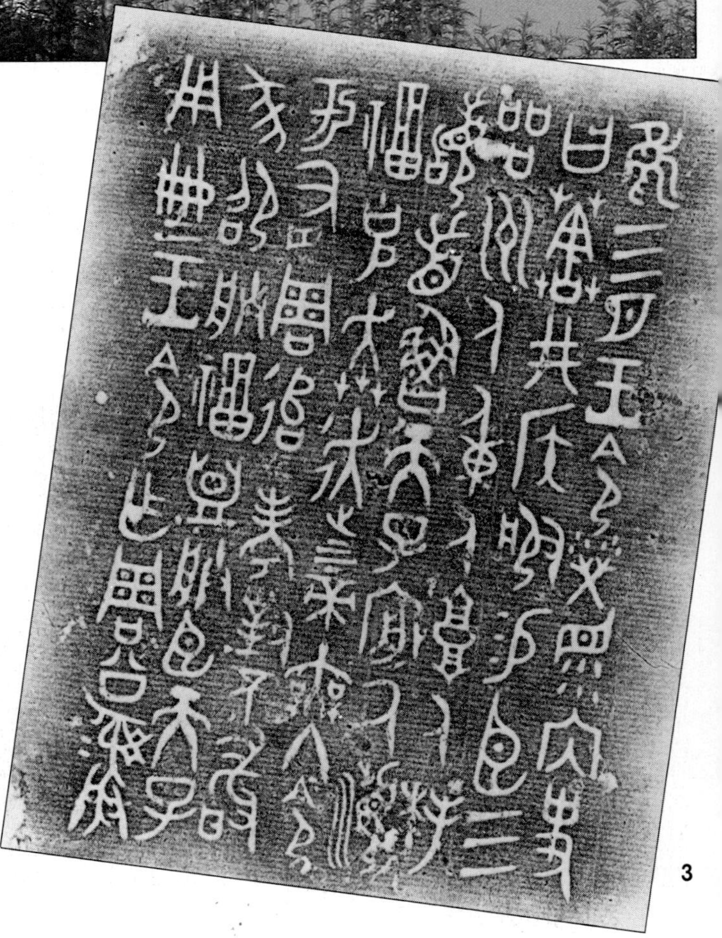

3

2
Japanese script is based on Chinese. This sign has an important message, but would a foreigner know? Where are the clues and what might they mean?

3
Early Chinese writing – small pictures turning into symbols, which are quicker and easier for many people to understand.

4
Once again we're returning to pictures. but now these are meant to be 'read' by all peoples. They're mainly found in public places such as airports and in the high street, where many cultures mix.

4

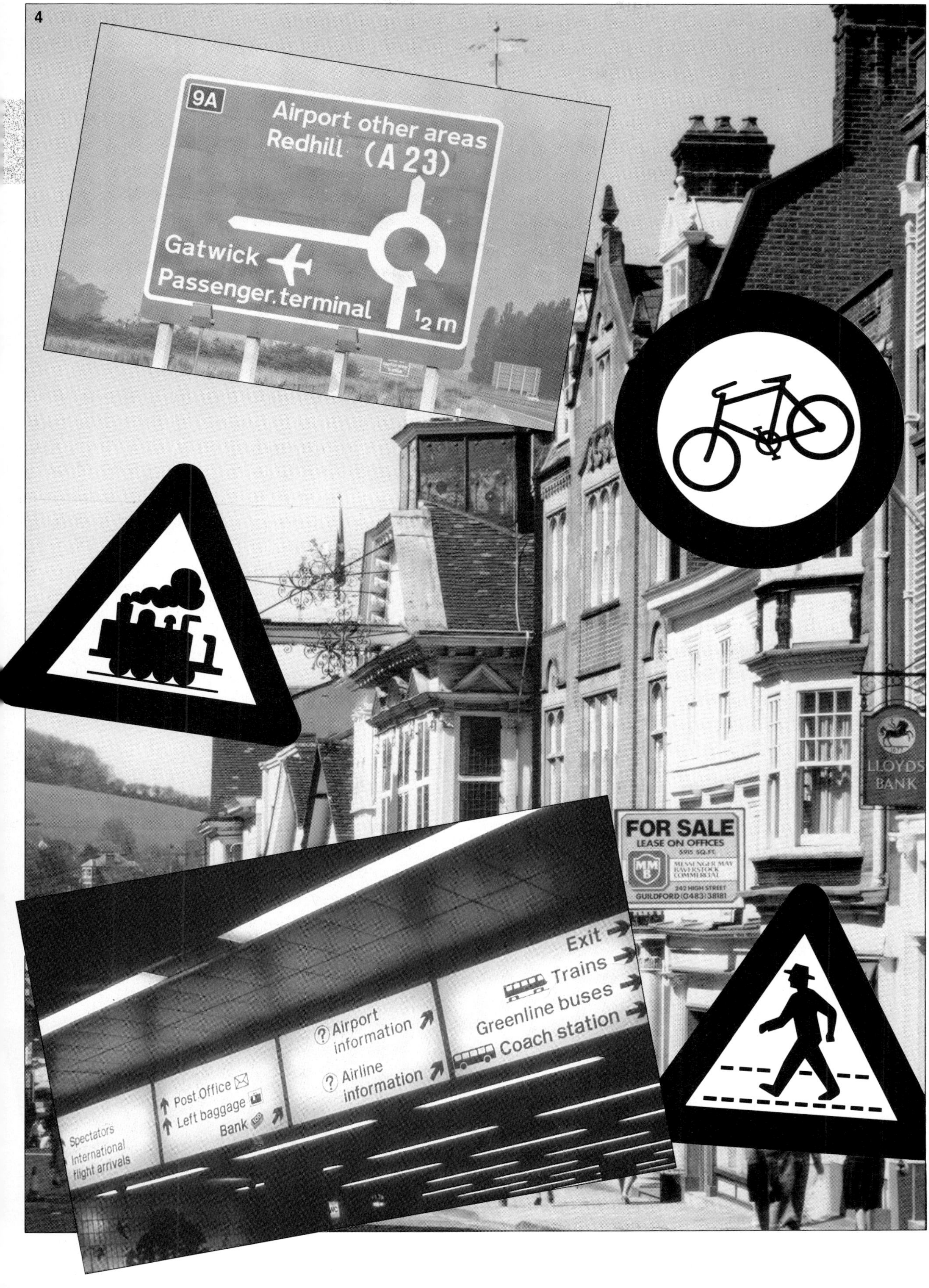
9A
Airport other areas
Redhill (A 23)
Gatwick
Passenger. terminal
½ m
LLOYDS
BANK
FOR SALE
LEASE ON OFFICES
Exit
Trains
Greenline buses
Coach station
Airport
information
Airline
information
Post Office
Left baggage
Bank
Spectators
International
flight arrivals

The Reader in Mind

Writing is an easy and efficient way of getting ideas and messages across to people. In societies like ours where millions can read and write, mechanised writing – printing, that is – has overtaken speech as the most effective way of reaching and influencing people. But like painting, sculpture and other forms of art it depends on people *looking*. How do you encourage people to look and then take in what they see? First, you make the writing *clear*. That means you use styles of writing which are simple and quick to grasp. But of course there are many ideas about what is clear and easy to understand. If you look at any piece of printing, say a newspaper, you will see how many typefaces there are. But of course there's something else too: our eyes and brains don't like monotony and a piece of printing stands out better if it looks different from the other printing round it. So there are thousands of typefaces to choose from.

There are other ways of attracting attention for one piece of writing when there are so many others around. Size, or underlining, or the use of colour, or a distinctive layout, or the addition of eye catching symbols or illustrations – all of these will help to draw the reader's attention. Using such tricks the lettering can be given meanings beyond what is in the words. Letters in the gothic style, say, are likely to indicate that the subject is about something old. Letters made out of leaves will probably carry a message about the environment. But as well as this, informational messages may work best as part of a concept – if they are co-ordinated. Many commercial organisations try to make sure all their graphics – the writing they produce – has the same look or 'identity'. Then the reader may begin to recognise who wrote it each time they see the same style. For centuries and in many cultures writing has been used as part of decorative schemes to make the total impact greater and to convey important information.

1

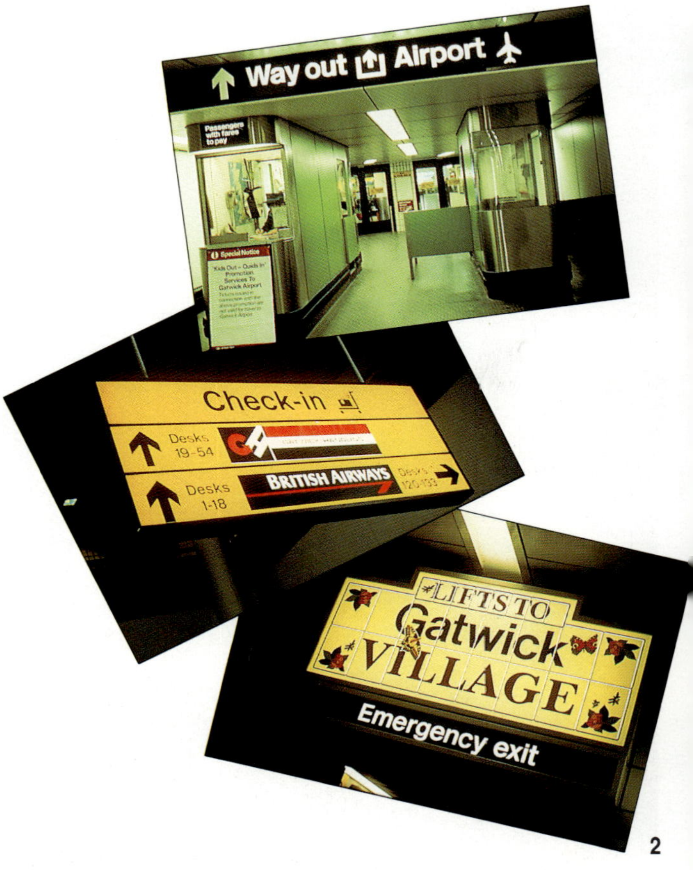

2

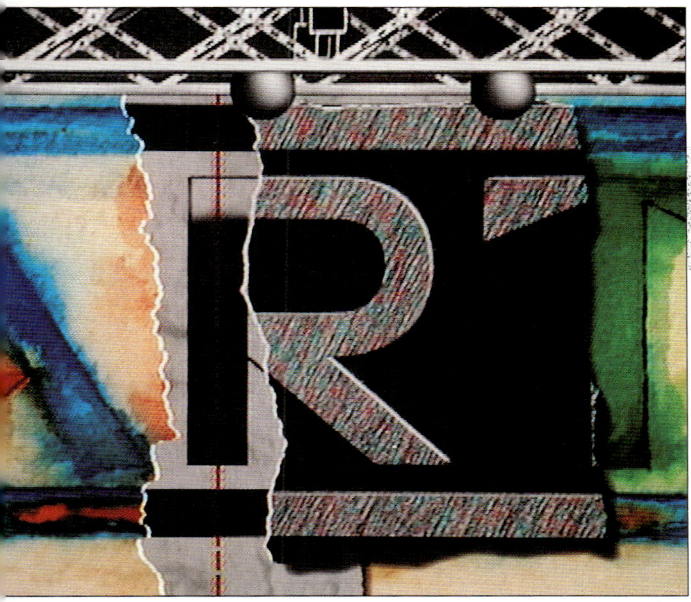

3△

5

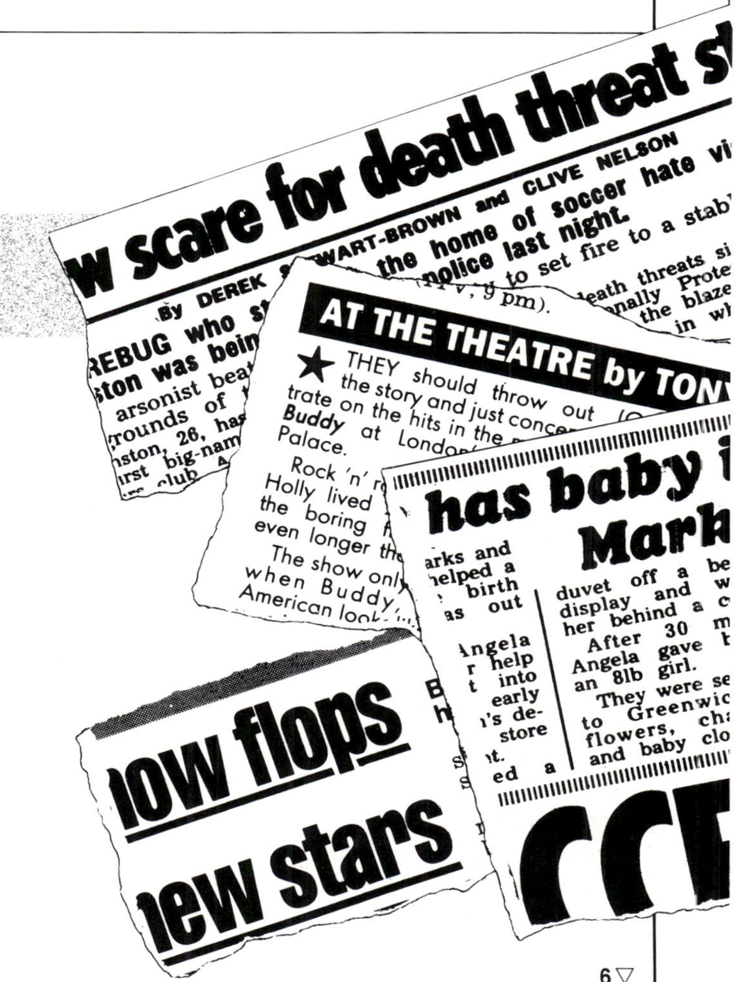

1
There are thousands of typefaces: what messages would suit these examples best?

2
Distinctive typefaces and layouts with pictures make the different functions of these airport signs clearer.

3
The 'Art work' television series logo. Why are there so many versions? Why do they move and change from one to another in the animated television version?

4
Arabic script decorates a mosque. If you read Arabic you'd be reading as you enjoyed the shapes of the design. What kind of thing is this likely to say, and what feeling is it likely to put into the minds of visitors?

5
Modern tabloid typefaces.

6
Toulouse-Lautrec often designed posters with the written message as part of the poster design. Does this one work for you? Do you think graphics such as this could ever be 'art'?

6▽

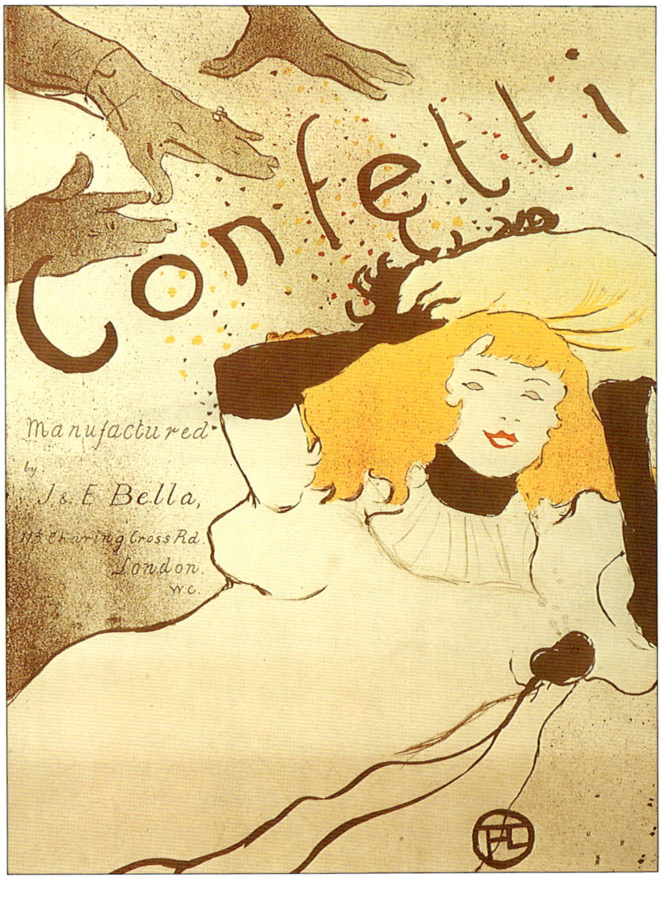

4▽

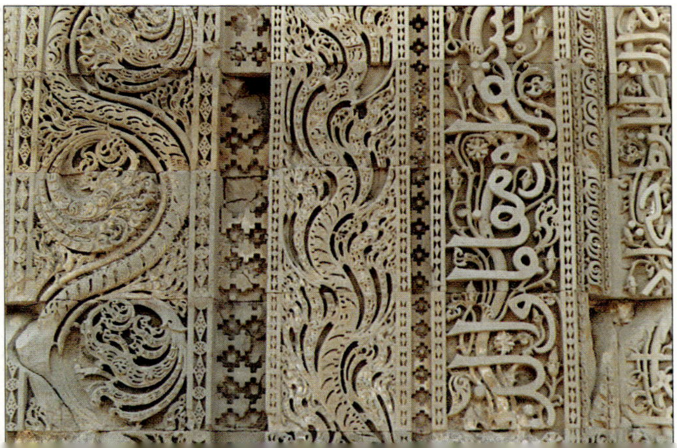

A Style Develops

The increased demand for using print effectively and attractively for publicity information and the promotion of the identity of a company or public organisation has meant much work for graphic designers. They have to go about it very like interior designers, getting to know the product being sold, or the ideas being promoted and the target audience. Something they have to keep in mind all the time is that, while a graphic identity usually needs to appeal to the public by being up to date, at the same time a style which is too trendy is likely to date very quickly. But despite this, from time to time the management of a large organisation may take a new direction and take on new ideas, and it may want to signal this with a change of image without the public forgetting the best of its past achievements.

One of the jobs graphic designers do is the updating of a well-known image, and this may happen a number of times over the years. The London Symphony Orchestra felt the need to update its graphics in 1987, and it employed the design partnership 'Assorted Images' to do the job. The orchestra was founded in 1904 and is well established as one of the world's great orchestras. But because it is so busy with concerts, tours, recordings and broadcasts, its graphic identity had become confused. Added to this, its most recent logo included a stylised picture of St Paul's Cathedral – fine to symbolise a London orchestra except that its new home was the Barbican Arts Centre. Also with developing rivalry between major orchestras in Britain for audiences and sponsorship, the LSO felt it was time to signal afresh to the public that it was still in business.

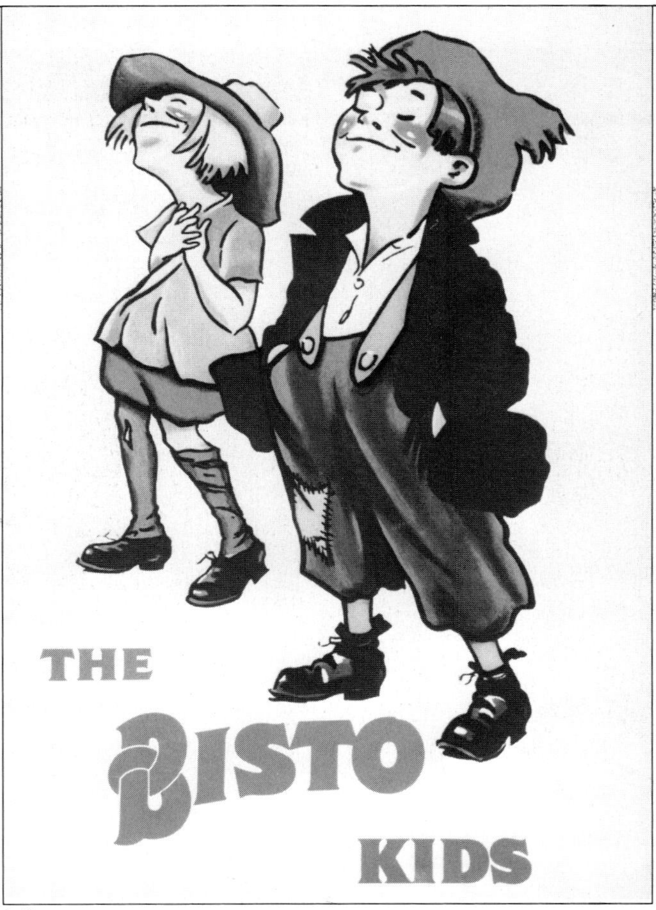

1–2

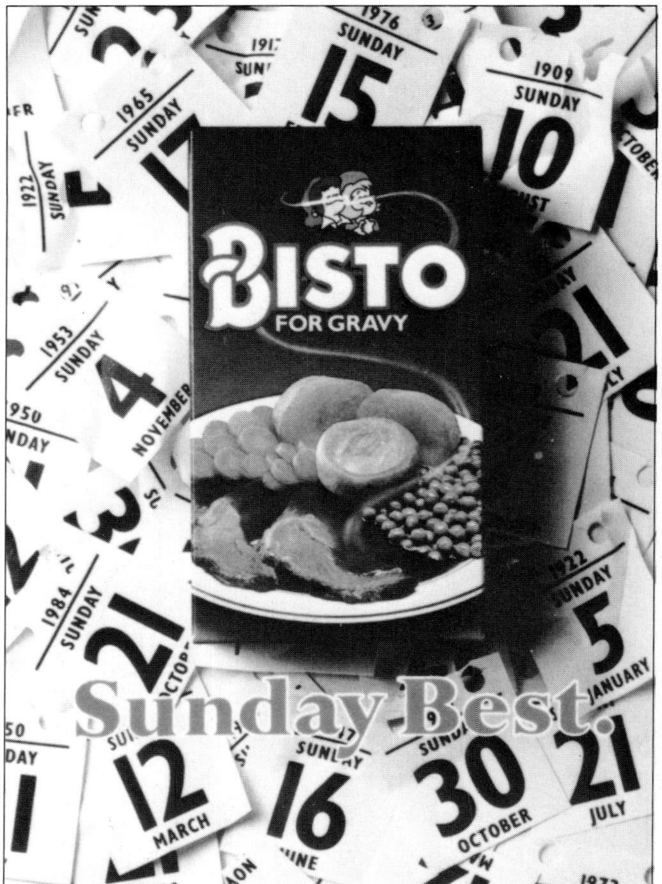

1–2
Early and current Bisto advertising art.

3–6
Stages in the updating work by Assorted Images' artistic director Malcolm Garrett. He selects a new face, Futura, and reduces it to its bare essentials. He puts back some of the more elegant features of Futura, including serifs. But the problem of balance remains. The 'L' and 'O' must be of similar weight. Why?

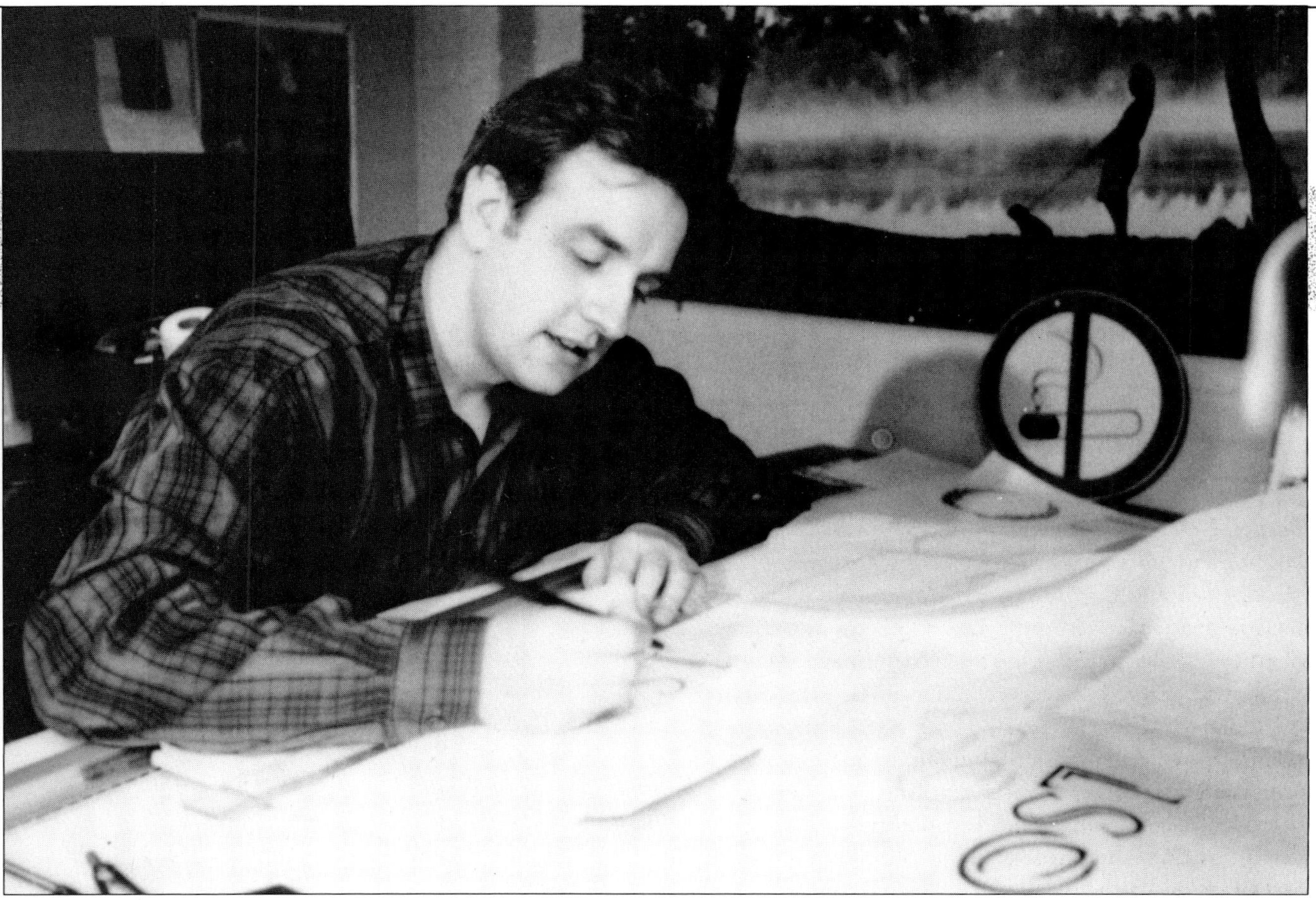

3-6

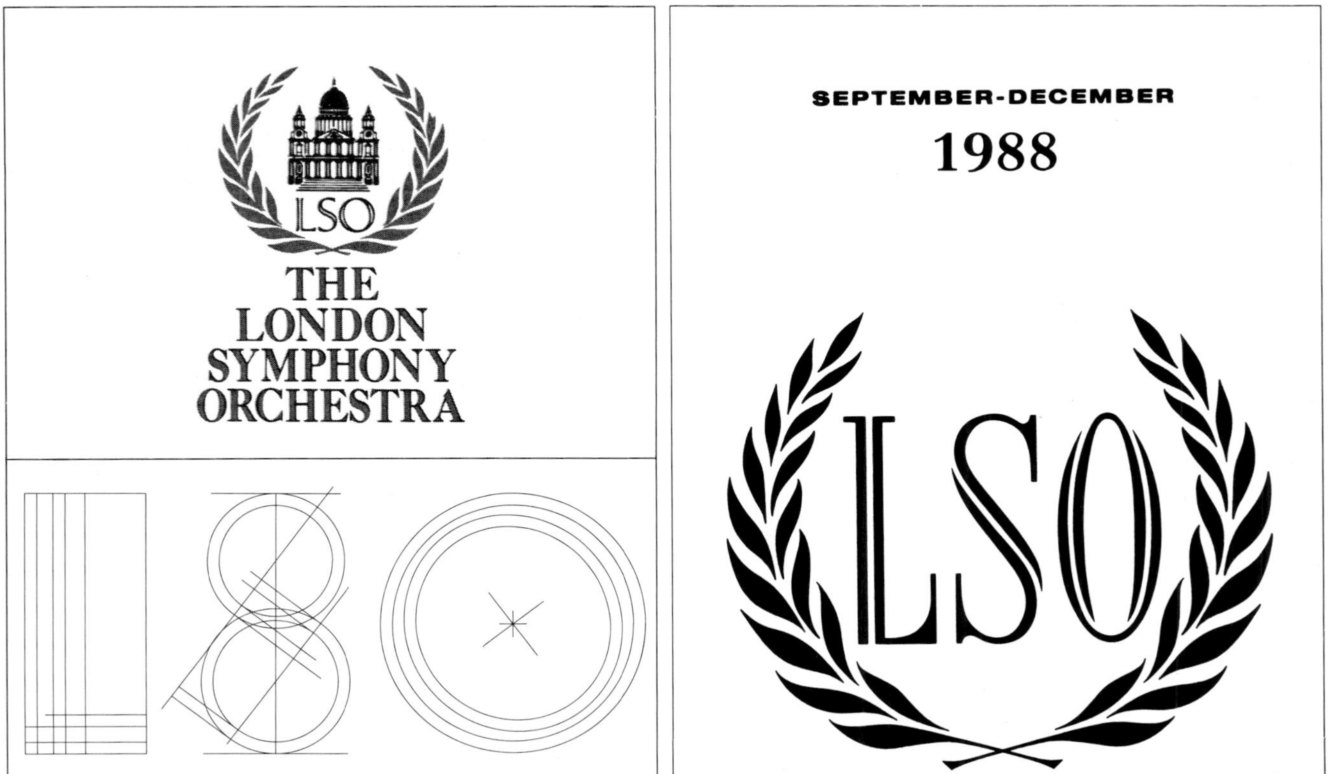
LSO
THE
LONDON
SYMPHONY
ORCHESTRA
SEPTEMBER-DECEMBER
1988
LSO
LSO

The Identity in Use

The final versions of the LSO logo were presented to the clients several weeks after the brief was agreed. The three letters which made up the initials of the orchestra's name had taken a great deal of work before graphic designer Malcolm Garrett was happy with them. As often happens no existing typeface was suitable, and he adapted Futura, an oldish typeface which has great clarity. Along the way Malcolm and his partners had experimented with a computer-designed typeface, before rejecting it. But the main problem lay in the 'L' and 'O'. 'L' starts with a vertical line while 'O' ends with a curve, and the two seemed unbalanced. The 'L' couldn't be curved so the 'O' had to be flattened, but without too much distortion. So the solution to the problem lay not in the mechanical choice of off-the-peg lettering, but in careful judgement and skilful drawing.

A second solution with square lettering was presented to the clients and rejected. While Malcolm spent much time on this problem (after all the three letters would lie at the centre of every use of the logo), colleagues wrestled with the wreath. Should it be an upright or horizontal oval, or circular? How heavy should the individual leaves be? What could be found to replace the St Paul's dome? The wreath was finally drawn almost round with what the graphic designers decided by eye was the right emphasis, but the symbol remained a problem. The Barbican is a new complex and although the site and the name indicates fortifications (part of the defences of medieval London), no one alive has seen them. Simple drawings of battlements seemed too forgettable, but the deciding factor was that any symbol seemed likely to be too heavy and a distraction from the three letters. So no symbol was included.

The new logo now seems to work in the many places it is seen – posters, leaflets, advertisements, on record sleeves and on the diary of engagements. The LSO has been complimented on it, and while it's difficult to be sure if it has increased knowledge of the orchestra, interest does seem to have grown.

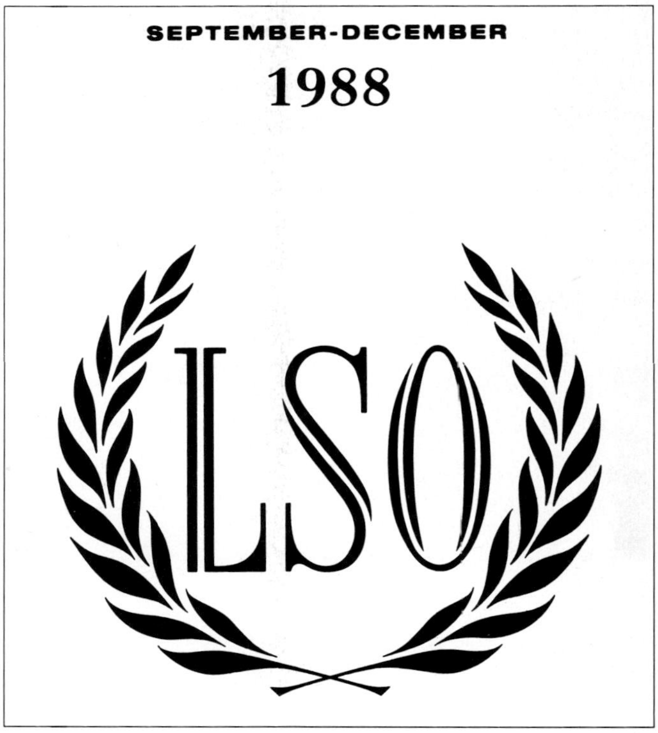

1△

2▽

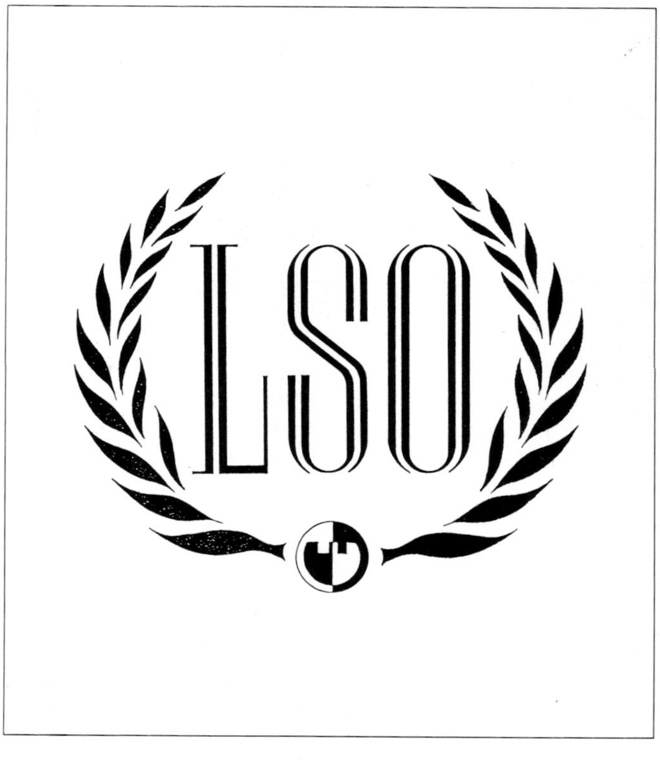

3

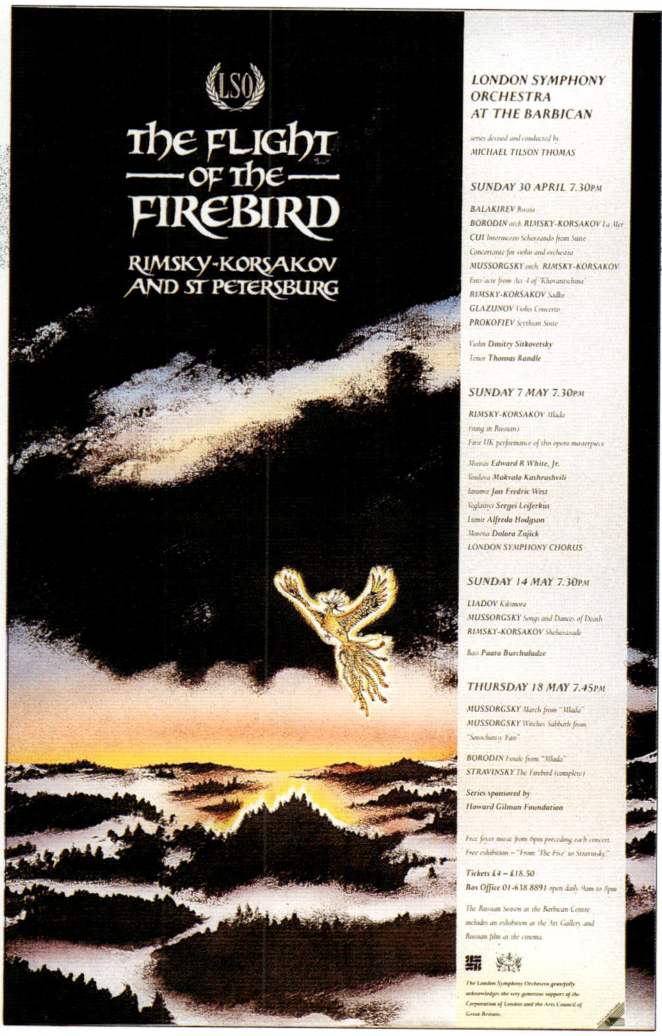

4

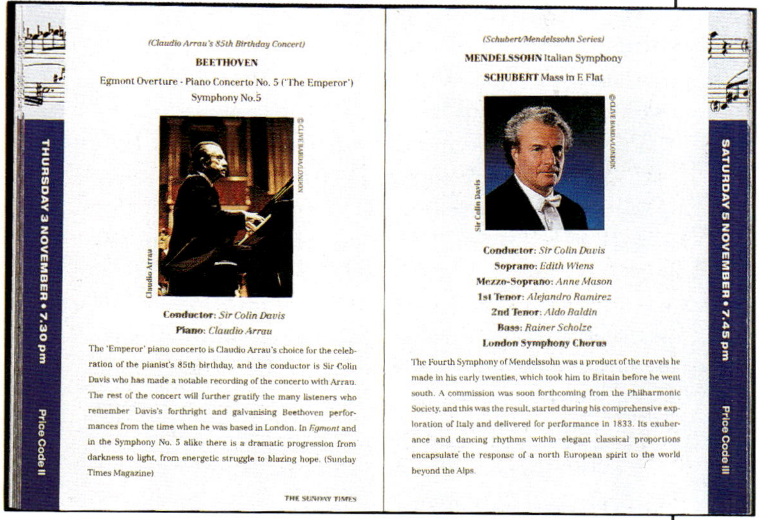

5

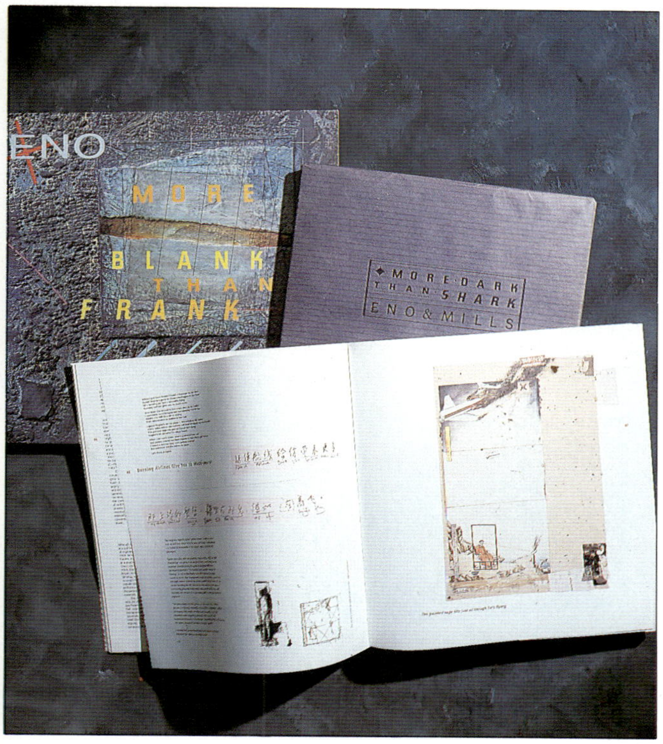

1
LSO logo: the new version as chosen by the clients.

2
LSO logo: alternative new logo with Barbican symbol.

3
LSO poster using the new logo.

4
The new LSO diary involves the clear arrangement of a great deal of information. To get this right involved trying it out from the point of view of someone anxious to find out about concerts on particular dates, and also looking for appearances of particular conductors, soloists or music. Much of Assorted Images' other work is to do with music.

5
Graphics promotion package for a Brian Eno album by Assorted Images.

POINT OF VIEW

Ideas for You

The printed word has become so important in our lives that making it work well is an established skill for the designer.

Here are things to do which are similar to the work of graphic designers:

1 Have a go at designing your own typeface. The two letters in *Pictures 1* and *2* above are examples from history. Yours need not be so elaborate, but you should say what your typeface is intended for and make sure it fits. Adapt one from a typeface book and draw two or three words in it.

2 Collect examples of logos. Say what each is for and how each is meant to work. Do you think it does in every case? Think of an organisation and design your own logo for it.

3 Use potato or linocut, monoprint, silkscreen or one of the other print techniques to produce your own symbols in the form of a picture. Ask someone else to describe its mood and meaning. Have they got your intention right?

4 The style magazine the *Face* and its chief graphic artist Neville Brody set a pace for original graphic design over the last ten years. Get a copy and see if you agree. If you do, why? With a typeface directory try to identify some of the faces used. With the rest of the group write and design spreads for your own magazine. You may need to use a typewriter for the words, but make the layout and the decoration special.

5 Choose a favourite record, or book or magazine. Think of two or three spin-offs from it (perhaps a poster, a giveaway sound cassette or some souvenir) and design them as part of a co-ordinated package. Use the same faces, colours and general style. Someone could produce the storyboard for a promotional video (and even record a rough version, if you have a school video camera).

6 Design some informational graphics for your home, school or high street, or a piece of electronic wizardry. Produce a sketch or still or storyboard for a commercial which fantasises on one of these everyday locations.

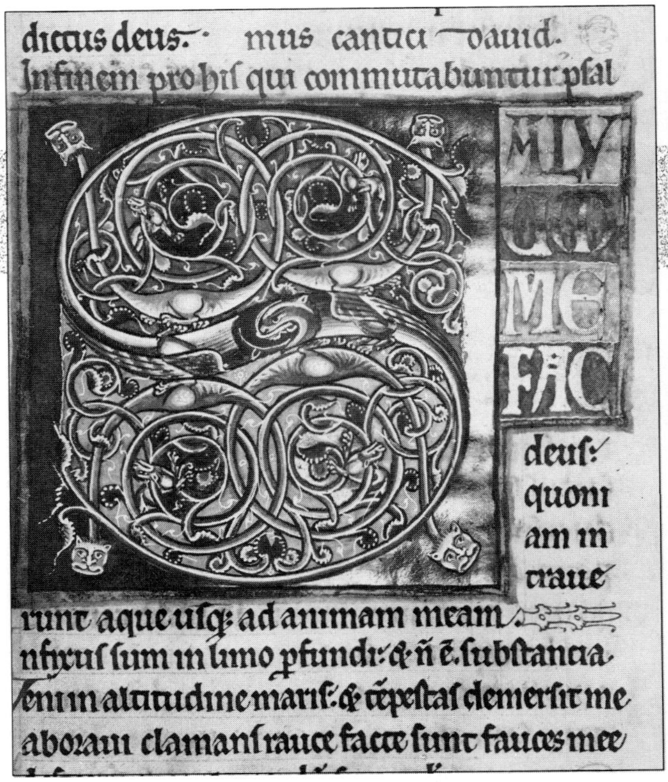

1-2

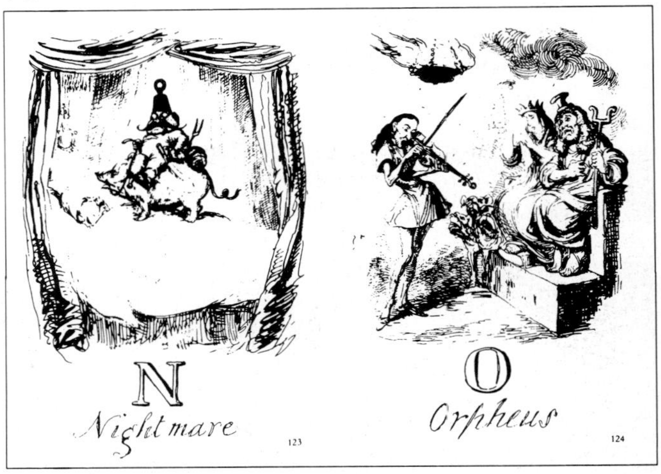

1-2
Medieval capital, Europe. Illuminated capitals by George Cruikshank, circa 1840.

3
Commercial logos.

4
A classic *Face* cover.

5
The National Westminster Bank produced this commercial for television and cinema. If you have seen it, describe what happens and discuss what was behind the concept. They built their own bank facade on an existing film studio 'High Street' lot. Why do you think they decided to go to all that trouble and expense?

3

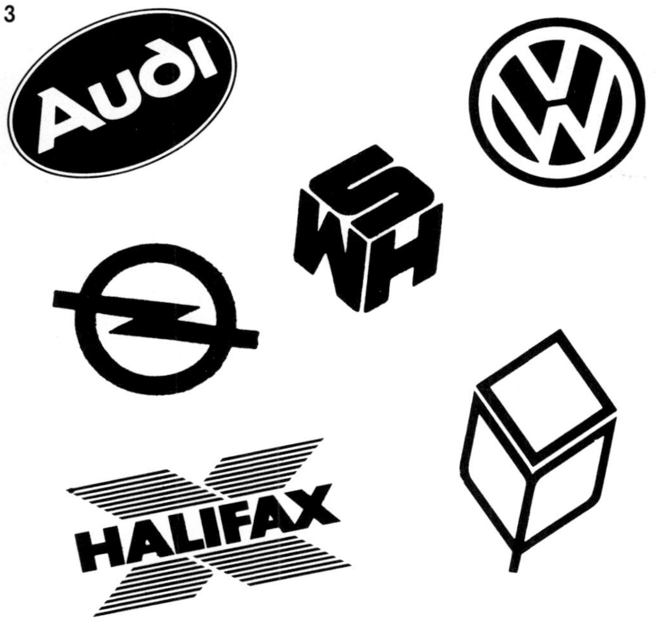
Audi
HALIFAX

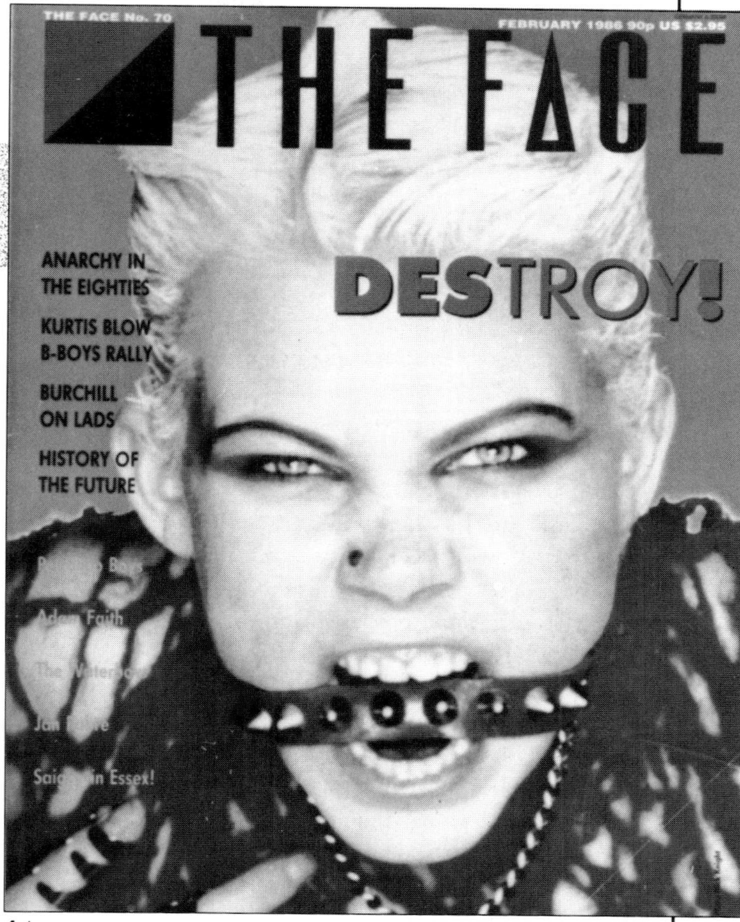
THE FACE No. 70
FEBRUARY 1986 90p US $2.95
THE FACE
ANARCHY IN THE EIGHTIES
KURTIS BLOW B-BOYS RALLY
BURCHILL ON LADS
HISTORY OF THE FUTURE
DESTROY!

4△

5▽

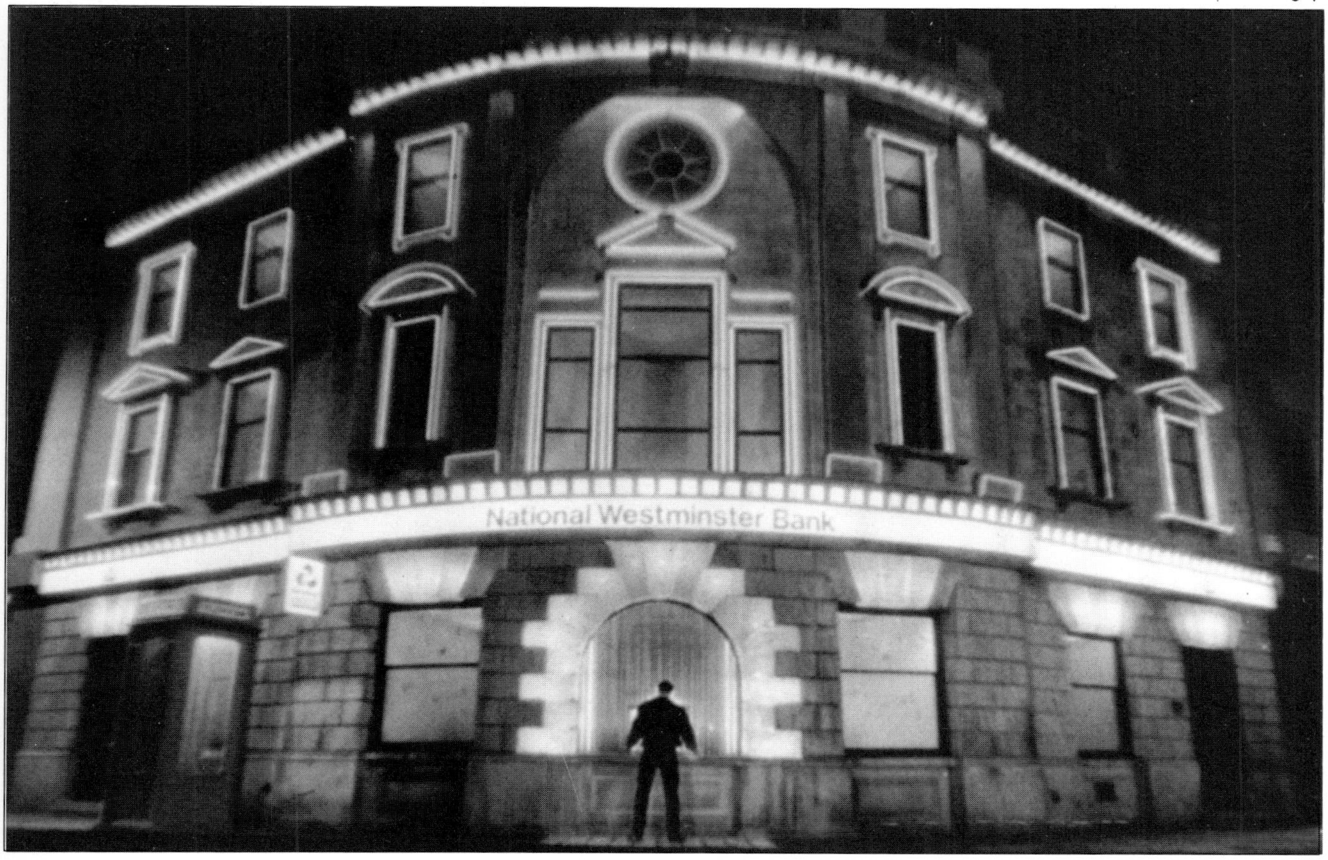
National Westminster Bank

POINT OF VIEW

Symbols in Art and Design

Artists have seen that written words don't just have importance because of what they mean, but for what they look like. Often meaning and appearance can be made to play off with or against one another, and artists have had fun making pictures of the results. Symbols are also important for artists, for they provide a powerful way of putting across an idea which is often complicated.

Here are some ways of looking at what artists and graphic designers do with words and symbols.

1 Draw or paint a picture based on your name, or address, or the name of your school or town. Make it symbolic or pictorially similar to the place or the person.

2 Research a few words or names in Arabic, Greek, Russian, Chinese or any Indian script or ancient Egyptian hieroglyphics. Can you discover the origins of any of the letters or characters? Write up and illustrate the results.

3 Produce a poster in the style of Hollywood or Indian films promoting yourself, your school, your town or a friend. Colour it, and use letters cut from newspapers or photographs.

4 Make a collage picture using printed paper and card. Discuss its meaning.

5 Paint a mystery picture using symbols. Can a friend discover what it means? A dictionary of symbols may help you and the audience, but think up some new ones too!

Bull

Electric light

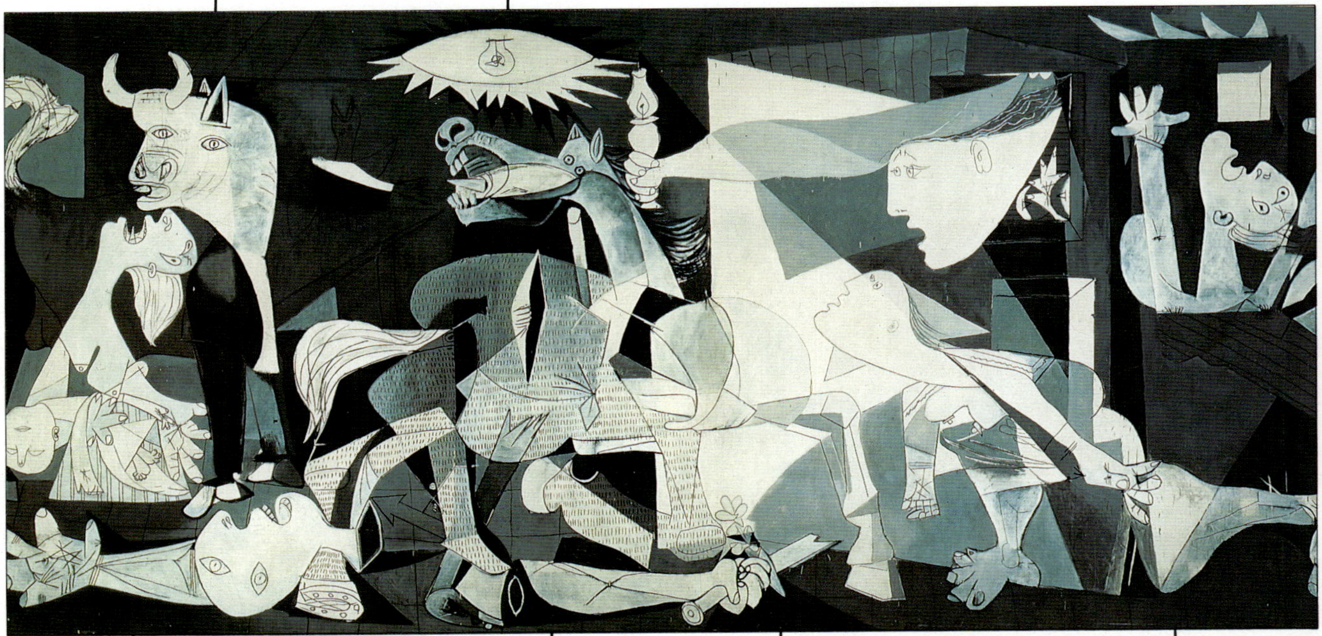

1

Woman with a child in her arms

Horse

Broken sword and flower

Figure with outstretched arms

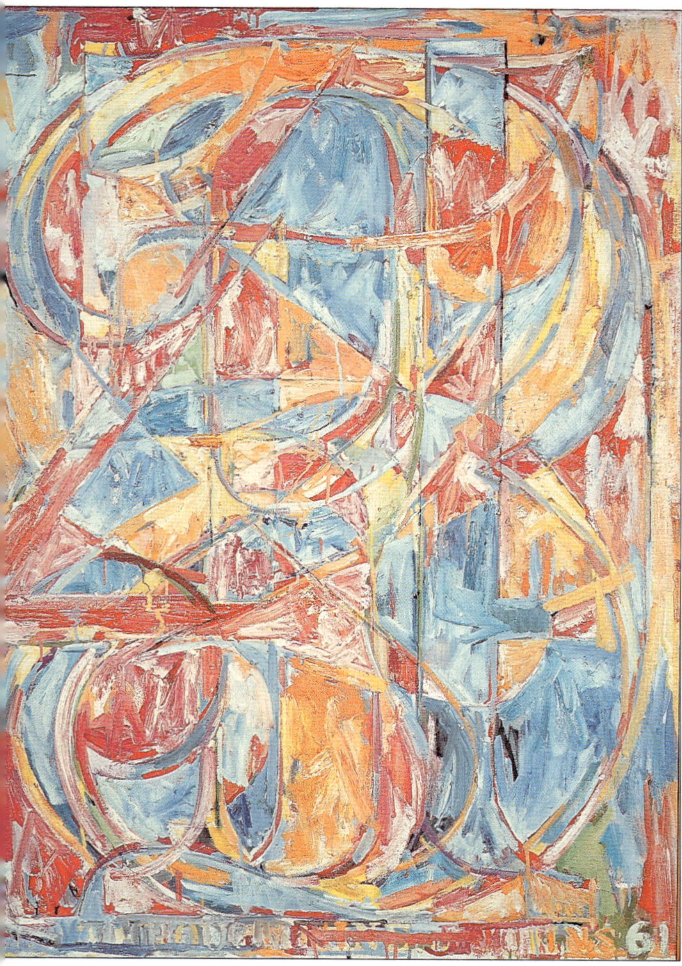

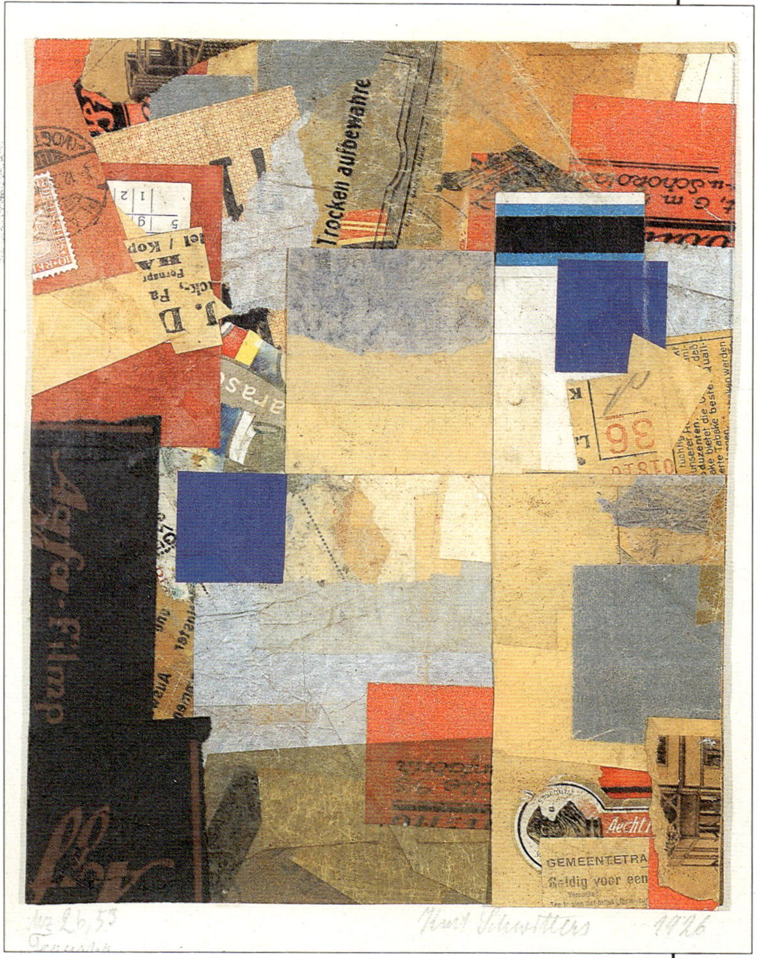

3

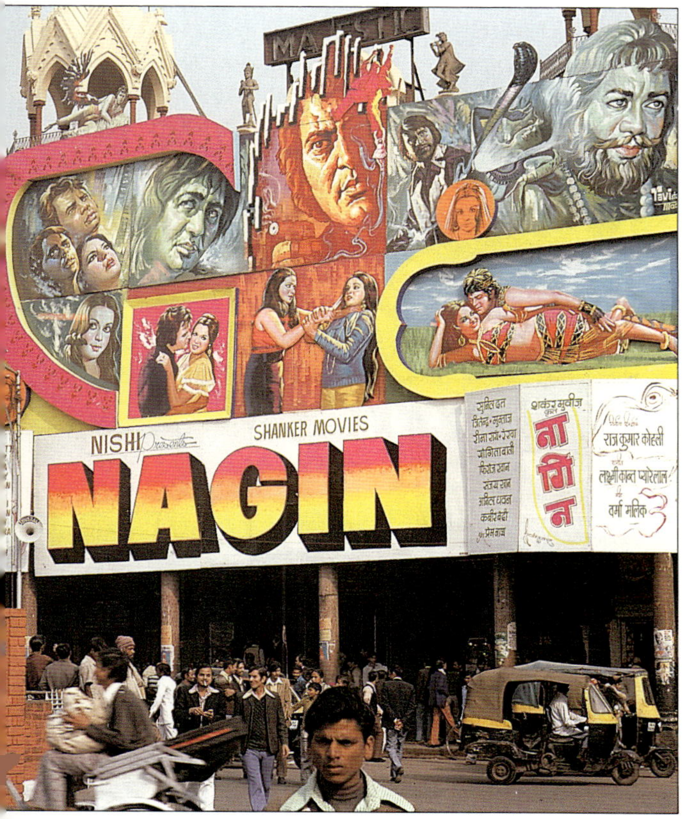

4

1
'Guernica' by Picasso, 1936. A painted protest at the bombing of a town during the Spanish Civil War. At first sight it may appear to be a wild jumble (that is deliberate, a symbol in itself). Look at the picture and unravel some of the visual elements. Then use reference books and your own intelligence to work out their possible symbolic meanings. Remember one symbol may have more than one meaning. Here are a few to start you off.

2
'Zero Through Nine' by Jasper Johns, 1961.

3
'Fernspr.' by Kurt Schwitters, 1926 (collage).

4
A film poster, New Delhi, India. In India the designing and hand painting of posters like this is big business, though they originated from the printed posters for the theatre and early cinema in Europe and America as well as local traditions of mural paintings. Notice that this one tries hard not to look like a single rectangular 'picture' or in any one style. Why? Find other advertising art and compare styles. Look for symbols in them.

REFLECTIONS: A WORLD O

The Environment

Few people are unaware of environmental issues today. Most of us have been taught about the balance between natural phenomena and living things, including mankind. It literally makes us what we are and we tamper with it at our peril. An artist is someone who makes objects which appeal to our senses and through them suggests ideas to us. Those ideas may be to do with religion, or war, the position of women, great men, love or the seven deadly sins. In our age when we worry about the ozone layer and acid rain, chemicals on the land and nuclear fall-out, why shouldn't artists think about the environment?

Today a number of artists set out to explore this subject in their work. They examine the landscape and record it in paint and photographs. They draw attention to it by placing man-made objects in it so that through them we are forced to think about them both and look more closely at each. Andy Goldsworthy makes shapes with 'natural' objects – leaves, moss, twigs, earth, water and even snow and ice. In this way he draws our attention to their qualities and beauty, their strengths and weaknesses. He always respects living things and makes sure that little is disturbed. His work seldom leaves the place it came from for long. He usually puts the finished object into its own background again, and having photographed it he leaves it to the forces of nature to decay and perhaps form a home for new generations of life. The objects themselves are seldom displayed in a gallery or bought and sold – this would be to treat his art as a commodity and this he doesn't want.

1

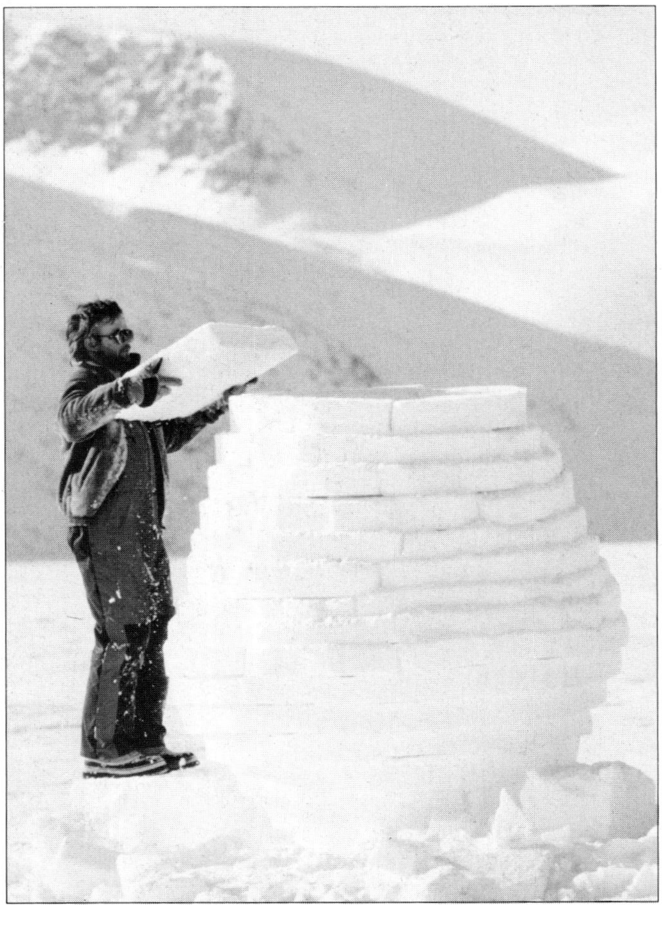

1
Andy Goldsworthy creating a snow sculpture in the Arctic.

2
Andy Goldsworthy used earth movers to create this pattern of earth banks and water. It is in a semi-urban area, where construction work is part of the scene. Man and his work are part of the environment, and here reflected in this interesting shape are forms which could be natural or man-made. People walking past it, or along the top, will be provoked into wondering 'why?' and 'by whom?' Already they'll be thinking about its shape, effect and mood, as well as the ideas in the artist's mind.

3
'29 August 1987. Calm overcast laid iris blades on pond pinned together with thorns filled in five sections with rowan berries, fish attaching (sic) from below difficult to keep all the berries in nibbled at by ducks' – Andy Goldsworthy's notes on this work. Try to imagine the brilliant greens and reds of the leaves and berries in this work.

4
Sahara sand dunes form entirely natural patterns.

5
Moy Keightley's 'Icelandic Stones', 1987 (water colour), painted on an Icelandic beach.

6
An aerial photograph of human-made prehistoric earth lines, Peru, at least a thousand years old.

DEAS

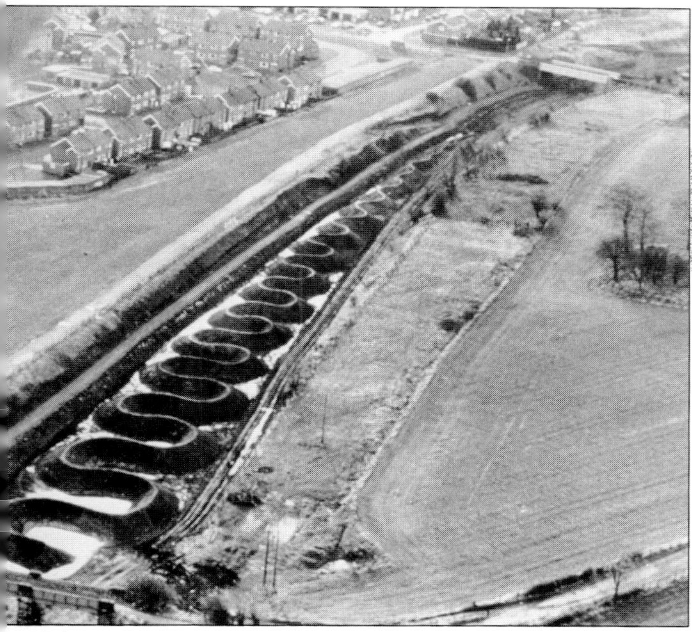

2△

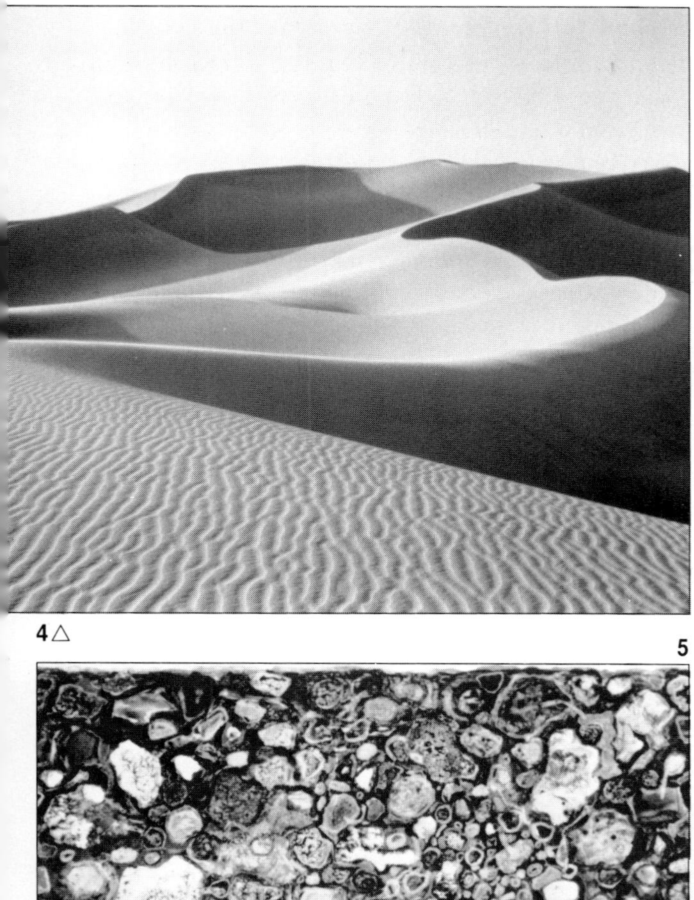

4△

5

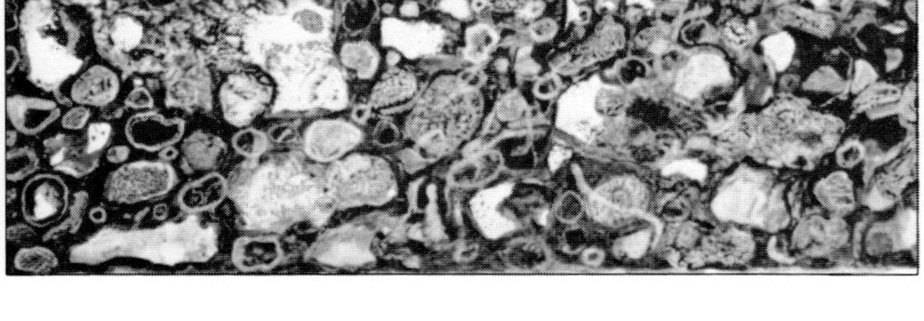

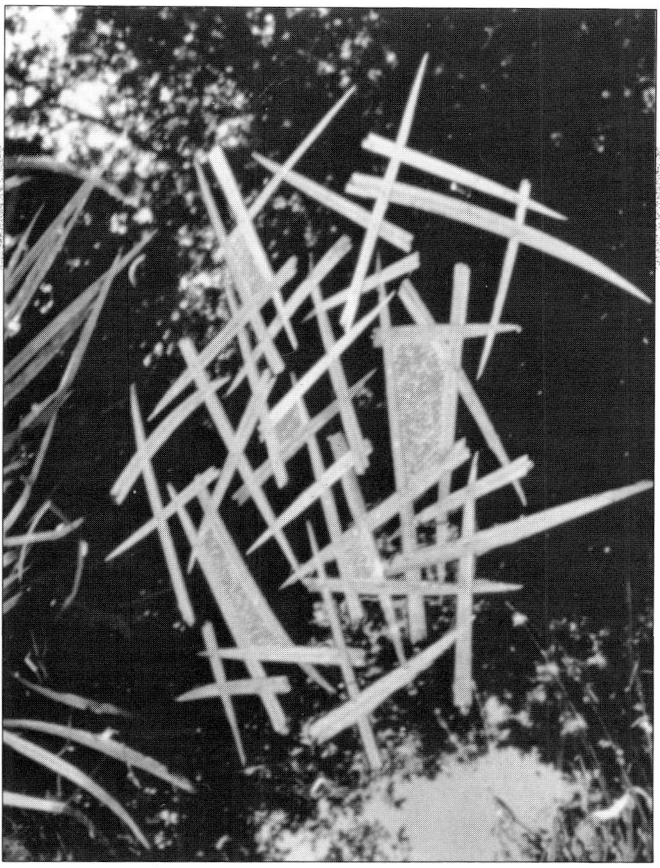

3△

6

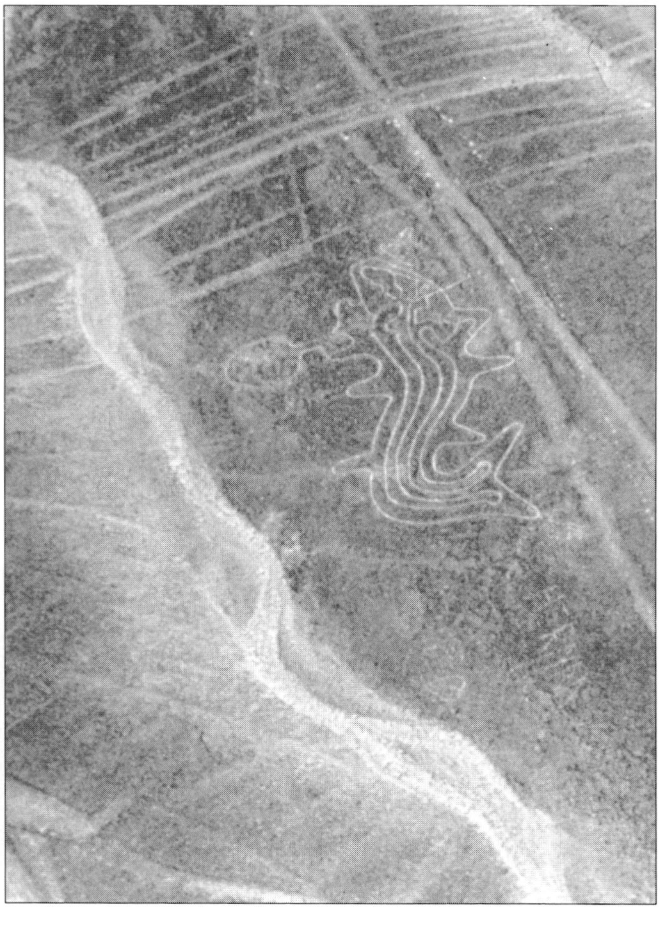

A Load of Rubbish?

Ann Carrington is a young sculptor who works with rubbish – or rather with what you and I would call rubbish. But to her it is a wonderful resource, because it contains interesting shapes, colours, patterns and surface decoration that remind her of the tools and possessions of modern life. With it she makes fantastic objects which help us look again at our world and ask questions about it. But first and foremost Ann's sculptures are funny. Italian Mortadella sausage is laughingly supposed to be made from dead horses and broken-down donkeys. So why not reverse the process and make a magnificent horse's head from salami? It's a humorous idea but it also makes us consider the way we think of animals – they're supposed to be noble, beautiful and intelligent, but we treat them badly and then we eat them – and also what's behind great art. Can you call it art if it's made out of meat and not marble? Should we be hypocritical enough to display only the best qualities of animals and their relationship to us? At a time of increased air travel (and by all accounts reduced air safety) shouldn't we rethink our attitude to flying? Ann's rebuilding of a plane as a tattily ingenious bird is funny and eye-catching, but it's also thought-provoking. Part of the trick is thinking about her materials as something of value, of potential use, rather than something to be thrown away. As a food tin the piece of metal she collects may be worthless, but by thinking about its shape and colours, its value as an art object and not a container, it may have plenty of useful life to come. It was the surrealist painters of the early twentieth century who first had the idea of finding other meanings for ordinary objects. Paul Klee's paintings often look like the work of young children, but he felt that in their freshness and energy they taught older people things about life they had perhaps forgotten. When children play they have the knack of building into their toys a fantasy world which is often more revealing than what older people believe is reality.

1

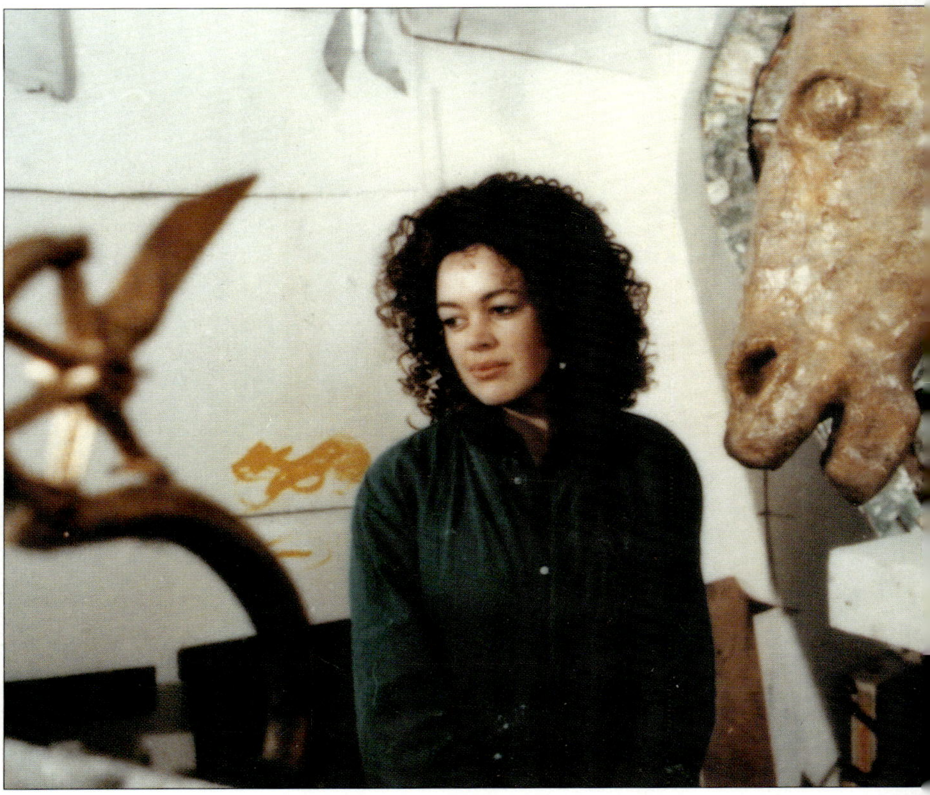

1
Ann Carrington and her real salami horse: art that will certainly not last forever!

2-3
Which of these is the truer portrait of a horse?

4
Another of Ann's planes has feathers, a beak instead of a nose and claws instead of an undercarriage.

5
A handmade third world toy, where our rubbish is prized for its usefulness.

6
'Temple Gardens' by Paul Klee, 1920.

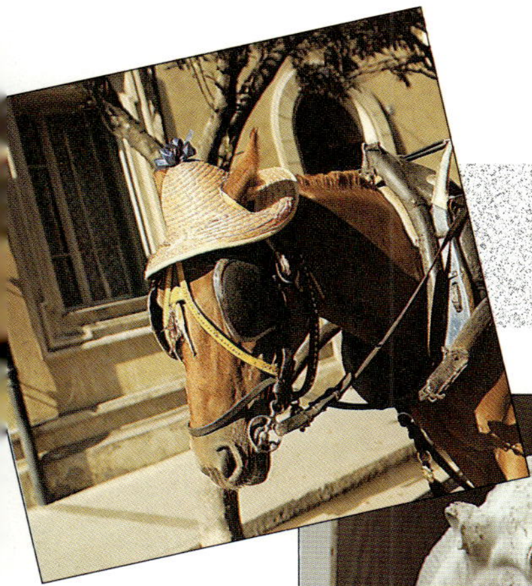

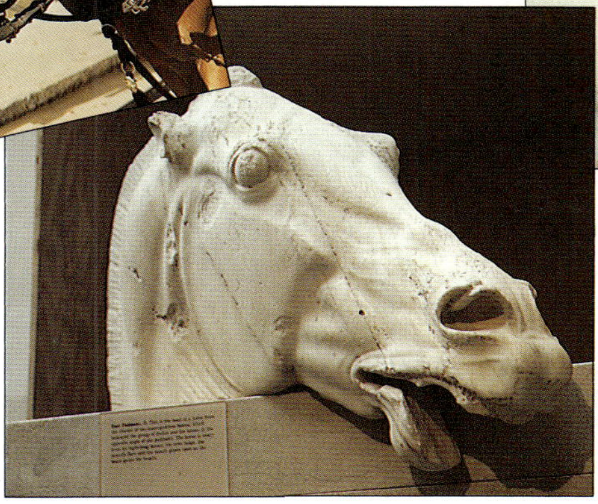

2–3

4

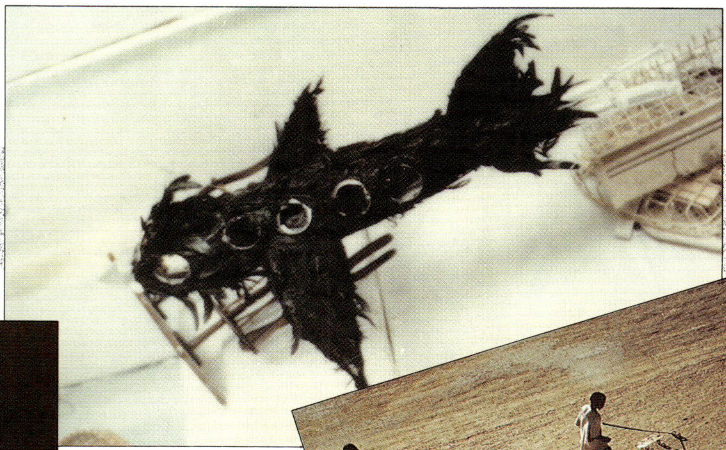

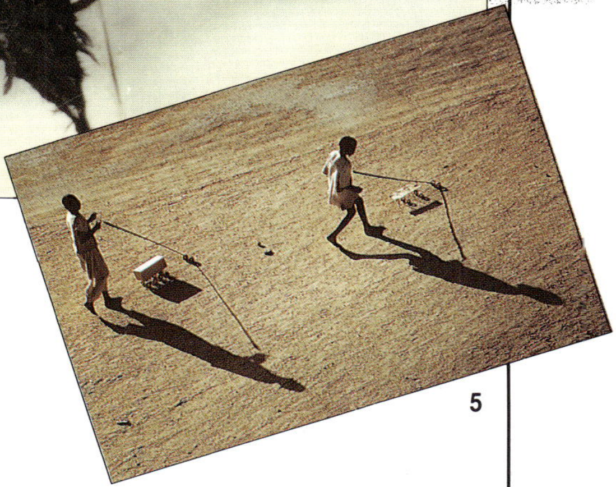

5

6

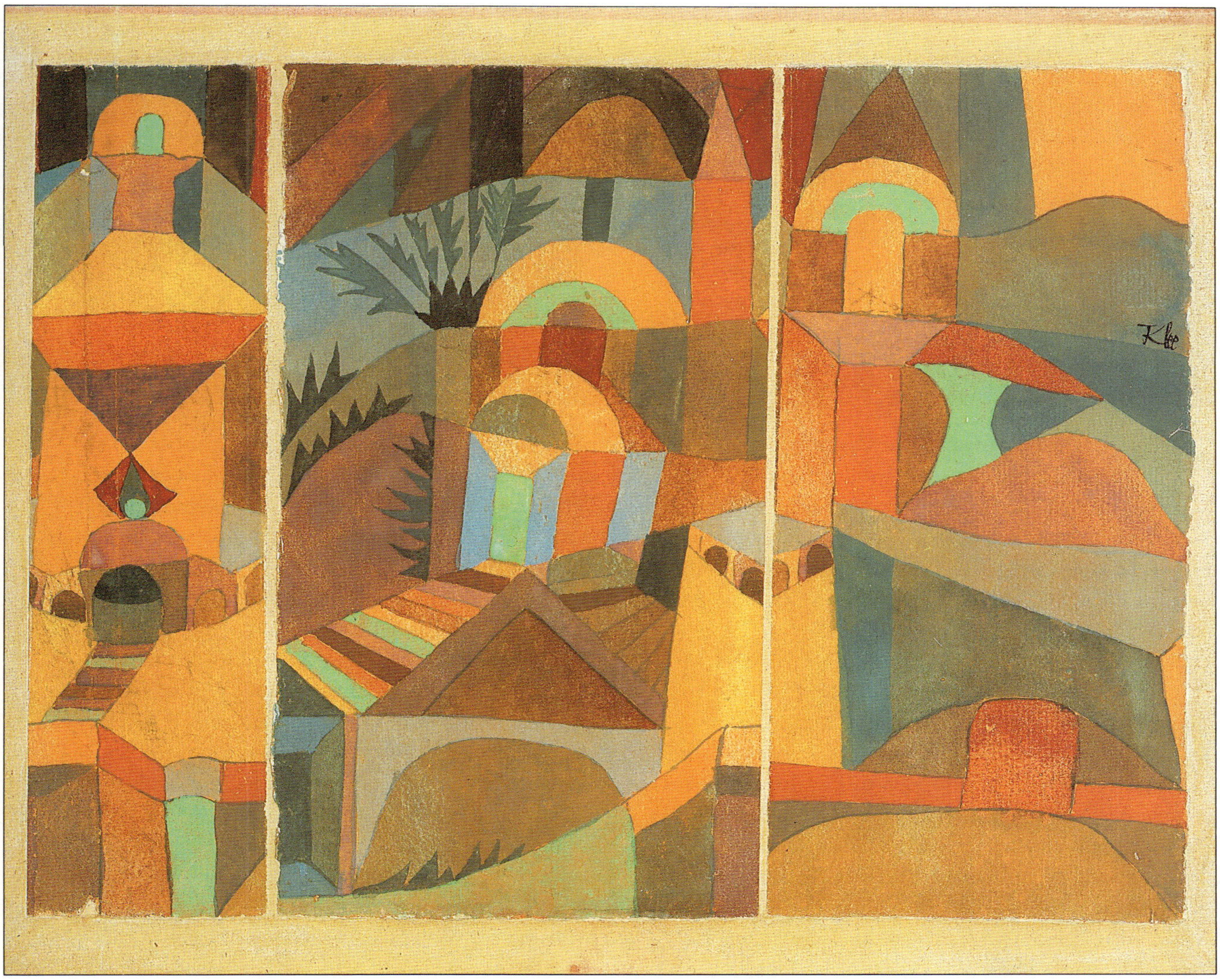

Street Theatre

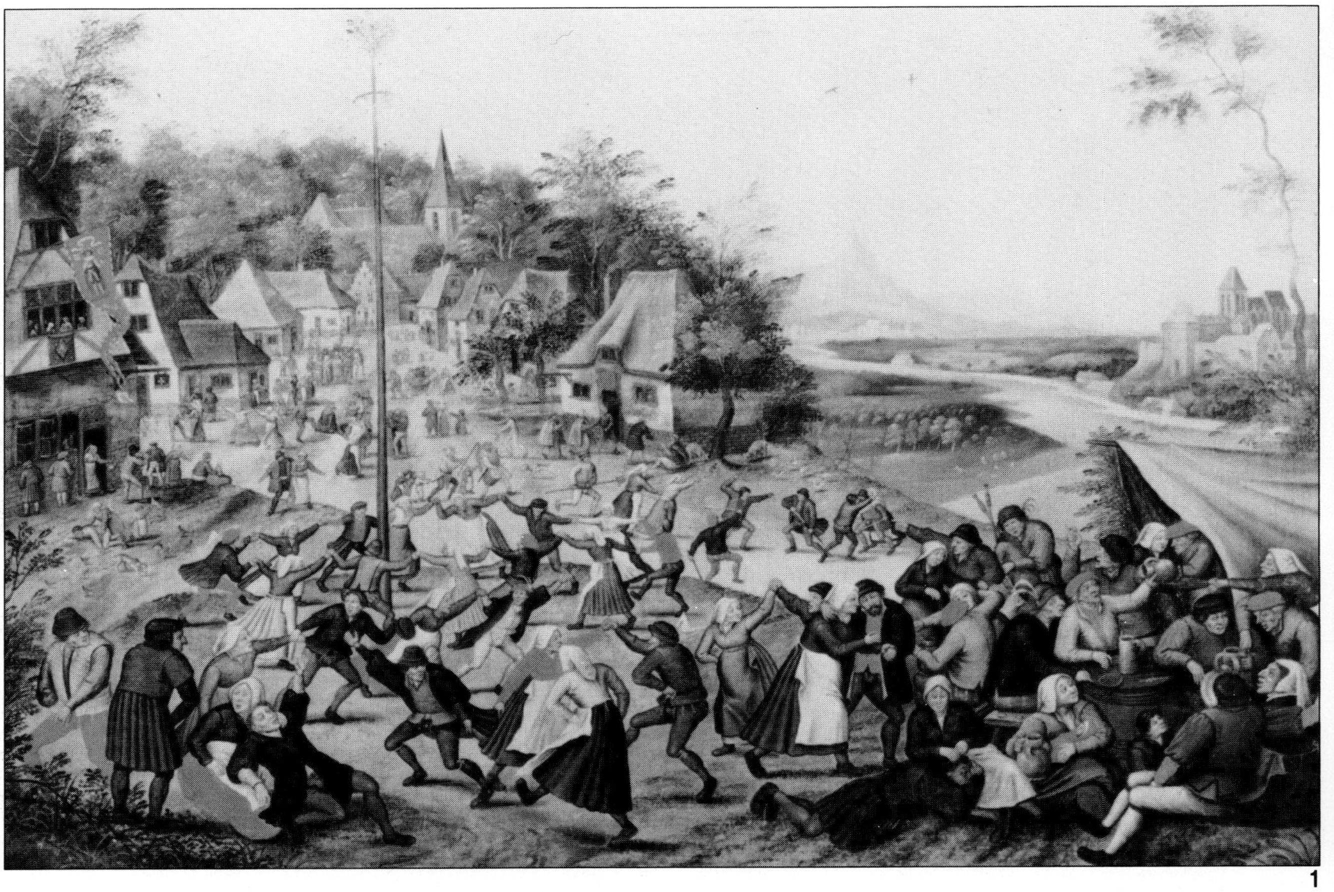

1

The word carnival comes from two Latin words meaning 'goodbye to meat'. From ancient times carnival was a festival in which Europeans had one last fling before the long fast of Lent. 'Mardi Gras', the French for 'Fat Tuesday', was the last and wildest day of all. All we have left in this country on 'Shrove Tuesday' is the custom of eating pancakes – even eggs were forbidden in Lent – but in Europe, in Venice and Madrid particularly and in the new world in Rio de Janeiro and in Trinidad it still goes on. The Trinidad carnival has been re-imported again to London and they sometimes call it 'Mas' (short for Masquerade) because it isn't just a time for eating, drinking, singing and dancing but for dressing up. In the past when there were laws about what each social class could wear dressing up, especially disguise, was frowned upon, except at Carnival time. Then people could do anything and break most taboos under a leader often called the 'Lord of Misrule'. While he reigned established customs could be mocked and overturned and the powerful and their servants changed places. Complaints and awkward questions could be voiced without fear of punishment, all in the spirit of fun.

Even today carnival is a mixture of two things. It's a magnificent spectacle with processions of dancers in co-ordinated costumes and floats produced by teams of workers and their designers. There is music, movement and a great deal to see in a wonderful feast of street theatre. The second idea is that each dance team and float has a theme – colours, shapes and symbols reflecting an idea. You are meant to enjoy the effect but think about the meaning for society as you enjoy it.

1
'A Village Kermesse and Peasants Dancing round a Maypole' by Pieter Brueghel the Younger, circa 1550.

2
The violence of the behaviour of Punch and Judy gives the show an atmosphere – joy and excitement mixed, like a carnival. Why is this?

3-4
Notting Hill carnival scenes.

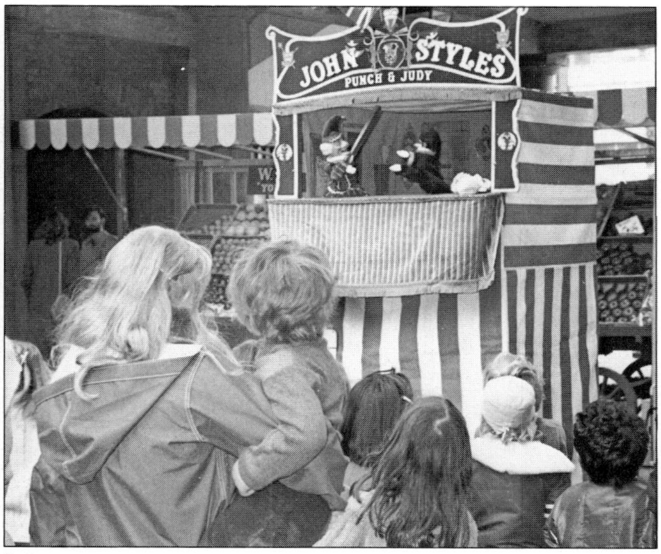

2△

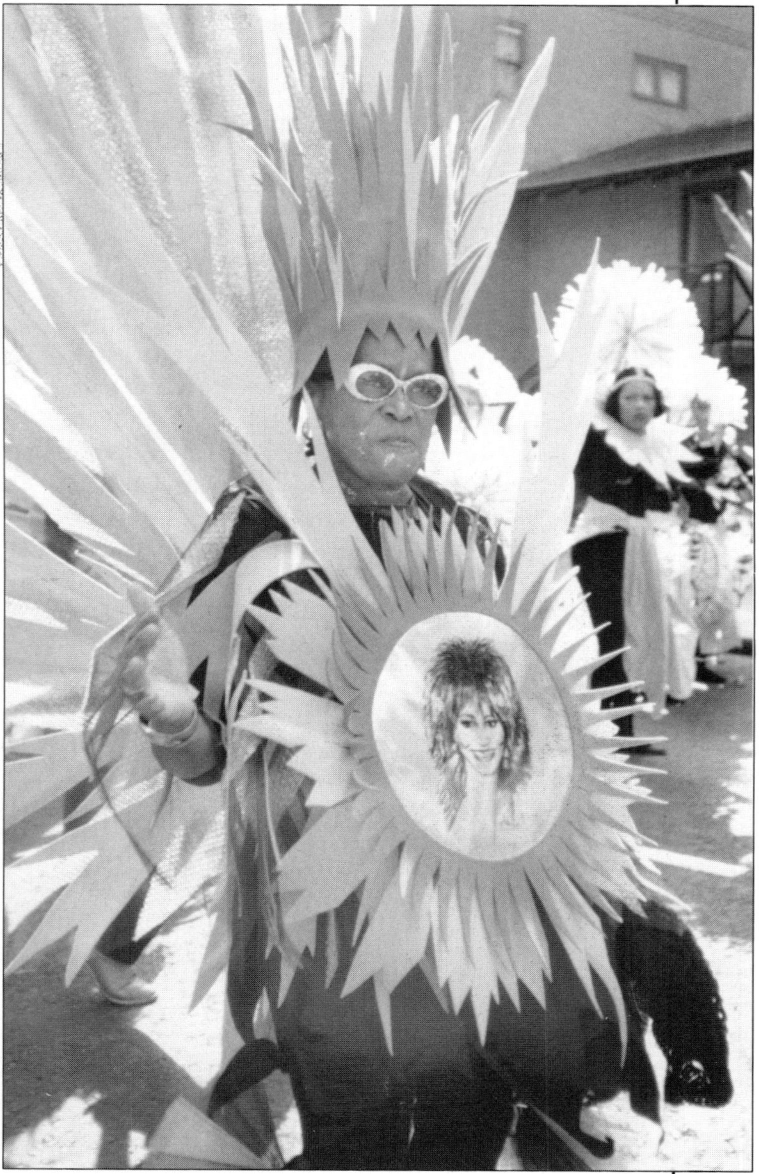

3-4

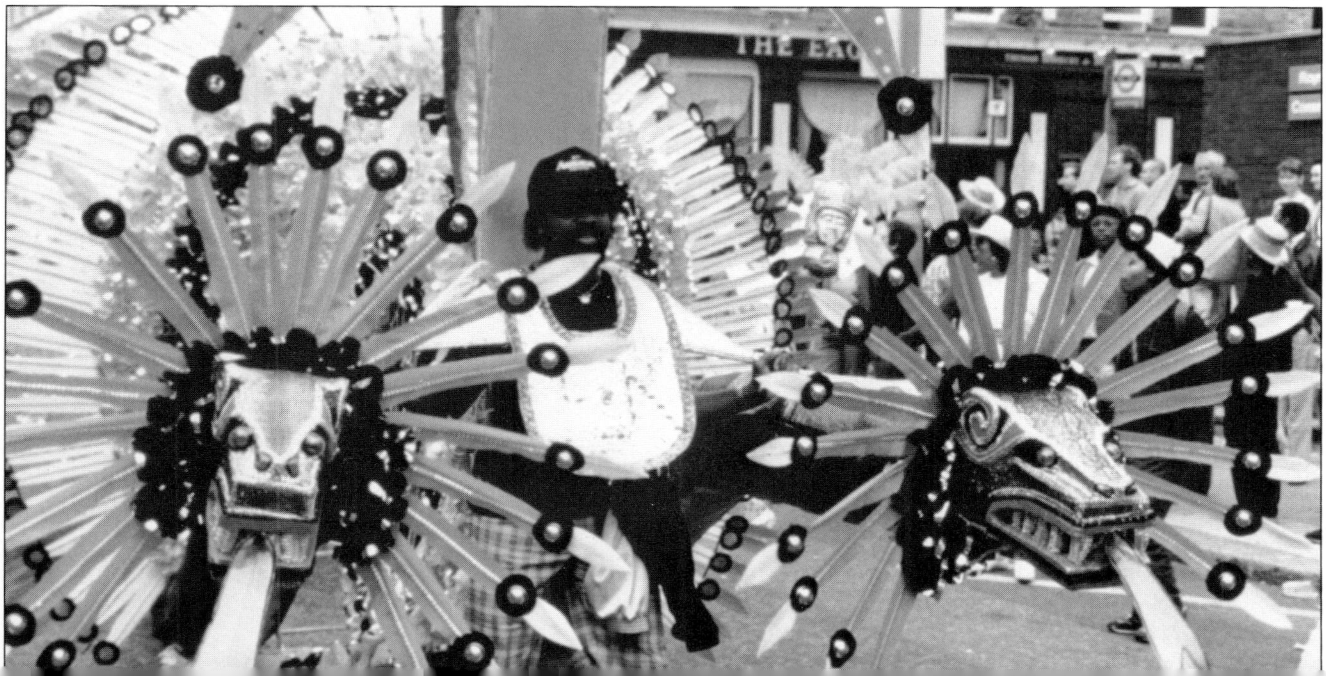

REFLECTIONS: A WORLD O

Telling Stories

Mankind has always liked stories. Not only are they fun to read or hear, but they are often used to pass on the history and the ideas of a society. In that way we know who we are and how we are supposed to behave. This doesn't mean that the stories or the images in which the ideas are wrapped up have to be dull, or the same as previous stories with the same ideas. Art isn't just an exciting way of telling stories, it's a good way of getting the idea across – 'a picture is worth a thousand words'. But the skill of the artist is in getting everything into an understandable form. The story may need a lot of characters and a great deal may happen. Another problem is finding a way of getting across thoughts and feelings, ideas which can't be seen. Sometimes the expression on a face or a gesture is enough, but sometimes colours, poses, symbols or imaginary figures or actions may come into it.

With such a lot to think about, story art needs careful advance planning. Individual figures and groups may need to be sketched first. The inspiration for them may come from a real event or photographs or videotape, or they may mean organising models to pose, dressed in improvised costumes and with improvised props and background. Stories often mean facial expressions and movements, and these also need to be studied first.

1

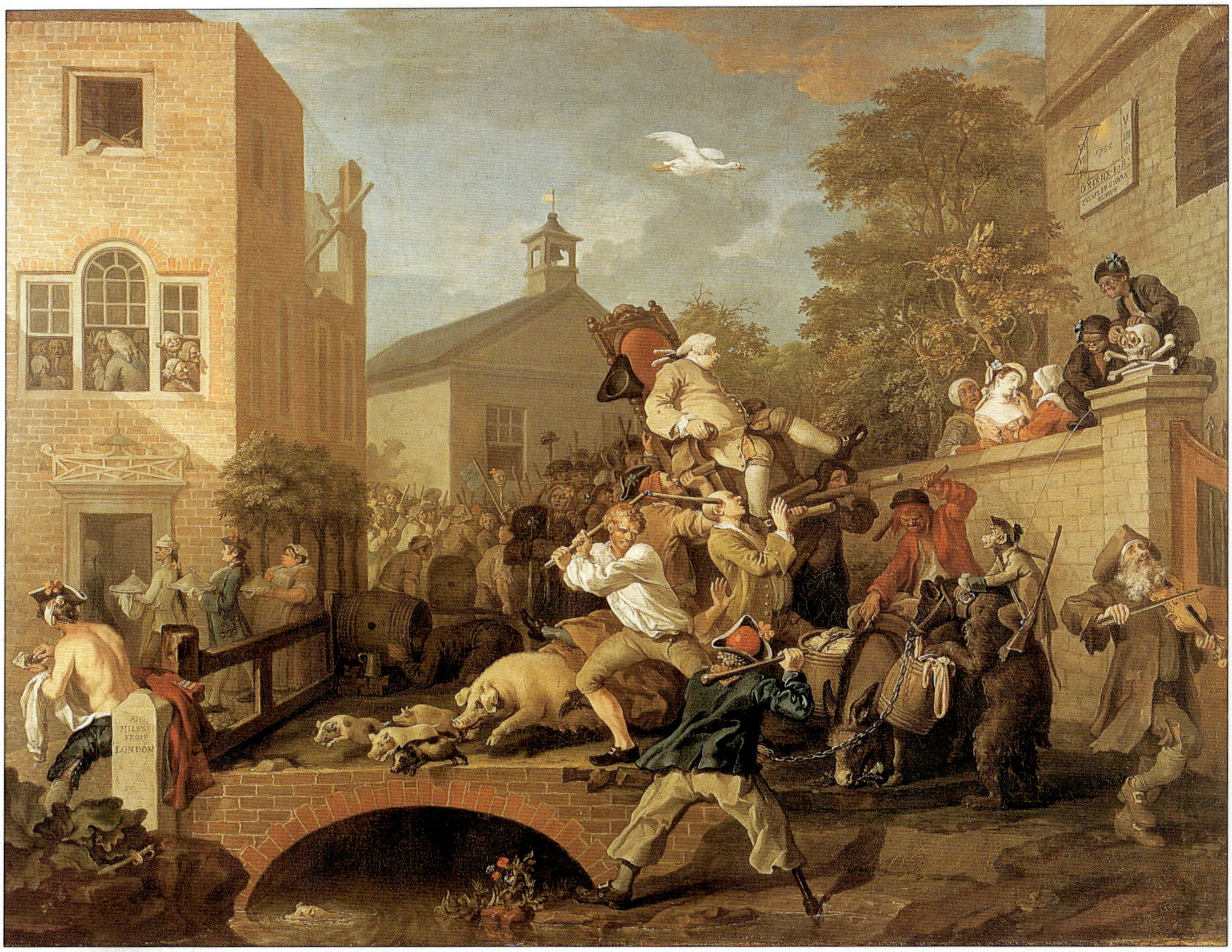

1
'Chairing the Member' by William Hogarth, 1755.
Hogarth probably saw a number of British general elections, and he knew the brutality and the fuss that went with them. He may have seen many of the incidents in his painting separately, but he has arranged them deliberately to tell his story, so that the procession is coming dramatically towards us. But he's also put in his own meaning. The new MP's procession is being led by a blind fiddler. He's being cheered by a performing monkey. His chair is upset by panicking pigs. Why?

2

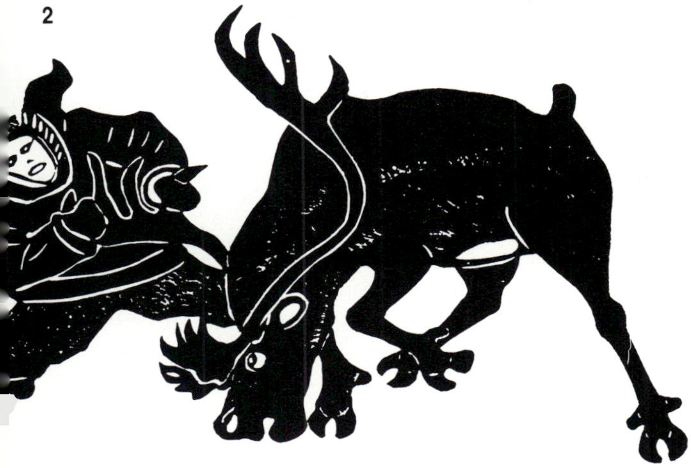

2
'Hunting for Caribou' by Tivi Etook, 1974.
This picture is printed from a stone carving by the Inuit artist. He writes: 'When I was young I saw my father fight the great animals with only his knife and I was filled with fear. I knew that if he won the battle we would have food but if he lost then we would all perish. That was the way of our life in those days . . .'

3
Rodin's group of characters from medieval European history ('the Burghers of Calais') show their despair in the way they stand. Find out their story. Why is the statue close to the Houses of Parliament in London?

3

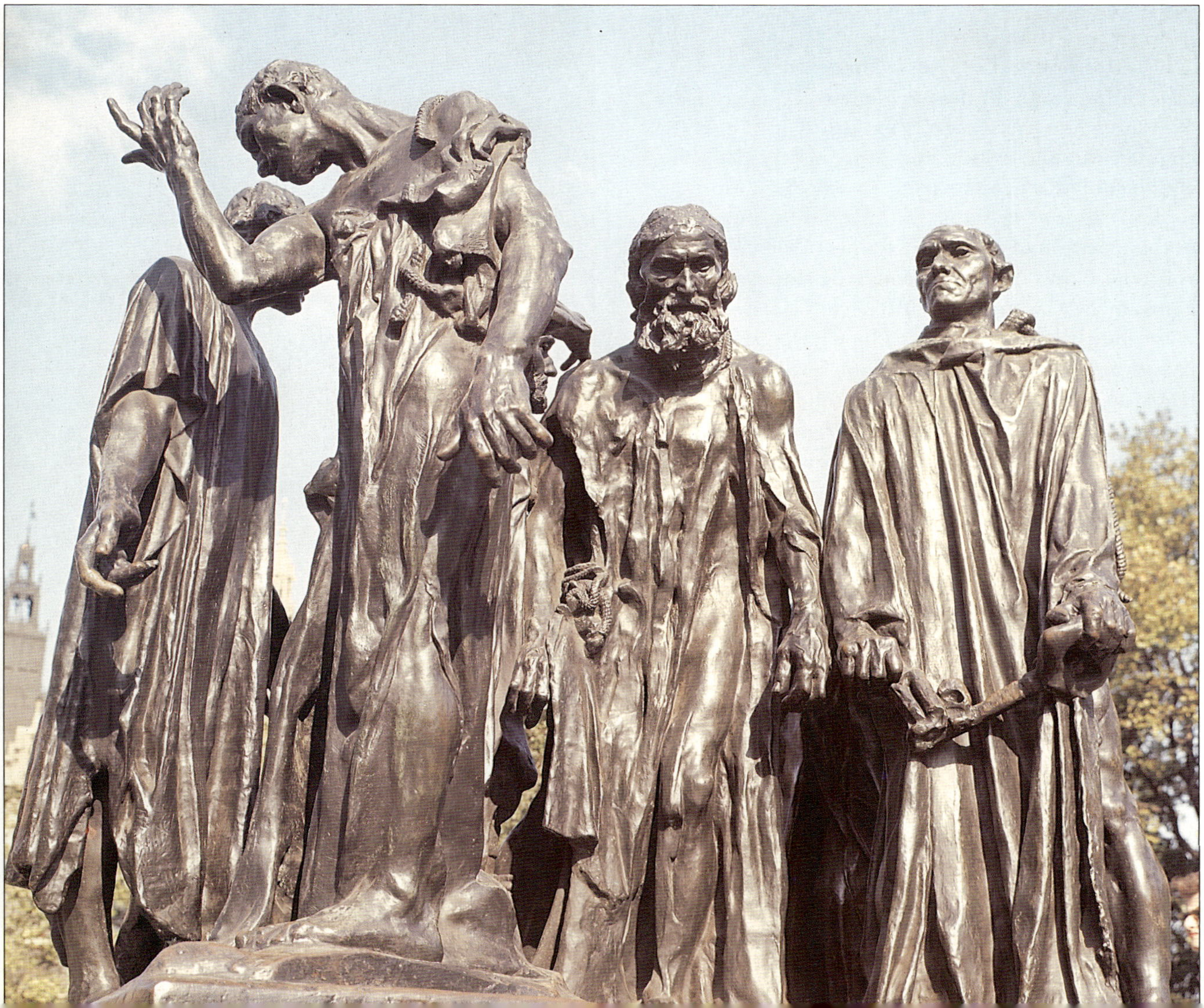

REFLECTIONS: A WORLD OF

Comics

Adventure comics are fun. The best of them have exciting stories and pictures and layout to match. Jim Baikie is one of the artists that draw Judge Dredd and other comic heroes. Like him, most comic artists are supplied with the story and the dialogue. But it's important for him to be up with the characters and the fictional world they live in. For most it's one of great courage and strength for the good men and beauty for the women. But this doesn't stop their enemies from being almost as brave and strong, and ruthless and cunning too. There are remarkable fights and chases, escapes and captures. There are spaceships and other exotic vehicles and unheard-of weapons and buildings that look as if they come from far into the future.

It is Jim Baikie's job to make the look of a page in the comic fit the excitement. Long gone are the days when each scene fitted neatly into a rectangular frame. Now Jim and other artists make the action spread across the page, in any direction that suits the pace of the story. Colours are strange and unexpected – and so are the points of view – until you realise that they're reproducing the strange circumstances in which adventure really happens. Jim is constantly being influenced by what we see in the papers and on the television news. Emergencies really do happen in odd places, at odd times of the day and night, where cameras can't get a good framing and the lighting doesn't show our faces with 'natural' flesh colours.

But all this fantasy doesn't mean Jim can treat his work casually. Every drawing is done by hand and the colouring is painted in layer upon layer. Jim has very strict deadlines to keep to, because printing can't wait when editions of the comic appear every week all through the year. To keep the layout, the colours and the angles fresh needs careful thought and a lively imagination.

1

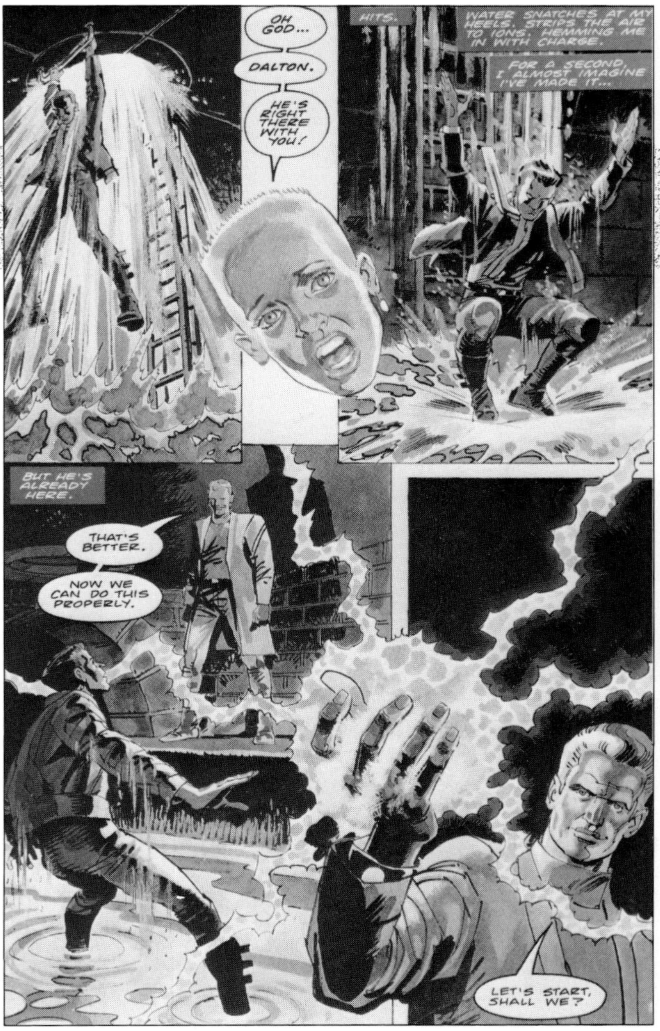

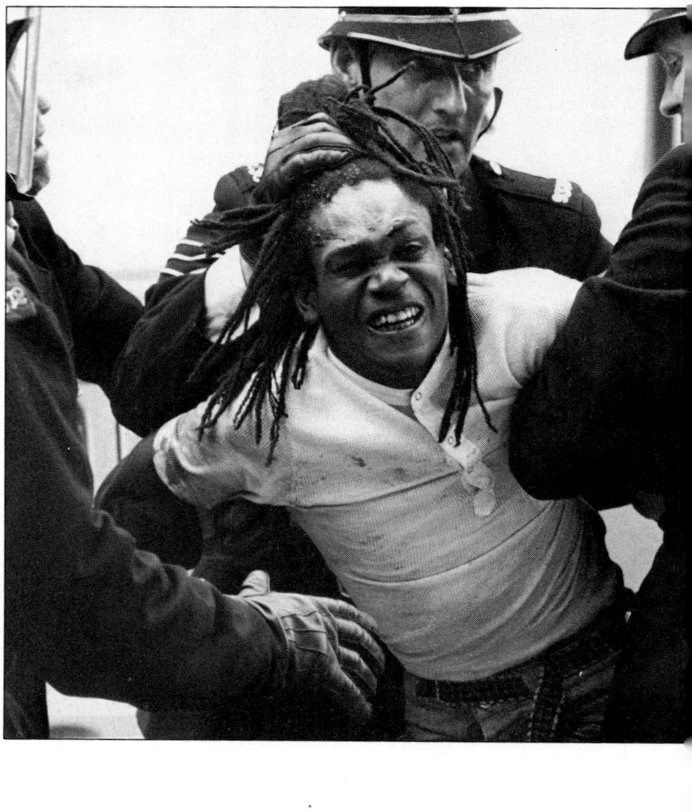

2

1
A page from *Crisis* magazine, by Jim Baikie, 1988. Note how far his organisation of the page has moved from strips or rectangular frames, also the unusual angles and poses he has given the characters.

2
This journalist's action photo has many of the same characteristics as a modern comic illustration.

3
Graffiti art may not be to everyone's taste, but at least it gives expression to people frustrated by boring and soulless environments. At worst it is vandalism, at best it is uplifting public art.

4
'Suburban Train Arriving in Paris' by Gino Severini, 1915. The artist was a Futurist, one of a group of artists about the time of the First World War who attempted to paint the speed and technological power of the modern world.

3

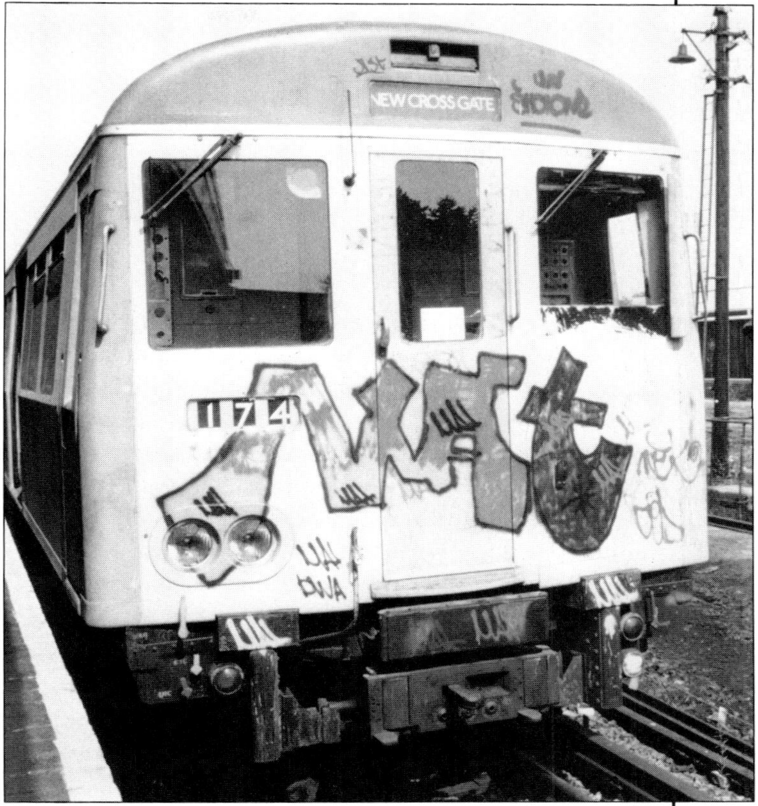

4▽

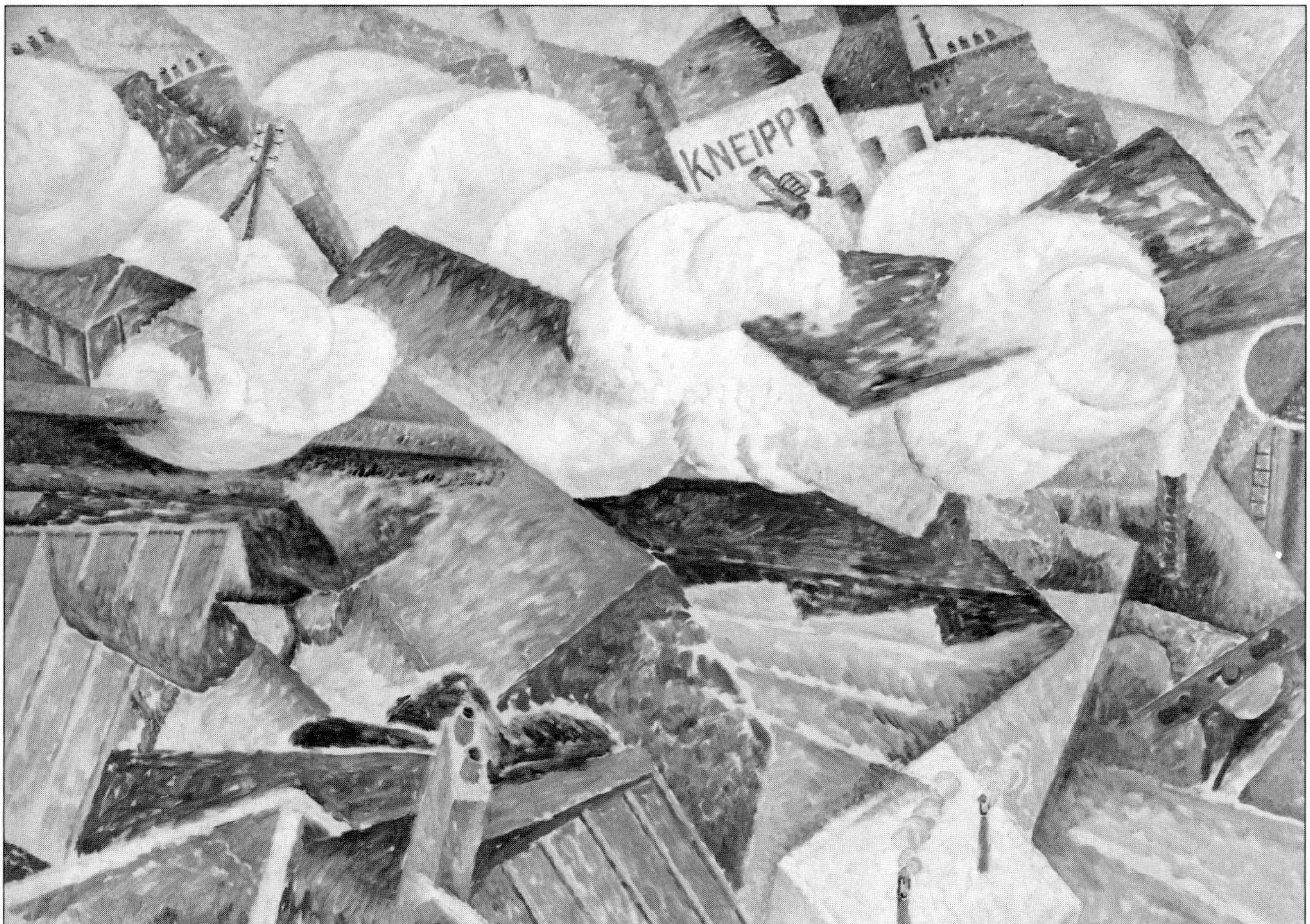

Landscapes

There are good and bad things about picturing landscape. You can record the main outlines at any time though they will change as the light changes, and concentrate on whatever takes your interest – the details of nature, the effect of distance, the cloudscape, ways of showing the make-up of mountains, woods and valleys in the view – what artists call the 'structure'. Or you can think about what goes on in such a place, or what *might* go on. For some artists that means the everyday activities of farmers and country people, or perhaps travellers, hunters and pleasure seekers. But already these seemingly normal activities begin to take us farther in time and place and our imagination.

Every landscape conjures up stories. What if the travellers are on the way to find treasure? What if the pleasure seekers are lovers? What if the lovers can only find happiness when they escape from a world that is against them? Suppose the hunters are heroes from some ancient legend, or even gods. Suppose the quarry is something extraordinary – a tiger perhaps. Wilder landscapes might conjure up wild stories. John Martin's landscapes were inspired by wild European mountain scenery, but he made the people tiny and the weather violent to serve his stories from the Bible. The unusual but realistic colours and shapes of modern fighting have often been arranged by artists to produce an effect which seems disjointed and shocking, in keeping with the horrors of war in our century.

1

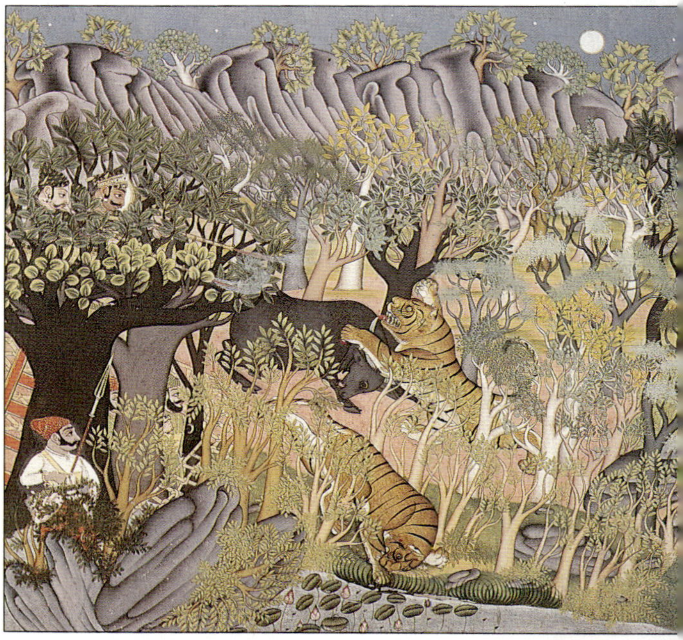

2▽

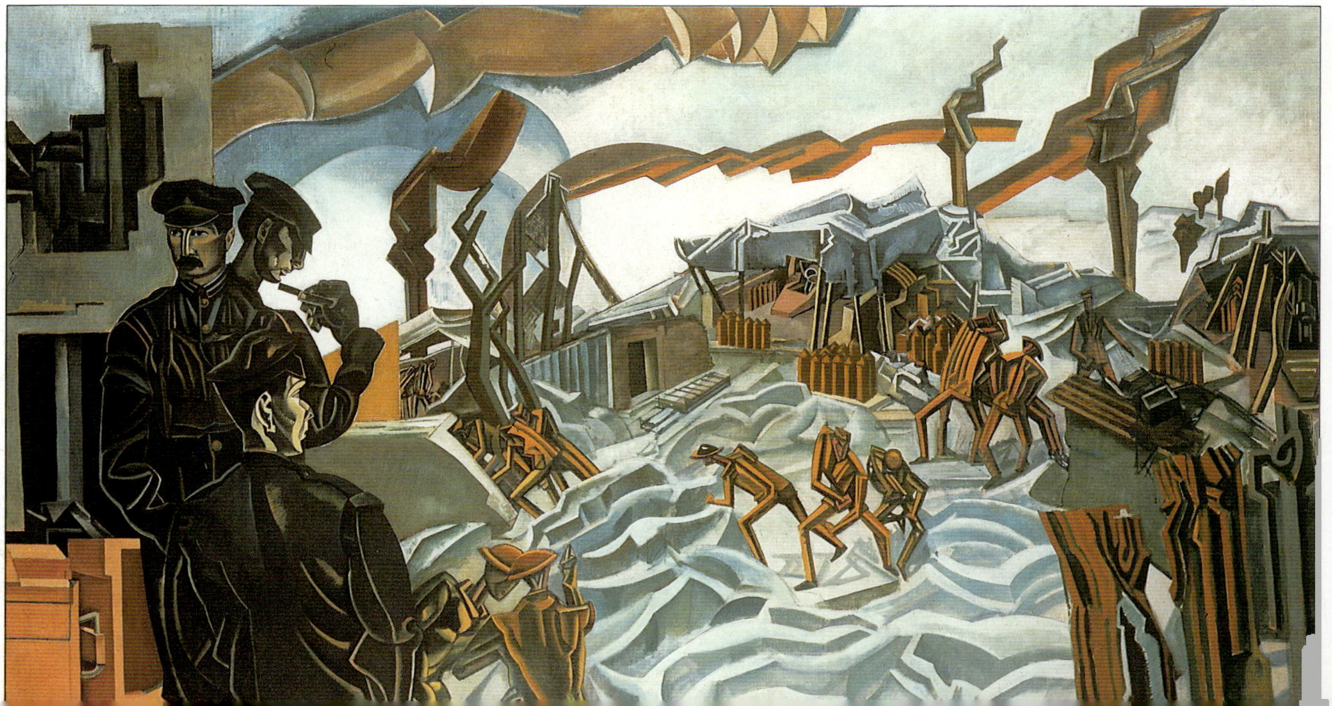

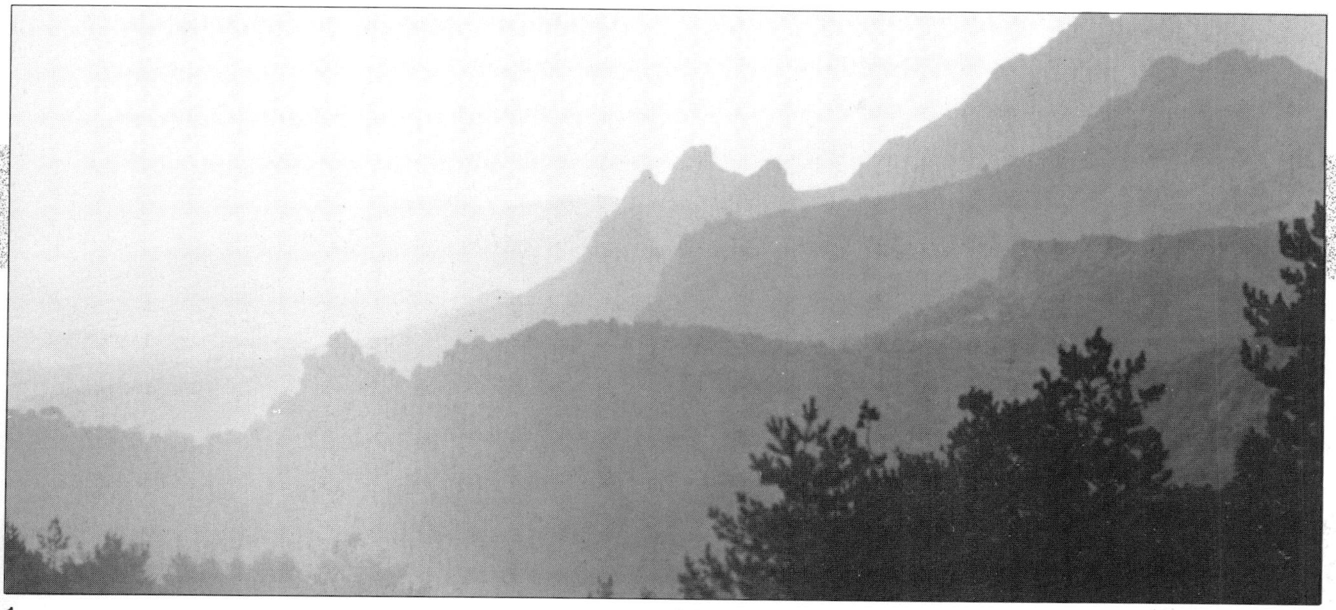

1
'Shooting Tigers' by Kaja Ummed Singh of Kotah, India, sixteenth century. The countryside, the men and the event are probably real, and known to the artist, but for him they are largely an excuse to enjoy the painting of colours and patterns. Notice the criss-cross of parallel lines, in the rocks, the trees and the stripes on the tigers. Notice too how much trouble the artist has taken to include many species of trees and plants. Would the earth and the rocks really be in those colours? Before you say, look at some photographs of Indian landscapes.

2
'A Battery Shelled' by Percy Wyndham Lewis, twentieth century. The colours are the greys and khakis of modern war, the shapes jagged and related to those of the Cubist movement which began just before the First World War. But the shapes and colours also relate to the mood. Look carefully at the picture and decide what everything is, and what the overall message might be.

3
The Pyrenees, Spain. A photograph demonstrates the effect of the atmosphere on distance. The furthest mountains are the haziest and bluest (useful to remember when you are trying to introduce depth into a picture). This can make an interesting exercise in colour and tone.

4
'Joshua Commanding the Sun to Stand Still' by John Martin, nineteenth century. An over-the-top picture of an earth-shattering story. Think of the ways John Martin uses the landscape to create his mood. Think particularly of perspective, lighting, viewpoint. Perhaps someone could find out what happened!

5
'Landscape with the Arrival of Aeneas' by Claude Lorrain, seventeenth century. The distance effects are produced by the same methods as in Picture 1, but the artist uses them here to give an idea of how far Aeneas may have travelled. Who was Aeneas? In which period does Lorrain set the legend?

3△ 4▽

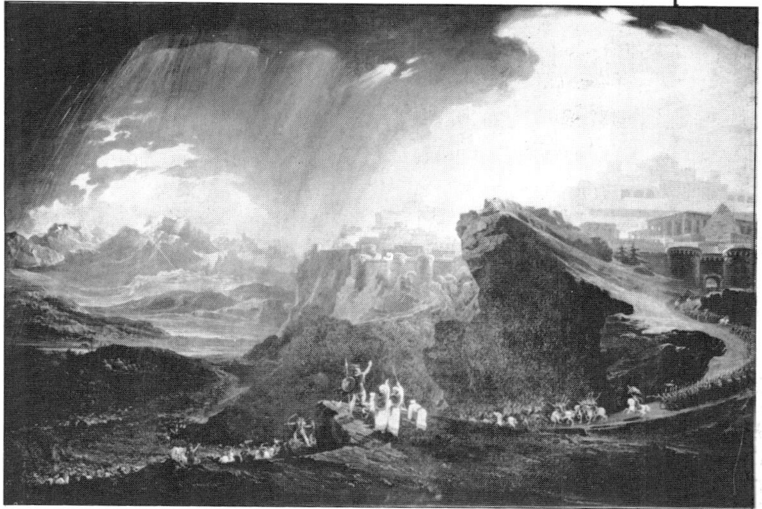

5▽

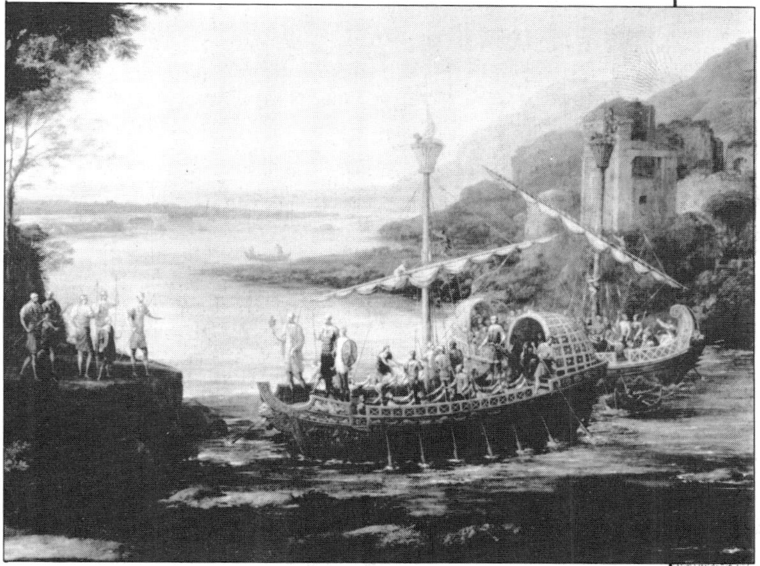

WHERE DO WE GO FROM H

Another Medium

1

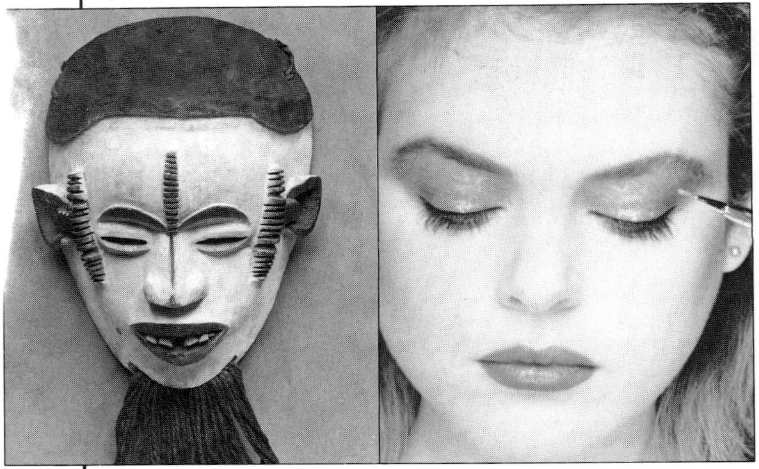

2

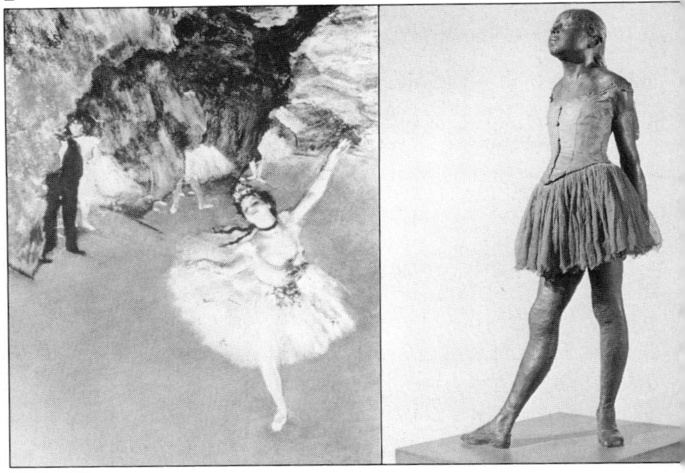

For a large part of this book we've been thinking about the normal forms art takes. If it is to interest us, art has to be about us or things we know, and if it is to do its job, design has to fit our physical needs and appeal to our ideas of what looks and feels right. Art and design work covers many activities, but we tend to think only of one or two. There is painting, drawing, sculpture and printmaking, and we use those media most for making portraits and figures and telling stories.

But it's a useful exercise to stretch our ideas of what art is, to see if new effects and ideas emerge. Try to think what would happen to your work if it was in other colours or in another medium. Degas, for instance, was so keen on making the subjects he painted and drew seem solid – almost touchable – that he was led to make sculptures of them as well as flat pictures. In many ways the sculptures and the pictures tell us about each other in a way neither form does independently. Raoul Dufy was a French painter who enjoyed the light bright colours of the summer countryside and the sea. His paintings are full of the excitement of being alive and so too are his fabrics, which match the happy mood of the paintings and yet work well as material for furnishings and elegant women's clothes. Pablo Picasso's pottery looks and feels useful, with simple patterns and figures to match, but it is like sculpture too and it bears being looked at for its own sake.

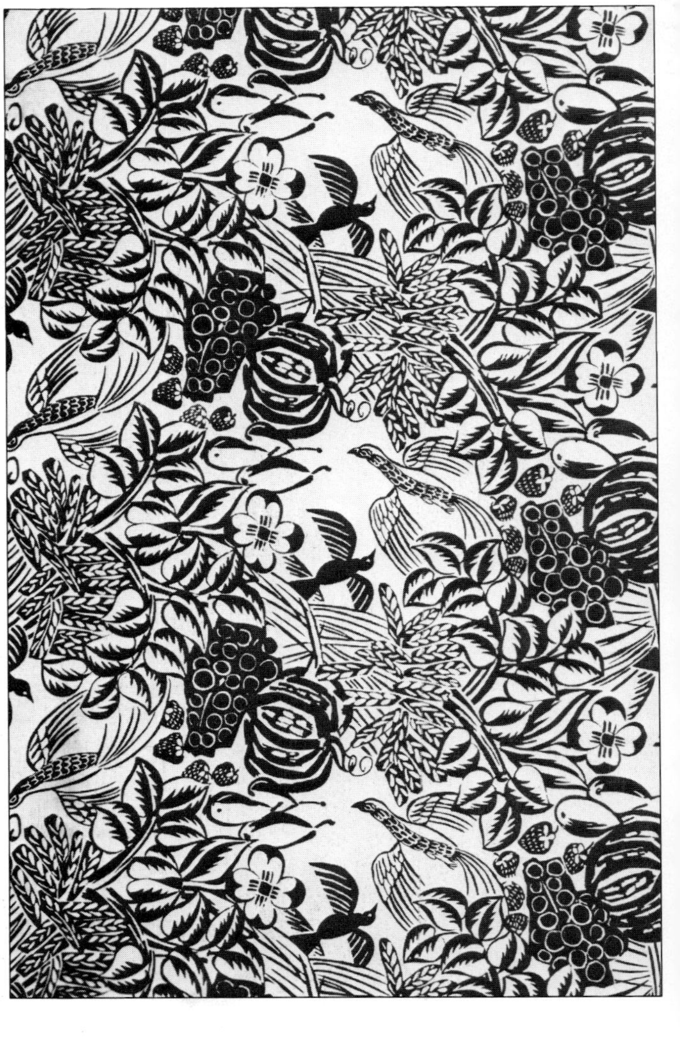

3

E?

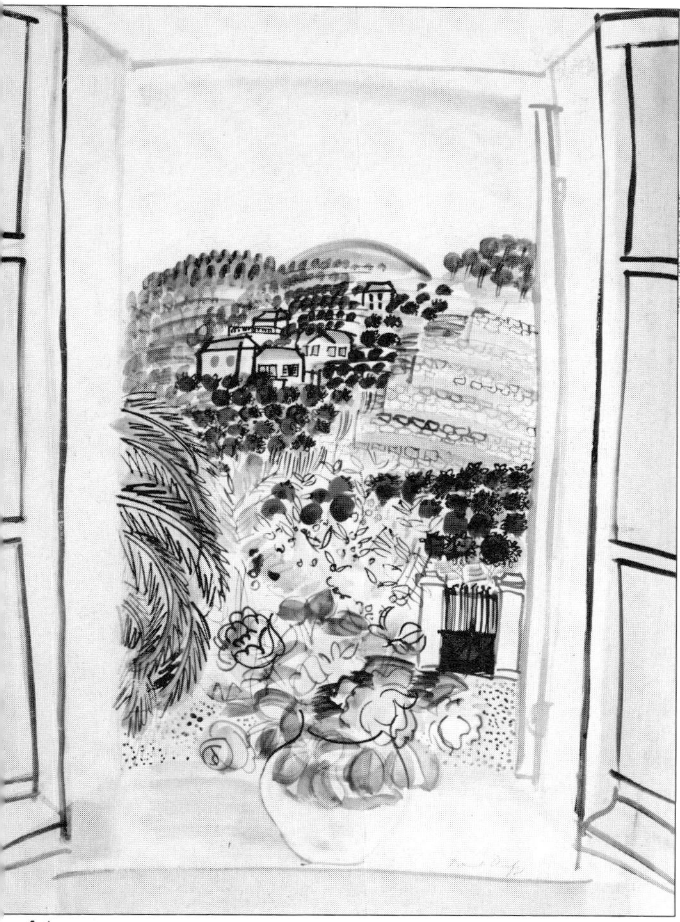

4△

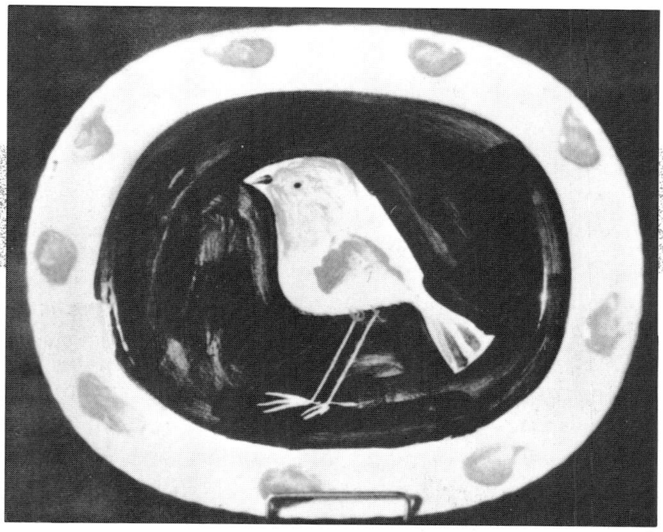

5

1
A mask from Northern Nigeria and party make-up from Europe. What is make-up for? What is the mask for? Are there any differences?

2
'Dancer' (painting and bronze sculpture) by Edgar Degas, late nineteenth century. The artist Degas haunted dance studios and theatres trying to absorb the atmosphere surrounding his favourite subject. What are the differences between the painting and the sculpture?

3
A sophisticated and lively fabric design by the French painter Raoul Dufy, circa 1920.

4
Dufy's 'Open Window at Saint-Jeannet'.

5
Ceramic plate by Pablo Picasso, twentieth century. A child-like design which fits its purpose well. Why might one of Picasso's other works not fit here, and why might this design not count as 'art'?

6
'D Day Landings, 1944' (black and white photograph) and The Overlord Embroidery, 1968 (needlework in colour). Which works best as a portrayal of the scene? What other media might be used for telling the story?

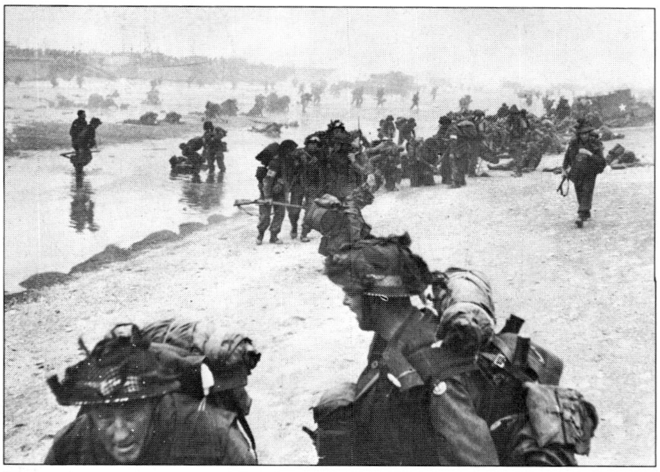

6

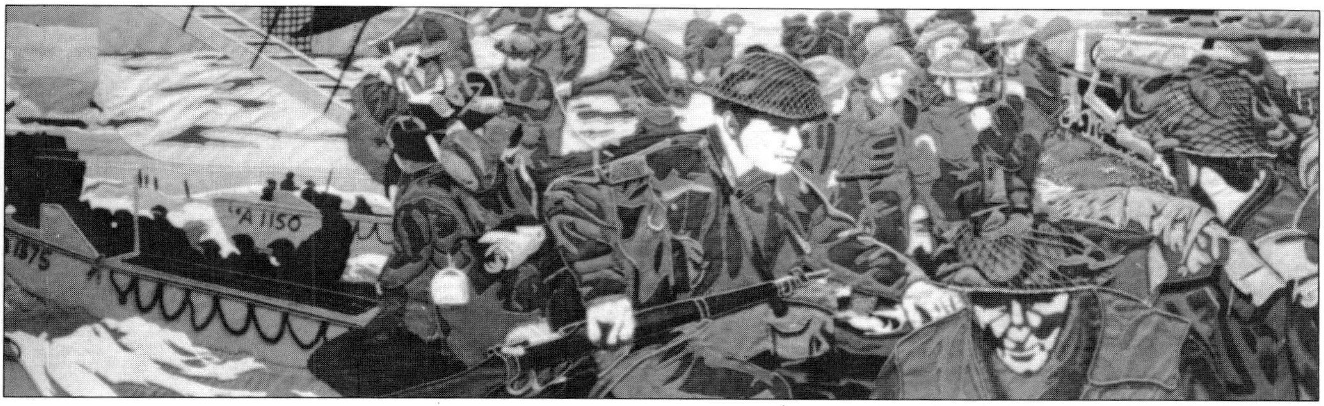

Another Time, Another Place

Humans have grown up looking around them and making art work for others to look at. Sometimes across the centuries, or in places very distant from one another, you can find art which is similar even though the artists could not possibly have seen each other's work. Why might that be?

What is your 'culture'? Think about the way *your* world looks and produce a display or folder to show how it is the same, and different, from others. Pick a period, or a culture different from your own, and again make a display or make an object or work of art to fit it. Watch out for the right shapes, colours, materials etc. Take an object from your culture and redesign it for the other culture. If it refuses to fit, you may have to design something completely new to do the same job.

Invent a culture for the future and design objects or art for it. You must have reasons for why everything fits. These may relate to the culture's trade, natural resources, weather, religion, politics, work and leisure activities, mode of transport and its history. You might try to invent and perform some of its music and literature and produce a play showing life there.

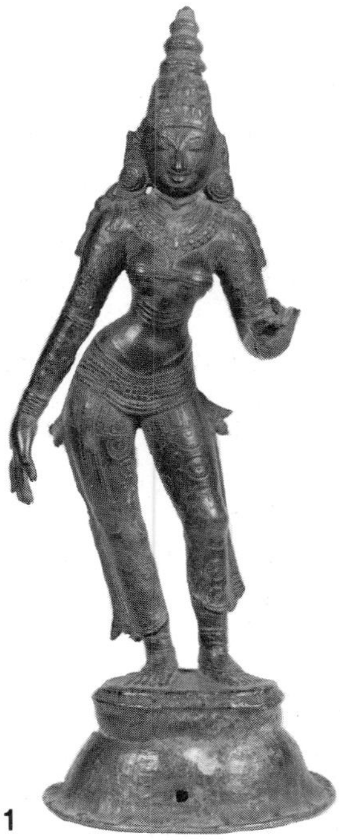

1

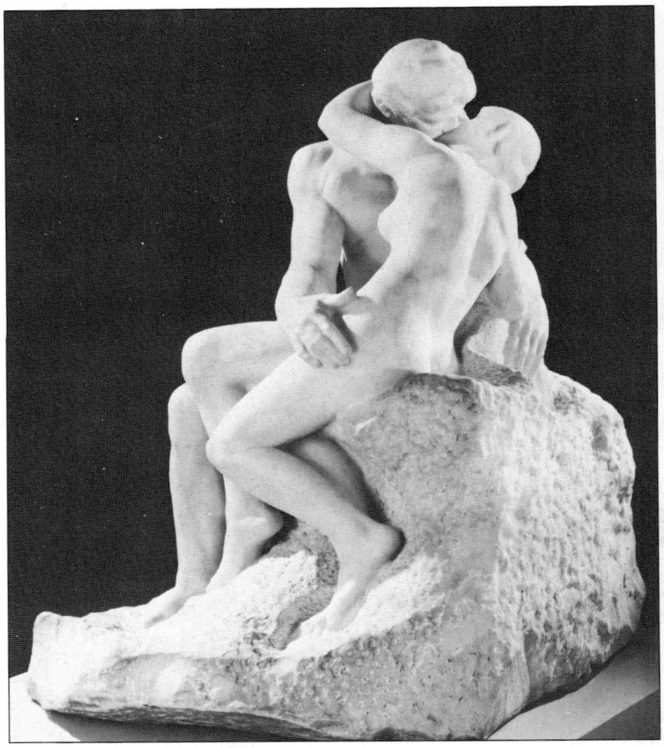

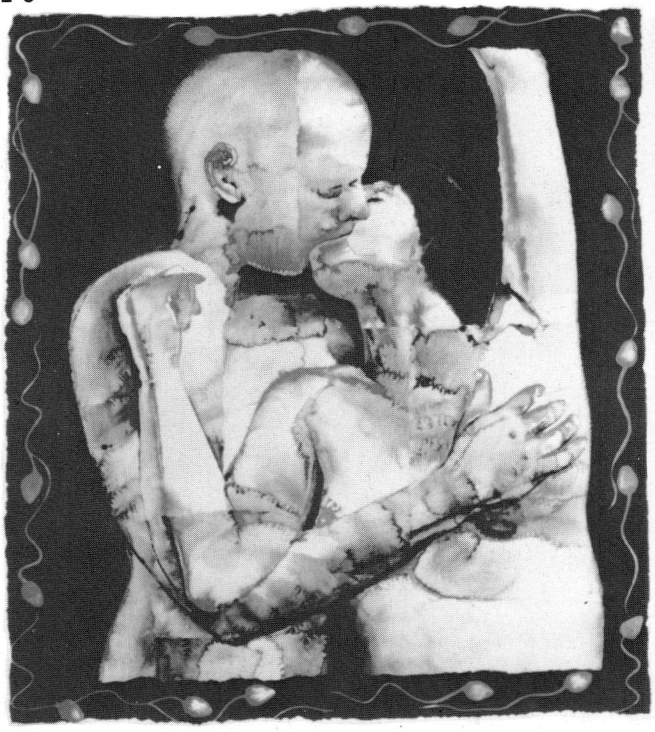

2-3

RE?

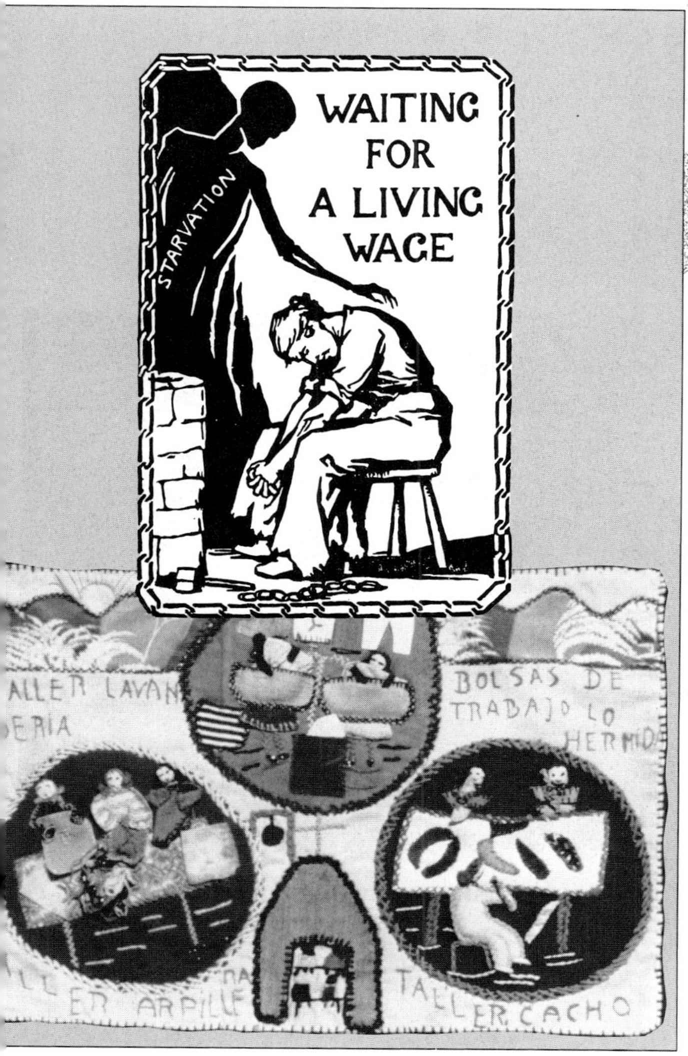

6▽

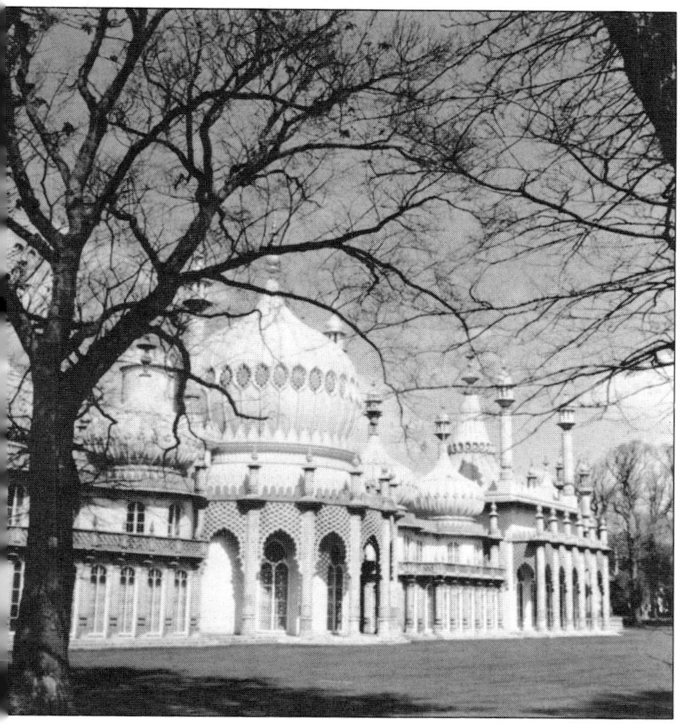

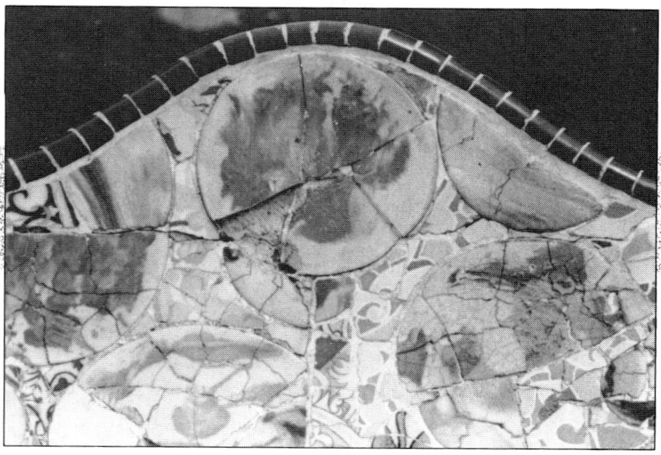

7-8

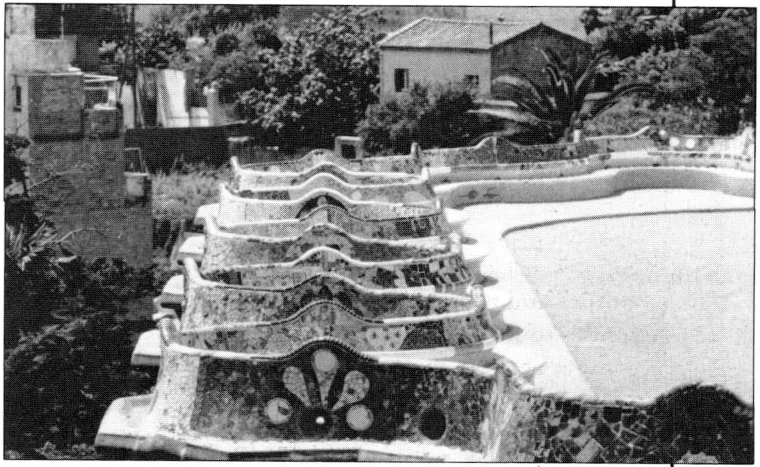

1
Degas could have seen sculptures of Indian dancers like this one, but he didn't copy them. What might he have liked about them? (See pages 82/83)

2-3
'The Kiss' by Auguste Rodin, nineteenth century, and Graham Dean, 1987. Graham Dean was certainly recalling Rodin's sculpture, now a hundred years old. Each of these is startling, but in different ways. What are they?

4-5
Two protests by women in different times and places. How are they the same, and different? Why the different media? If you were persecuted here and now what would be your safest and most effective way of protesting through art?

6
Brighton Pavilion by John Nash, 1822. An 'Indian' building in Sussex. Why did the patron commission this style? How is it different from Indian palaces, and how is it 'British'?

7-8
Park seating, Barcelona by Antonio Gaudi, c. 1890. Interesting to look at *and* very practical. Find out why Barcelona in his time might be the place for Gaudi's designs. Why use jumbled tile fragments for decoration?

Another Point of View

Another way of thinking about what you see is to take another point of view. Salvador Dali shows us the most important image in Christian art from an unusual point of view, but from a viewpoint which makes total sense to a dedicated Christian. Piranesi was an Italian writer about architecture. Since in his time the buildings of ancient Rome were considered the best, he used them as the basis for his dreams of grand cities of the future. But sometimes the dreams became nightmares. In his series of 'prison' pictures he showed the inside of other huge buildings which were depressing mazes designed to shut out justice and mercy. The tiny figures help to make us feel how hopeless and helpless we would be without law. Grandeur becomes tyranny, hope becomes despair.

It's a useful trick to look at a subject from a distance and the close-up produces interesting effects too. A number of 'abstract' works turn out to be the result of the artist looking at just one small part of something larger, and the question 'what on earth is it?' is the trigger to careful looking and appreciation of the colours, shapes and textures.

It helps, in the mind's eye, to look round the edge of works of art. The smile on the face of Leonardo da Vinci's 'Mona Lisa' has baffled viewers for centuries. What is she smiling about? By changing the point of view, perhaps by looking over her shoulder, or seeing beyond the picture frame, we might learn the real answer . . .

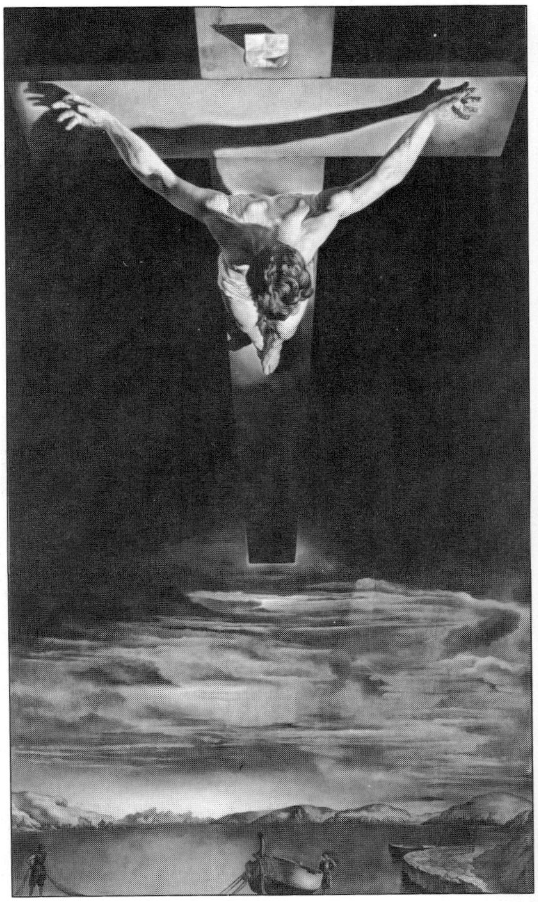

1△

2▽

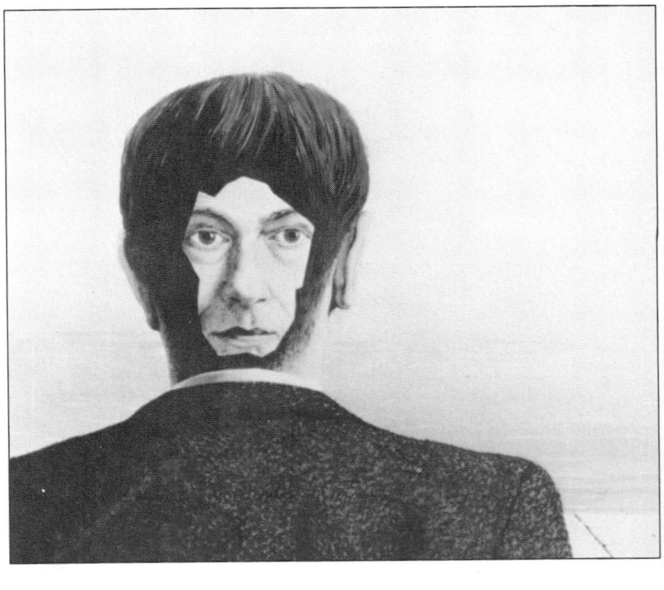

1
'Christ of St John of the Cross' by Salvador Dali, twentieth century. There is a conventional position from which to view most scenes. If you take another, you can wake up tired eyes and brains, and make the viewer look and think again.

2
Self-portrait by René Magritte. This surrealist work is a puzzle. What does it mean?

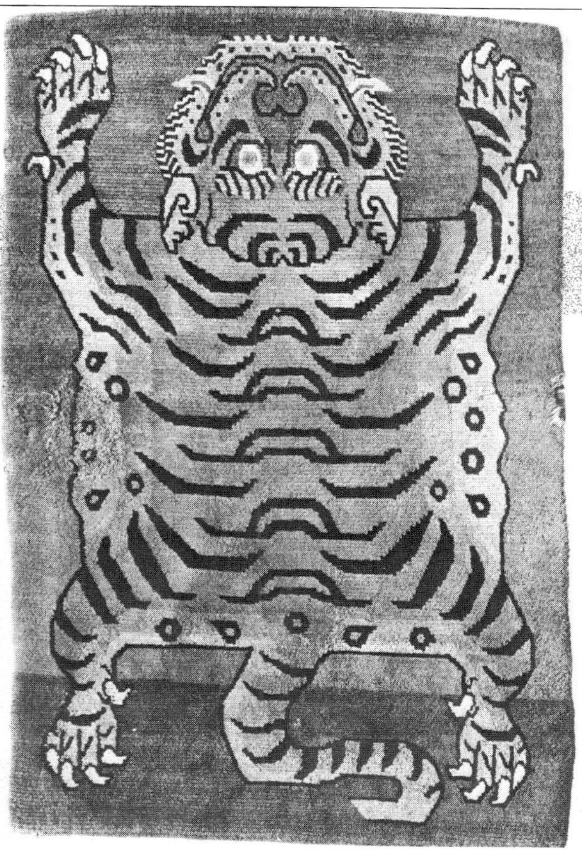

3-4

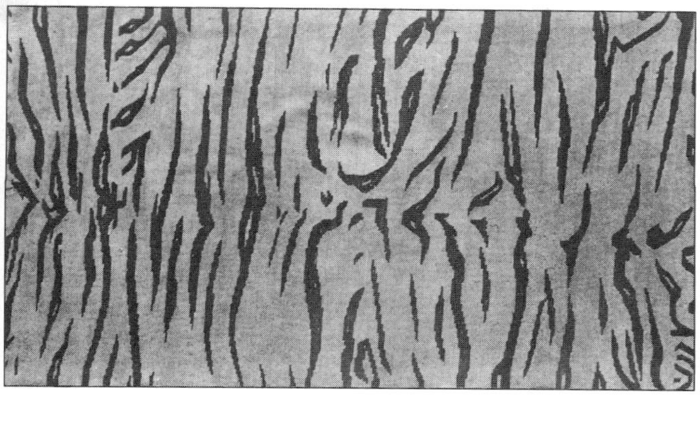

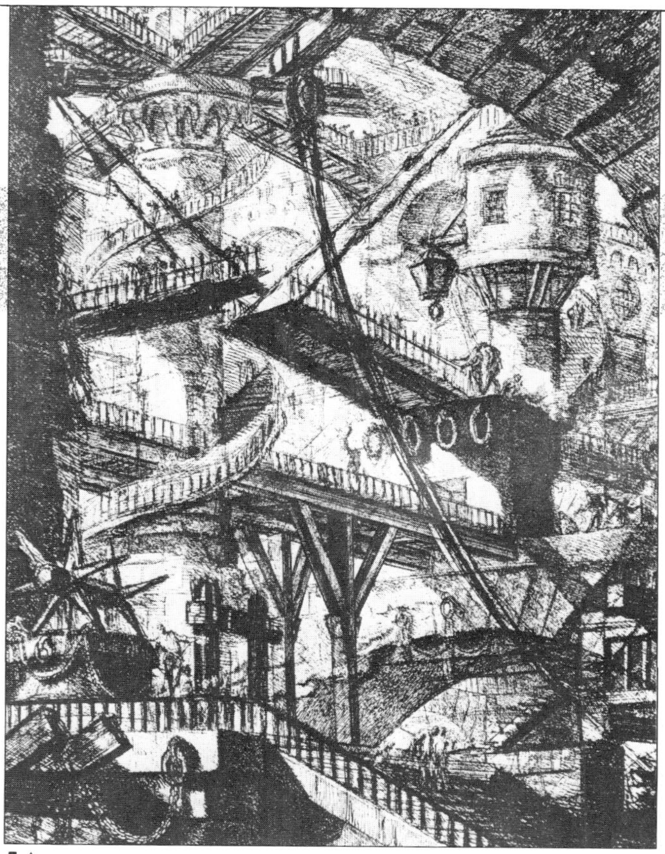

5△

6▽

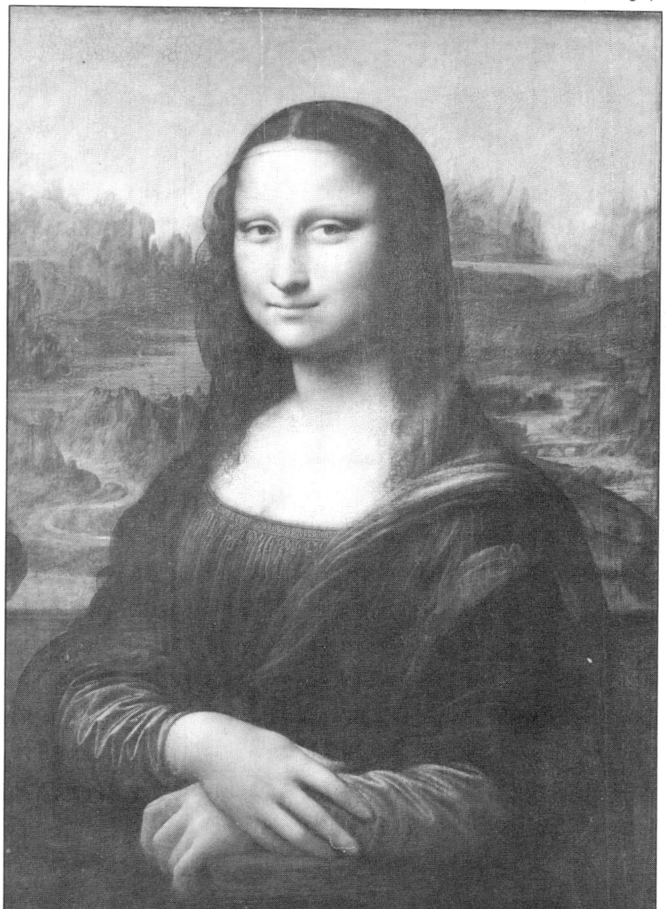

3-4

Tiger rugs from Tibet. Without the rug showing paws, head and tails, they become an unusual piece of abstract art.

5

Giovanni Piranesi was an Italian writer about architecture, working in the eighteenth century. This is one of his 'Prisons' prints.

6

What – for you – is the solution to the puzzle of Leonardo da Vinci's 'Mona Lisa'?

WHERE DO WE GO FROM H

Extend the Story

Some art work seems complete as it is. In fact, a picture may rely on its frame to give it impact as a well-directed shock of colour, movement or story on a plain wall would lose its power if it went on and on. But it's a useful exercise to think about where a piece of art or design fits. It helps us to appreciate what it meant to people when it was first seen or used, and why the artists chose certain ways of expressing themselves – to contrast with what already existed, or to ask people to compare his idea with something or even some already well-known work of art. We have to ask questions like 'what happened before the picture or after it? What was that person or view like at other times, in other moods? What would they be like if circumstances were completely altered? What if the artist had been interested in other colours, other shapes, other ways of putting across the ideas they saw in the scene?' You can try all these variations and more. Pick one scene, event or piece of design and rethink it for different circumstances – perhaps several different circumstances. You can extend the possibilities by asking questions like 'what if?'

Of course, this doesn't help our first reactions to art or design. We want to know if they're useful or if they appeal to us. But anything that helps us think about the ideas behind art and design, and why it's made the way it is, increases our experience of looking and thinking about what we see and helps us make better judgements.

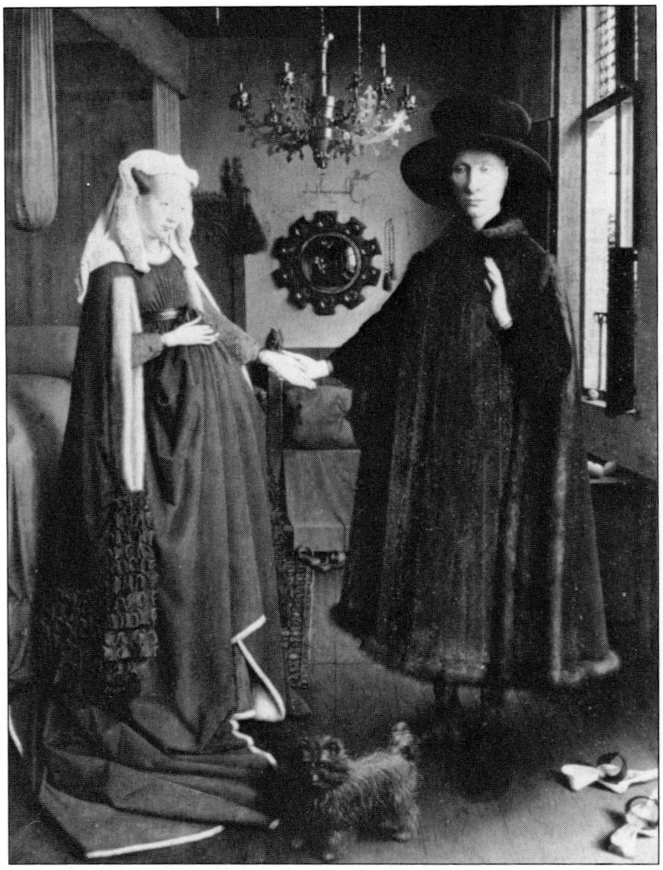

1-2

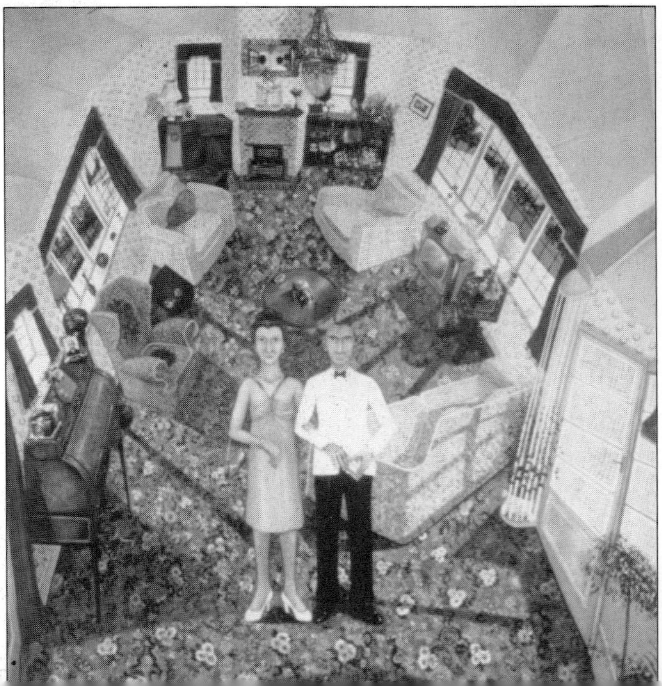

1-2
'Arnolfini and his Wife' by Jan van Eyck, fifteenth century and 'Mr and Mrs Stanley Joscelyn' by Anthony Green, 1972. Anthony Green knows Van Eyck's painting well, and though marriage 500 years ago must have been very different from today, there will be similarities too. You could talk about what marriage means, and why we want pictures of weddings and other important events. But look at the detail, and particularly the mirrors. There is much more to the story in both paintings.

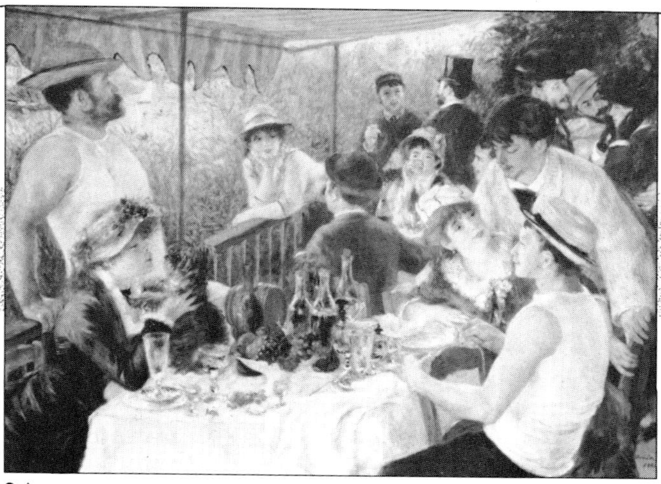

3△

3

'Luncheon of the Boating Party' by Auguste Renoir, nineteenth century. What if this happy summer view by Rencir was seen in winter? Or by night? Or after a nuclear attack? Or in tropical Africa? How would it look then?

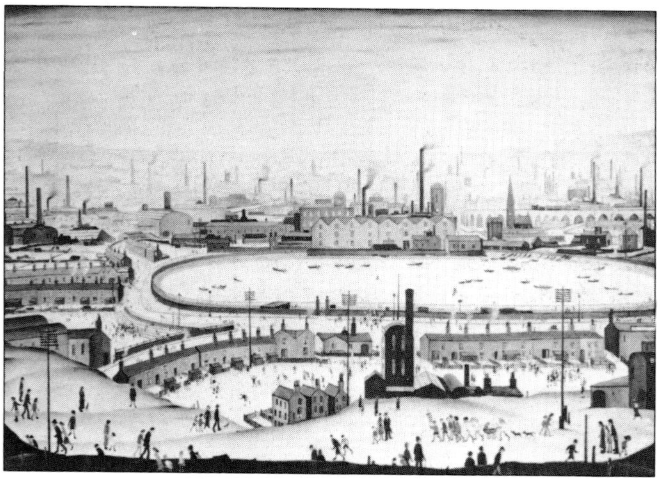

4–5

4–5

'The Pond' by L. S. Lowry, twentieth century and 'Stephen's Lowry', a version by a ten-year-old boy, London Borough of Brent. L. S. Lowry's view means different things to its viewers, but he doesn't tell us what he thinks. Stephen McKenzie thinks he knows, and he's extended the story from the original.

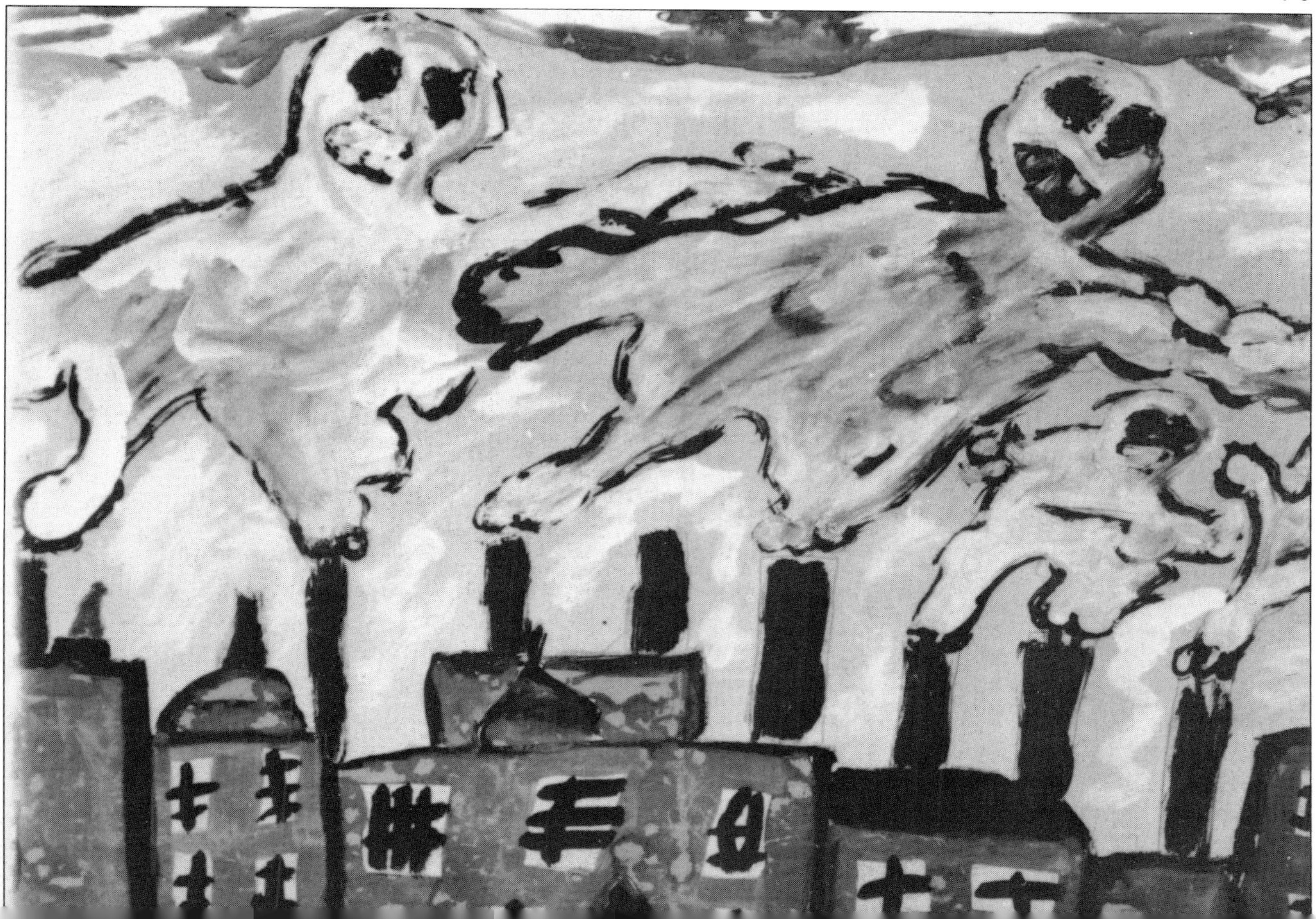

STUDY

Themes

You may be interested in following-up ideas you have had to deepen your knowledge of the subject and fatten up your folder, or you may be looking for an interesting theme to start off some artwork. Here's a list, only to be used if your own imagination isn't working for some reason!

There are several good ways of thinking round an idea. You could take your theme across cultures to see how people in different places and points in history have dealt with it. Or you could look at the single culture surrounding the idea you have chosen and think about the art, music, literature or design associated with it. Or you could consider the development through history of a single object (shoes for instance). If your idea has been considered by a particular artist or designer before, it might be interesting to see how she/he tackled the problem and how her/his solutions could help you.

The lists below also add to the suggestions elsewhere in this book for starting points for practical art and design work.

Artists, Art Movements and Art Themes to Study and Adapt

Abstract Art
Bauhaus
Bosch
Cubists
David Hockney
Impressionists
Italian Renaissance
Kandinsky
L. S. Lowry
Nude
Portraiture
Pre-Raphaelites
Turner and the Romantics
Stanley Spencer
Still Life
James Whistler
Vermeer and the Dutch School

Suggested Themes for Design Projects

A publicity campaign: promoting our city
Bedsitter
Car dashboards
Clothes
Designing for the old and young
Hats
I protest!
Packaging
Record sleeves
Robots
Shoes
Seating
Street style
Toys

Other Cultures:
Suggestions for Research Projects on a Particular Period or Place

Ancient Egypt
Aztec
Benin
Berber
Borneo
China
Classical Greece
Classical Rome
Dogon
Indian
Indonesian
Inuit
Islamic
Japan
Masai
Medieval/Gothic
Mongol
Red Indian
Turkish
Victorian

Suggestions for Themes for Your Own Artwork

Carnival
Cartoonists
Celebrations
Cities of the future
Clothes
Comic characters
Dragons and dinosaurs
Fear/horror
Friendship
Happiness
Meeting
Nightlife
Noise
Over the rainbow
Posters/Labels/Logos
Puzzle
Reflections
Rhythm
Shadows
Shoes
Shops
Splash
Speed
Star quality
They're almost human
Under the sea
Weddings
Weekly self-portrait

Materials and Techniques

This could never be a complete list of materials and what you could make of them, and it is in the spirit of GCSE for you to think up your own ideas and experiments until you find the best way of achieving the effect you are after or find a new one which pleases you. But sometimes it is hard to start or you may be interested in trying something new to you, and this is a list to help you get going. Always discuss your plans with a teacher to make sure what you are doing is safe and that there aren't any hidden pitfalls. If you are involved in designing or working on an assessed project, a limited time – and budget – may be a crucial factor.

1 Drawings on paper with pencil (soft), charcoal, felt-tip, pen and brush, black or coloured inks, wax crayons and pastels.

2 Painting on paper with brush, blowing, running, etc.; with powder, tempera block, water colour, oil and other sorts of ready-mixed paints. Also smoke from a candle, permanganate of potash, water, oil or oil mixed with paint on paper.

3 Types of paper – different sizes, colours, shapes, textures, degrees of fineness and coarseness. Paper making – transparent, tissue and cellophane.

4 Drawing or painting on many surfaces – stone, wood, cloth, card and metal.

5 Photography as observation or as 'art'. Trick photography, direct exposure printing ('photogramming'), scratched still negatives, scratched movie positives. Photography as research evidence.

6 Embroidery, soft toys and collage in fabric. Appliqué. Sewing cloth, felt, paper and foil.

7 Sculpture – clay, plaster, wire, metal, metal foil, wood, papier mâché, paper, cloth, puppets, mobiles, string and masks.

8 Cut paper – collage, silhouette, split silhouette, folded and cut patterns, split photograph, paper foldback, shadow puppets and paper sculpture.

9 Prints on cloth, paper blocks made from wood, lino, potato cuts, ends of fruit, vegetables, plastic/wood blocks, rods, shapes, paper, polystyrene, string, woodgrain and cut card. Monoprinting, screen printing, leaves, tie and dye, batik and combing with thickened colours.

10 Metal – foil as texture, welded/twisted/soldered as sculpture. Wire, foil as sculpture, foil/metal lace as decoration.

11 Lighting effects – colour, angle, soft or hard focus, patterned, through transparent paper/celluloid.

12 Model making (see sculpture) – of buildings, figures, natural objects and scenery. With clay, wood, paper folded and screwed up wire, metal foil, sponge plaster, polystyrene blocks, matchsticks, cardboard tubes and boxes, buttons, old socks and tights stuffed and tied to shape.

13 Rubbings – of cast or cut metal, bark, cloth, tyre mould, back of hardboard with heelball/wax crayons.

14 Resist – any substance, e.g. paper, cloth, wood, lino, pottery, stone, metal, with candle wax applied to it (by rubbing through, free drawing, etc.) to form a picture/patterns, etc., will resist paint and form a negative pattern, tie and dye batik, marbling.

15 Stencils – done with stipple, wax, paint, pencil and ink.

16 Stipple – mouth spray, brush spatter, blowing with straw.

17 Collages/mosaics – any material that can be stuck to a base. Photo montage.

18 Scrape back – of wax, and also patent two-colour board. See especially black on silver.

19 Mirrors and reflections.

20 Wood and plastic carving, moulding, bending and fretting.

21 Computer paint box.

Study Sources

There is something to look at and learn from almost everywhere and everything. If they're well chosen, well arranged, well lit and well mounted, with good viewing space, exhibitions can be exciting to organise or to visit.

At home you can keep on space on the wall – or in a scrapbook for postcards and souvenirs – anything from magazines to strange or colourful objects that have caught your eye. Start a collection of some ordinary items like pencil sharpeners and see how many different sorts you can find. At school you might try some of the following ideas:

1 Displays arranged by students to fit certain suggested themes or moods, or to supplement a particular picture ('Summer Holidays' or 'Sadness' or a photograph of a Joe Tilson sculpture).

2 A display of objects from your local museum lending service. Stuffed animals are extremely popular and despite the sad fact that they are lifeless, they do stay still long enough to be carefully observed and drawn!

3 A display of pictures and other linked objects from books and postcards in the school's collections and library, perhaps with the idea of 'trailing' new work.

4 A 'view of the week'. Set up a project relating, for example, to the view from a particular school window, and surround the frame with a display of objects, research, artwork and writing related to that view. Alternatively, how about a display of views of school dinner being eaten?

5 Doodle of the week. Provide a graffiti board for (sensible) sketches, patterns, scribbles and/or pin-ups.

6 Arrange a public display of class work and suggest to other classes that they do the same. Posters could be produced to direct other members of the school to each display.

7 For some years a scheme has existed in the East End of London (based on the part locally-funded Whitechapel Art Gallery) for artists to visit schools to work for a term. In this case all the school provides is the work space. The interest generated among the children (and the artists) has apparently been enormous. Could your nearest gallery be persuaded to look for money to fund a similar project? Indeed, does it do so already? Another idea might be to persuade a local artist to bring a selection of work in for a display period and talk about it to class groups.

Galleries, Museums and Art Centres

One of the most exciting ways of getting to know more about art and design is to see what artists and designers have done in the past, and in other parts of the world. Galleries and museums are sometimes very grand places, but these days more and more of them think of their job as being to welcome and help people who are a bit nervous and don't know where to start. Many have Education Departments staffed by people who may talk to students or adults about a single artist or designer, or set up a trail of discovery around the collections, or invite living artists to come in and work in the galleries, or even get actors to portray artists of the past and give us a taste of their working methods.

Many people visit museums and galleries first with their school and when they have found how interesting the collections can be they often come back at the weekends or during holidays and bring friends or family with them. You can often join a club and get to know your 'own' gallery or museum really well.

Knowing about what you see will come, with time. *Enjoying* what you see is something anyone can do, right from the first visit. Remember – your view is as important as anyone else's.

Don't forget the commercial galleries which are run as businesses selling art. They're almost always free to look round and glad to welcome serious viewers who aren't interested in buying.

Galleries and Museums with Education Departments (A Short List)

London	Museum of Mankind, Design Museum (Butlers Wharf), Science Museum, Crafts Council, Dulwich College Picture Gallery, Hayward Gallery, Museum of London Commonwealth Institute, British Museum, Geffrye, Bethnal Green, National Army Museum, National Maritime Museum, National Gallery, National Portrait Gallery, Tate Gallery, Victoria and Albert Museum, Whitechapel
Aberystwyth	Dyfed Arts Centre
Aberdeen	City Art Gallery
Bath	Crafts Study Centre, Avon, American Museum
Bedford	Cecil Higgins
Belfast	Ulster Museum
Birmingham	City Museum
Bolton	City Art Gallery
Bradford	National Museum of Photography, Film and Television
Brighton	City Art Gallery
Bristol	City Museum, Arnolfini
Cambridge	Fitzwilliam, Kettles Yard
Doncaster	City Art Gallery
Edinburgh	National Gallery of Modern Art, National Portrait Gallery, National Museum of Scotland
Exeter	Royal Albert
Glasgow	Art Gallery
Halifax	Piece Hall
Huddersfield	City Art Gallery
Ipswich	City Art Gallery
Kendal	Abbot Hall
Lancaster	City Art Gallery
Leeds	City Art Gallery
Liverpool	Tate Gallery North, Merseyside Museums, Walker Art Gallery
Manchester	Museum, City Art Gallery, (also Whitworth)
Newcastle-upon-Tyne	Laing
Newport	City Art Gallery
Norwich	Castle Museum
Nottingham	Castle
Oxford	Ashmolean, Museum of Modern Art
Plymouth	City Museum, Arts Centre, Devon
Sheffield	Graves, Ruskin
Southampton	City Art Gallery
Sudbury	Derbyshire, Museum of Childhood
Swansea	Glyn Vivian
Warrington	City Art Gallery
Wigan	Drumcroon Art Centre
Worcester	City Art Gallery
York	City Art Gallery

Bibliography

For Students

(* denotes higher level books)

K. BAYNES, *About Design* (Design Council, 1976)
BBC PUBLICATIONS Look, Look and Look Again I and II (BBC, 1984 and 1985)
*G. BRETT, Through our own Eyes (Heretic Books, 1986)
I. BURDEN, J. MORRISON and J. TWYFORD, *Design and Designing* (Longman, 1988)
M. CASSIN, *More Than Meets the Eye* (National Gallery, 1988)
*K. CLARK, *The Nude: A Study of Ideal Art* (John Murray, 1956)
*K. CLARK, *Leonardo da Vinci* (Penguin, 1958)
M. COMPTON, *Looking at Pictures in the Tate Gallery* (Tate Gallery, 1979)
J. DAWSON, *Prints and Print Making* (Phaidon, 1981)
*E. GOMBRICH, *The Story of Art* (Phaidon, 1950)
*P. GREEN, *Design Education: Problem Solving and Visual Experience* (Batsford, 1974)
A. GREEN, *A Green Part of the World: Paintings* (Thames and Hudson, 1984)
*B. HILLIER, *Cartoons and Caricatures* (Studio Vista, 1970)
M. KEIGHTLEY, *Investigating Art: A Practical Guide for Young People* (Bell and Hyman, 1984)
S. G. KELLY and E. LUCIE-SMITH, *The Self Portrait: A Modern View* (Sarema Press, 1987)
F. KENNET and T. MEASHAM, *Looking at Paintings* (Marshall Cavendish, 1978)
*B. LAWSON, *How Designers Think* (Architectural Press, 1980)
C. McDERMOTT, *Street Style: British Design in the 1980s* (Design Council, 1987)
F. PALMER, *Themes and Projects in Art and Design* (Longman, 1988)
*R. PARKER, *The Subversive Stitch: Embroidery and the Making of the Feminine* (Women's Press, 1984)
R. PERRY, *The Writing on the Wall: Graffiti* (Elm Tree Books, 1976)
*N. PEVSNER, *Pioneer of Modern Design* (Penguin, 1974)
H. A. PLUCKROSE, *The Art & Craft Book* (Evans Brothers, 1969)
T. POLHEMUS and L. PROCTOR, *Pop Styles: Where Fashion Meets Rock 'N' Roll* (Vermilion, 1984)
H. READ, *Concise History of Modern Painting* (Thames and Hudson, 1974)
W. READ, *GCSE Art and Design* (Longman, 1988)
*K. ROWLAND, *History of the Modern Movement: Art, Architecture and Design* (Looking and Seeing, 1976)
*A. SCHARF, *Art and Photography* (Penguin, 1974)
J. WALKER, *Cross-Overs: Art into Pop, Pop into Art* (Comedia Publishing Group, 1987)
J. WOZENCROFT, *The Graphic Language of Neville Brody* (Thames and Hudson, 1988)
P. YORK, *Style Wars* (Sidgwick and Jackson, 1980)

For Teachers

BBC PUBLICATIONS *Art Work*, (Notes to TV Series, 1990)
CALOUSTE GULBENKIAN FOUNDATION *The Arts in Schools: Principles, Practice and Provision* (1982)
P. H. GOOCH, *Ideas for Art Teachers* (Batsford, 1972)
D. HARGREAVES, *The Teaching of Art and the Art of Teaching* (Falmer Press, 1983)
J. M. PICKERING, *Visual Education in the Primary School* (Batsford, 1971)
R. TAYLOR, *Educating for Art: Critical Response and Development* (Longman, 1986)

Index

abstract art 22–3, 86
Abu Dhabi 42–3
advertising art 62–3, 66–7, 68–9
animals 15, 72
approach 6–10, 22
Archimboldo 38, 39
architecture 54, 86
art and culture 84, 90
  centres 94
  definition 15
  galleries 20, 24, 94
  history 12, 22, 24, 84
Art and Design (Unendorsed) (GCSE) 12, 13
artists
  visits to schools 93
  at work 18, 20
  working in galleries 94
'Assorted Images' 62, 62–3, 64–5
awareness 6, 12, 13, 22

Baikie, Jim 16–17, 78, 78–9
Barker, Dale Devereaux 10–11
Bell, Steve 38
Benson, Gordon 44, 44–5, 46, 46–7, 48
Blake, William 28–9, 36
Bosch, Hieronymus 90
Bowery, Lee 34–5
Brennand-Wood, Michael
  'Construction' 22–3
Brody, Neville 66
Brueghel, Pieter (the Younger)
  'Village Kermesse and Peasants Dancing round a Maypole' 74–5
Buddha 28–9
Bugatti type 35 racing car 42–3

carnival 74
  Notting Hill 74–5
carpets 24–5
Carrington, Ann 6–7, 10–11, 72, 72–3
cartoon strips 16–17, 78–9
cave paintings 24–5
ceramics 12, 18, 18–19, 82
chairs 42–3
Christian art 24–5, 46–7, 48–9, 50–1, 86
clay 10, 22–3
collage 10–11, 68–9
colour 6, 8, 10, 12, 15, 18, 20, 52, 54, 60, 72, 74, 76, 78, 80, 82, 84, 86, 88
comics 16–17, 78, 78–9
computer paint box *see* Video Paintbox
cost of materials 6, 12, 44, 52
Crisis (magazine) 78–9
Cruikshank, George 66–7
Cubism 80–1
culture 34–5
cultures, for research projects 90

Dali, Salvador 86
  'Christ of St John of the Cross ' 86–7
Dean, Graham 32–3, 84–5
  'Compartments' 16–17
  'The Kiss' 32, 84
decoration 66, 72
Degas, Edgar 82, 84–5
  'Dancer' 82–3
design 12, 22
  of interiors 44
  nature of 41, 44
designers, clients of 50
Din, Rasshied 44, 46, 48, 50
display 10, 22, 54, 93
drawing 8, 12, 82
drawings 22, 24
Dufy, Raoul 82
  fabric design 82–3
  'Open Window at Saint-Jeannet' 82–3

embroidery 82–3
Eno, Brian 64–5
environment, the 70
ergonomics 52–3
Etook, Tivi
  'Hunting for Caribou' 76–7
exhibitions 93; *see also* art galleries

fabric 10, 82, 82–3
Face (magazine) 66, 66–7
fantasy 52–3, 66, 72
fashion 8–9, 34–5, 41, 52, 54, 62
Fluck and Law 38
form 12, 82
Forsyth, Alan 44, 44–5, 46, 46–7, 48
Freud, Lucien 10–11, 28–9
Futurism 78–9

galleries with education departments 94; *see also* art galleries
Garrett, Malcolm 62–3, 64
Gaudi, Antonio
  park seating 84–5
GCSE 92
  assessment objectives 12–13
  courses 12
  drawing and painting 12
  principles 12
  syllabus 12
  a teacher's view 12
Giotto 24
Goldsworthy, Andy 70
  earth banks and water 70–1
  snow sculpture 70–1
graffiti 16–17, 78–9
graphic design 57, 60, 62, 64, 66, 78–9
graphic identity 57, 60, 62; *see also* logos
graphics 22, 52, 58–9, 60–1, 62–3, 64–5, 66, 66–7, 68

Graphics (GCSE) 12
Greece Classical
  'The Wrestlers' 8–9
  Zeus statue 16–17
Green, Anthony 20, 42–3
  'La France au 14 Lissenden Mansions 1944–5' 20–1
  model of study 52–3
  'Mr and Mrs Stanley Joscelyn' 88–9
  'Paradise' 20–1

Hockney, David 90
Hogarth, William
  'Chairing the Member' 76–7
  'Servants' 36
humour 38, 72

ideas 6, 12, 52, 66, 88
ink 10–11, 92
interior design 54, 62
  costing 48, 52
  flat 54–5
  hospital chapel 44, 44–5, 46–7, 48, 48–9, 50, 50–1
  Japanese house 46–7
  restaurant 52–3
  shop 44, 44–5, 46, 48, 50
Inuit culture 76–7

Jackson, Michael 34–5
Jaipur, Amber Palace 54–5
Johns, Jasper
  'Zero Through Nine' 68–9

Keightley, Moy
  'Icelandic Stones' 70–1
Klee, Paul 8–9, 72
  'Colourful Architecture' 8–9
  'Temple Gardens' 72–3
Kossoff, Leon
  'In the Studio, I' 32–3

landscape 70, 80, 80–1
layout 60, 60–1, 62–3, 66
Le Corbusier
  a 'modulor' 52–3
lettering 60, 64, 66–7
Lewis, Percy Wyndham
  'A Battery Shelled' 80–1
light 44, 46, 48, 54, 80
logos 44–5, 46, 50–1, 57, 60–1, 62–3, 64, 64–5, 66, 66–7
London Symphony Orchestra logo 62, 62–3, 64, 64–5
London Underground map 22, 41, 42–3
Lord of Misrule 74
Lorrain, Claude
  'Landscape with the Arrival of Aeneas' 80–1
Louis Philippe, king 38
Lowry, L. S. 90 'The Pond' 88–9

McKenzie, Stephen
'Stephen's Lowry' 88-9
magazines 66
Magritte, René
self-portrait 86-7
Mardi Gras 74
Martin, John 80
'Joshua Commanding the Sun to Stand Still' 80-1
Martini, Simone
'The Annunciation' 16-17
'Mas' 74
Masai warriors 34-5
materials 6, 8, 12, 72, 84
media 6, 36, 82
metal sculpture 92
mirrors 54-5; *see also* reflections
models 22, 76
Mondrian, Piet 16-17
monoprint 66
Moore, Henry 30-1
mosaic 10-11
Mount Rushmore sculptures 32-3
Mughal portrait of an Indian prince 36
museums 93
with education departments

Nash, John
Brighton Pavilion 84-5
Navajo sand picture 24-5
Newton, Sir Isaac 36
'Next' shop interior 44-5, 46, 48, 50, 50-1
Nigerian art 82-3
note-taking 6-7

observation 12
op art 8-9

painting 12, 20, 60, 82
paintings 22, 24, 70
Paolozzi, Eduardo 10-11
pattern 6, 12, 15, 18, 20, 70-1, 72
pen and brush 92
photography 10-11, 29, 30-1, 36, 42-3, 52, 70, 70-1, 76, 78-9, 80-1, 82-3, 92, 93
Photography (GCSE) 12
Picasso, Pablo 82
ceramic plate 82-3
'Guernica' 68-9
Piranesi, Giambattista 86, 86-7
planning 6, 10
Pollock, Jackson
'Yellow Islands' 22-3
Pompidou Centre, Paris 42-3
portraits 10-11, 22-3, 28-9, 29, 30, 32-3, 34, 36, 38, 72-3, 82, 88-9
portraiture
and Islam 25
and Judaism 25
posters 68-9
potato printing 66
pottery *see also* ceramics
Pre-Raphaelites 90
print 60, 62
printing techniques 66
printmaking 12, 82
prints 92
protest through art 84-5
publicity 62
Punch and Judy 74-5
puppetry 38

reflections 92; *see also* mirrors
Renaissance, Italian 46-7
Renoir, Auguste
'Luncheon of the Boating Party' 88-9
research 8, 10, 12, 46, 48, 52
Riley, Bridget 8-9
Rio de Janeiro 74
Rodin, Auguste
'The Burghers of Calais' 76-7
'The Kiss' 84-5
Rogers, Richard 42-3

Schwitters, Kurt
'Fernspr.' 68-9
scrapbooks 6-7, 8, 93
screen printing 92
sculpture 8-9, 10-11, 20, 22, 24, 30-1, 60, 72, 82, 82-3, 84-5
Severini, Gino
'Suburban Train Arriving in Paris' 78-9
shape 6, 12, 15, 18, 20, 54, 72, 74, 80, 84, 86
Shiva 28-9
Shrove Tuesday 74
silkscreen printing 66
Singh, Kaja Ummed
'Shooting Tigers' 80-1
sketchbooks 6, 8
Smith, Clive 8-9, 34-5
sources 6
Spencer, Stanley 90
stained glass
'The Apostles Fishing' 24-5
still life 90
stipple 92
stories and art 76, 80, 82, 88
street theatre 74
structure 80
study 12
sources 93
subjects 6, 12
Surrealists 72, 86-7
symbols 18, 28-9, 30-1, 46, 57, 58-9, 60, 60-1, 64, 66, 68, 68-9, 74, 76

techniques 92
textiles 12; *see also* fabric
texture 6, 10, 12, 15, 54, 86
themes 12, 90, 93
Things to Come
still from film 54-5
3D Studies (GCSE) 12
Tibetan tiger rugs 86-7
Tilson, Joe 93
tools 6, 8
Toulouse-Lautrec, Henri de
poster 60-1
traditions, artistic and cultural 24; *see also* cultures for research projects
typefaces 60, 60-1, 62-3, 64, 66

USA 24

Van Eyck, Jan
'Arnolfini and his Wife' 88-9
Van Gogh, Vincent
'Sunflowers' 20-1
Velasquez, Diego
'Las Meninas' 32-3
Vermeer, Jan 90
video 36, 66, 76
Video Paintbox 18-19, 92
Vinci, Leonardo da 6-7, 8-9, 86
'Mona Lisa' 86-7
Vitruvius, Marcus Pollius 28-9

Watt, Alison
'The Last Supper' 30-1
Whitechapel Art Gallery 93
Wigan 18
Wilson, Nikki 18-19
Woon, Liam 10-11
writing 58-9, 60-1; *see also* graphic design, graphics